# The Active Side
## of Infinity

OTHER BOOKS BY CARLOS CASTANEDA

*The Teachings of Don Juan*

*A Separate Reality*

*Journey to Ixtlan*

*Tales of Power*

*The Second Ring of Power*

*The Eagle's Gift*

*The Fire from Within*

*The Power of Silence*

*The Art of Dreaming*

*Magical Passes*

*The Wheel of Time*

# The Active Side
# of Infinity

## CARLOS
## CASTANEDA

HarperCollins*Publishers*

HarperCollins books may be purchased for educational, business, or sales promotional use. For information please write: Special Markets Department, HarperCollins Publishers, Inc., 10 East 53rd Street, New York, NY 10022.

FIRST EDITION

*Designed by Eric Coates*

Library of Congress Cataloging-in-Publication Data

Castaneda, Carlos
    The active side of infinity / Carlos Castaneda. — 1st ed.
        p. cm
    ISBN 0-06-019220-8
    1. Juan, Don, 1891–. 2. Yaqui Indians—Religion. 3. Hallucinogenic drugs and religious experience. 4. Altered states of consciousness. I. Title
E99.Y3C26 1999
299'.7—dc21                                                                 98-19980

99 00 01 02 03 ❖/RRD 10 9 8 7 6 5 4 3

This book is dedicated to the two men
who gave me the impetus and the tools to do
anthropological fieldwork : Professor Clement
Meighan and Professor Harold Garfinkel.
Following their suggestions, I plunged into
a field situation from which I never emerged.
If I failed to fulfill the spirit of their teaching,
so be it. I couldn't help it. A greater force,
which shamans call *infinity*, swallowed me
before I could formulate clear-cut
social scientists' propositions.

# CONTENTS

"Syntax" ∾ ix

"The Other Syntax" ∾ xi

Introduction ∾ 1

**A Tremor in the Air** ∾ 27
A Journey of Power ∾ 29
The Intent of Infinity ∾ 43
Who Was Juan Matus, Really? ∾ 65

**The End of an Era** ∾ 75
The Deep Concerns of Everyday Life ∾ 77
The View I Could Not Stand ∾ 88
The Unavoidable Appointment ∾ 95
The Breaking Point ∾ 103
The Measurements of Cognition ∾ 115
Saying Thank You ∾ 128

**Beyond Syntax** ∾ 139
The Usher ∾ 141
The Interplay of Energy on the Horizon ∾ 160
Journeys Through the Dark Sea of Awareness ∾ 176
Inorganic Awareness ∾ 187
The Clear View ∾ 201
Mud Shadows ∾ 215

**Starting on the Definitive Journey** ∾ 235
The Jump into the Abyss ∾ 237
The Return Trip ∾ 263

## Syntax

A man staring at his equations
said that the universe had a beginning.
There had been an explosion, he said.
A bang of bangs, and the universe was born.
And it is expanding, he said.
He had even calculated the length of its life:
ten billion revolutions of the earth around the sun.
The entire globe cheered;
They found his calculations to be science.
None thought that by proposing that the universe began,
the man had merely mirrored the syntax of his mother tongue;
a syntax which demands beginnings, like birth,
and developments, like maturation,
and ends, like death, as statements of facts.
The universe began,
and it is getting old, the man assured us,
and it will die, like all things die,
like he himself died after confirming mathematically
the syntax of his mother tongue.

# The Other Syntax

Did the universe really begin?
Is the theory of the big bang true?
These are not questions, though they sound like they are.
Is the syntax that requires beginnings, developments
and ends as statements of fact the only syntax that exists?
That's the real question.
There are other syntaxes.
There is one, for example, which demands that varieties
of intensity be taken as facts.
In that syntax nothing begins and nothing ends;
thus birth is not a clean, clear-cut event,
but a specific type of intensity,
and so is maturation, and so is death.
A man of that syntax, looking over his equations, finds that
he has calculated enough varieties of intensity
to say with authority
that the universe never began
and will never end,
but that it has gone, and is going now, and will go
through endless fluctuations of intensity.
That man could very well conclude that the universe itself
is the chariot of intensity
and that one can board it
to journey through changes without end.
He will conclude all that, and much more,
perhaps without ever realizing
that he is merely confirming
the syntax of his mother tongue.

# INTRODUCTION

THIS BOOK IS a collection of the memorable events in my life. I gathered them following the recommendation of don Juan Matus, a Yaqui Indian shaman from Mexico who, as a teacher, endeavored for thirteen years to make available to me the *cognitive world* of the shamans who lived in Mexico in ancient times. Don Juan Matus's suggestion that I gather this collection of memorable events was made as if it were something casual, something that occurred to him on the spur of the moment. That was don Juan's style of teaching. He veiled the importance of certain maneuvers behind the mundane. He hid, in this fashion, the sting of finality, presenting it as something no different from any of the concerns of everyday life.

Don Juan revealed to me as time went by that the shamans of ancient Mexico had conceived of this collection of memorable events as a bona-fide device to stir caches of energy that exist within the self. They explained these caches as being composed of energy that originates in the body itself and becomes displaced, pushed out of reach by the circumstances of our daily lives. In this sense, the collection of memorable events was, for don Juan and the shamans of his lineage, the means for *redeploying* their unused energy.

The prerequisite for this collection was the genuine and all-consuming act of putting together the sum total of one's emotions and realizations, without sparing anything. According to don Juan, the shamans of his lineage were convinced that the collection of memorable events was the vehicle for the emotional and energetic adjustment necessary for venturing, in terms of perception, into the unknown.

Don Juan described the total goal of the shamanistic knowledge that he handled as the preparation for facing the *definitive journey*: the journey that every human being has to take at the end of his life. He said that through their discipline and resolve, shamans were capable of retaining their individual awareness and purpose after death. For them, the vague, idealistic state that modern man calls "life after death" was a concrete region filled to capacity with practical affairs of a different order than the practical affairs of daily life, yet bearing a similar functional practicality. Don Juan considered that to collect the memorable events in their lives was, for shamans, the preparation for their entrance into that concrete region which they called the *active side of infinity*.

Don Juan and I were talking one afternoon under his ramada, a loose structure made of thin poles of bamboo. It looked like a roofed porch that was partially shaded from the sun but that would not provide protection at all from the rain. There were some small, sturdy freight boxes there that served as benches. Their freight brands were faded, and appeared to be more ornament than identification. I was sitting on one of them. My back was against the front wall of the house. Don Juan was sitting on another box, leaning against a pole that supported the ramada. I had just driven in a few minutes earlier. It had been a daylong ride in hot, humid weather. I was nervous, fidgety, and sweaty.

Don Juan began talking to me as soon as I had comfortably settled down on the box. With a broad smile, he commented that overweight people hardly ever knew how to fight fatness. The smile that played on his lips gave me an inkling that he wasn't being facetious. He was just pointing out to me, in a most direct and at the same time indirect way, that I was overweight.

I became so nervous that I tipped over the freight box on which

I was sitting and my back banged very hard against the thin wall of the house. The impact shook the house to its foundations. Don Juan looked at me inquiringly, but instead of asking me if I was all right, he assured me that I had not cracked the house. Then he expansively explained to me that his house was a temporary dwelling for him, that he really lived somewhere else. When I asked him where he really lived, he stared at me. His look was not belligerent; it was, rather, a firm deterrent to improper questions. I didn't comprehend what he wanted. I was about to ask the same question again, but he stopped me.

"Questions of that sort are not asked around here," he said firmly. "Ask anything you wish about procedures or ideas. Whenever I'm ready to tell you where I live, if ever, I will tell you without your having to ask me."

I instantly felt rejected. My face turned red involuntarily. I was definitely offended. Don Juan's explosion of laughter added immensely to my chagrin. Not only had he rejected me, he had insulted me and then laughed at me.

"I live here temporarily," he went on, unconcerned with my foul mood, "because this is a magical center. In fact, I live here because of you."

That statement unraveled me. I couldn't believe it. I thought that he was probably saying that to ease my irritation at being insulted.

"Do you really live here because of me?" I finally asked him, unable to contain my curiosity.

"Yes," he said evenly. "I have to groom you. You are like me. I will repeat to you now what I have already told you: The quest of every nagual, or leader, in every generation of shamans, or sorcerers, is to find a new man or woman who, like himself, shows a double energetic structure; I *saw* this feature in you when we were in the bus depot in Nogales. When I *see* your energy, I *see* two balls of luminosity superimposed, one on top of the other, and that feature binds us together. I can't refuse you any more than you can refuse me."

His words caused a most strange agitation in me. An instant

before I had been angry, now I wanted to weep.

He went on, saying that he wanted to start me off on something shamans called the *warriors' way*, backed by the strength of the area where he lived, which was the center of very strong emotions and reactions. Warlike people had lived there for thousands of years, soaking the land with their concern with war.

He lived at that time in the state of Sonora in northern Mexico, about a hundred miles south of the city of Guaymas. I always went there to visit him under the auspices of conducting my fieldwork.

"Do I need to enter into war, don Juan?" I asked, genuinely worried after he declared that the concern with war was something that I would need someday. I had already learned to take everything he said with the utmost seriousness.

"You bet your boots," he replied, smiling. "When you have absorbed all there is to be absorbed in this area, I'll move away."

I had no grounds to doubt what he was saying, but I couldn't conceive of him as living anywhere else. He was absolutely part of everything that surrounded him. His house, however, seemed indeed to be a temporary dwelling. It was a shack typical of the Yaqui farmers; it was made out of wattle and daub with a flat, thatched roof; it had one big room for eating and sleeping and a roofless kitchen.

"It's very difficult to deal with overweight people," he said.

It seemed to be a non sequitur, but it wasn't. Don Juan was simply going back to the subject he had introduced before I had interrupted him by hitting my back on the wall of his house.

"A minute ago, you hit my house like a demolition ball," he said, shaking his head slowly from side to side. "What an impact! An impact worthy of a portly man."

I had the uncomfortable feeling that he was talking to me from the point of view of someone who had given up on me. I immediately took on a defensive attitude. He listened, smirking, to my frantic explanations that my weight was normal for my bone structure.

"That's right," he conceded facetiously. "You have big bones. You could probably carry thirty more pounds with great ease and no one, I assure you, no one, would notice. I would not notice."

His mocking smile told me that I was definitely pudgy. He asked me then about my health in general, and I went on talking, desperately trying to get out of any further comment about my weight. He changed the subject himself.

"What's new about your eccentricities and aberrations?" he asked with a deadpan expression.

I idiotically answered that they were okay. "Eccentricities and aberrations" was how he labeled my interest in being a collector. At that time, I had taken up, with renewed zeal, something that I had enjoyed doing all my life: collecting anything collectible. I collected magazines, stamps, records, World War II paraphernalia such as daggers, military helmets, flags, etc.

"All I can tell you, don Juan, about my aberrations, is that I'm trying to sell my collections," I said with the air of a martyr who is being forced to do something odious.

"To be a collector is not such a bad idea," he said as if he really believed it. "The crux of the matter is not that you collect, but what you collect. You collect junk, worthless objects that imprison you as surely as your pet dog does. You can't just up and leave if you have your pet to look after, or if you have to worry about what would happen to your collections if you were not around."

"I'm seriously looking for buyers, don Juan, believe me," I protested.

"No, no, no, don't feel that I'm accusing you of anything," he retorted. "In fact, I like your collector's spirit. I just don't like your collections, that's all. I would like, though, to engage your collector's eye. I would like to propose to you a worthwhile collection."

Don Juan paused for a long moment. He seemed to be in search of words; or perhaps it was only a dramatic, well-placed hesitation. He looked at me with a deep, penetrating stare.

"Every warrior, as a matter of duty, collects a special album," don Juan went on, "an album that reveals the warrior's personality, an album that attests to the circumstances of his life."

"Why do you call this a collection, don Juan?" I asked in an argumentative tone. "Or an album, for that matter?"

"Because it is both," he retorted. "But above all, it is like an album of pictures made out of memories, pictures made out of the recollection of memorable events."

"Are those memorable events memorable in some specific way?" I asked.

"They are memorable because they have a special significance in one's life," he said. "My proposal is that you assemble this album by putting in it the complete account of various events that have had profound significance for you."

"Every event in my life has had profound significance for me, don Juan!" I said forcefully, and felt instantly the impact of my own pomposity.

"Not really," he replied, smiling, apparently enjoying my reactions immensely. "Not every event in your life has had profound significance for you. There are a few, however, that I would consider likely to have changed things for you, to have illuminated your path. Ordinarily, events that change our path are impersonal affairs, and yet are extremely personal."

"I'm not trying to be difficult, don Juan, but believe me, everything that has happened to me meets those qualifications," I said, knowing that I was lying.

Immediately after voicing this statement, I wanted to apologize, but don Juan didn't pay attention to me. It was as if I hadn't said a thing.

"Don't think about this album in terms of banalities, or in terms of a trivial rehashing of your life experiences," he said.

I took a deep breath, closed my eyes, and tried to quiet my mind. I was talking to myself frantically about my insoluble problem: I most certainly didn't like to visit don Juan at all. In his presence, I felt threatened. He verbally accosted me and didn't

leave me any room whatsoever to show my worth. I detested losing face every time I opened my mouth; I detested being the fool.

But there was another voice inside me, a voice that came from
a greater depth, more distant, almost faint. In the midst of my
barrages of known dialogue, I heard myself saying that it was too
late for me to turn back. But it wasn't really my voice or my
thoughts that I was experiencing; it was, rather, like an unknown
voice that said I was too far gone into don Juan's world, and that
I needed him more than I needed air.

"Say whatever you wish," the voice seemed to say to me, "but
if you were not the egomaniac that you are, you wouldn't be so
chagrined."

"That's the voice of your other mind," don Juan said, just as if
he had been listening to or reading my thoughts.

My body jumped involuntarily. My fright was so intense that
tears came to my eyes. I confessed to don Juan the whole nature
of my turmoil.

"Your conflict is a very natural one," he said. "And believe you
me, I don't exacerbate it that much. I'm not the type. I have
some stories to tell you about what my teacher, the nagual Julian,
used to do to me. I detested him with my entire being. I was very
young, and I saw how women adored him, gave themselves to
him like anything, and when I tried to say hello to them, they
would turn against me like lionesses, ready to bite my head off.
They hated my guts and loved him. How do you think I felt?"

"How did you resolve this conflict, don Juan?" I asked with
more than genuine interest.

"I didn't resolve anything," he declared. "It, the conflict or
whatever, was the result of the battle between my two minds.
Every one of us human beings has two minds. One is totally ours,
and it is like a faint voice that always brings us order, directness,
purpose. The other mind is a *foreign installation*. It brings us conflict, self-assertion, doubts, hopelessness."

My fixation on my own mental concatenations was so intense
that I completely missed what don Juan had said. I could clearly

remember every one of his words, but they had no meaning for me. Don Juan very calmly, and looking directly into my eyes, repeated what he had just said. I was still incapable of grasping what he meant. I couldn't focus my attention on his words.

"For some strange reason, don Juan, I can't concentrate on what you're telling me," I said.

"I understand perfectly why you can't," he said, smiling expansively, "and so will you, someday, at the same time that you resolve the conflict of whether you like me or not, the day you cease to be the *me-me* center of the world.

"In the meantime," he continued, "let's put the topic of our two minds aside and go back to the idea of preparing your album of memorable events. I should add that such an album is an exercise in discipline and impartiality. Consider this album to be an act of war."

Don Juan's assertion—that my conflict of both liking and not liking to see him was going to end whenever I abandoned my egocentrism—was no solution for me. In fact, that assertion made me angrier; it frustrated me all the more. And when I heard don Juan speak of the album as an act of war, I lashed out at him with all my poison.

"The idea that this is a collection of events is already hard to understand," I said in a tone of protest. "But that on top of all this, you call it an album and say that such an album is an act of war is too much for me. It's too obscure. Being obscure makes the metaphor lose its meaning."

"How strange! It's the opposite for me," don Juan replied calmly. "Such an album being an act of war has all the meaning in the world for me. I wouldn't like my album of memorable events to be anything but an act of war."

I wanted to argue my point further and explain to him that I did understand the idea of an album of memorable events. I objected to the perplexing way he was describing it. I thought of myself in those days as an advocate of clarity and functionalism in the use of language.

Don Juan didn't comment on my belligerent mood. He only shook his head as if he were fully agreeing with me. After a while, I either completely ran out of energy, or I got a gigantic surge of it. All of a sudden, without any effort on my part, I realized the futility of my outbursts. I felt embarrassed no end.

"What possesses me to act the way I do?" I asked don Juan in earnest. I was, at that instant, utterly baffled. I was so shaken by my realization that without any volition on my part, I began to weep.

"Don't worry about stupid details," don Juan said reassuringly. "Every one of us, male and female, is like this."

"Do you mean, don Juan, that we are naturally petty and contradictory?"

"No, we are not naturally petty and contradictory," he replied. "Our pettiness and contradictions are, rather, the result of a transcendental conflict that afflicts every one of us, but of which only sorcerers are painfully and hopelessly aware: the conflict of our two minds."

Don Juan peered at me; his eyes were like two black charcoals.

"You've been telling me on and on about our two minds," I said, "but my brain can't register what you are saying. Why?"

"You'll get to know why in due time," he said. "For the present, it will be sufficient that I repeat to you what I have said before about our two minds. One is our true mind, the product of all our life experiences, the one that rarely speaks because it has been defeated and relegated to obscurity. The other, the mind we use daily for everything we do, is a *foreign installation*."

"I think that the crux of the matter is that the concept of the mind being a *foreign installation* is so outlandish that my mind refuses to take it seriously," I said, feeling that I had made a real discovery.

Don Juan did not comment on what I had said. He continued explaining the issue of the two minds as if I hadn't said a word.

"To resolve the conflict of the two minds is a matter of *intending* it," he said. "Sorcerers beckon *intent* by voicing the word *intent* loud and clear. *Intent* is a force that exists in the universe. When sorcerers beckon *intent*, it comes to them and sets up the path for attainment, which means that sorcerers always accomplish what they set out to do."

"Do you mean, don Juan, that sorcerers get anything they want, even if it is something petty and arbitrary?" I asked.

"No, I didn't mean that. *Intent* can be called, of course, for anything," he replied, "but sorcerers have found out, the hard way, that *intent* comes to them only for something that is abstract. That's the safety valve for sorcerers; otherwise they would be unbearable. In your case, beckoning *intent* to resolve the conflict of your two minds, or to hear the voice of your true mind, is not a petty or arbitrary matter. Quite the contrary; it is ethereal and abstract, and yet as vital to you as anything can be."

Don Juan paused for a moment; then he began to talk again about the album.

"My own album, being an act of war, demanded a super-careful selection," he said. "It is now a precise collection of the unforgettable moments of my life, and everything that led me to them. I have concentrated in it what has been and will be meaningful to me. In my opinion, a warrior's album is something most concrete, something so to the point that it is shattering."

I had no clue as to what don Juan wanted, and yet I did understand him to perfection. He advised me to sit down, alone, and let my thoughts, memories, and ideas come to me freely. He recommended that I make an effort to let the voice from the depths of me speak out and tell me what to select. Don Juan told me then to go inside the house and lie down on a bed that I had there. It was made of wooden boxes and dozens of empty burlap sacks that served as a mattress. My whole body ached, and when I lay on the bed it was actually extremely comfortable.

I took his suggestions to heart and began to think about my past, looking for events that had left a mark on me. I soon realized that my assertion that every event in my life had been meaningful was nonsense. As I pressed myself to recollect, I found that I didn't even know where to start. Through my mind ran endless disassociated thoughts and memories of events that had happened to me, but I couldn't decide whether or not they had had any meaning for me. The impression I got was that nothing had had any significance whatsoever. It looked as if I had gone through life like a corpse empowered to walk and talk, but not to feel anything. Having no concentration whatsoever to pursue the subject beyond a shallow attempt, I gave up and fell asleep.

"Did you have any success?" don Juan asked me when I woke up hours later.

Instead of being at ease after sleeping and resting, I was again moody and belligerent.

"No, I didn't have any success!" I barked.

"Did you hear that voice from the depths of you?" he asked.

"I think I did," I lied.

"What did it say to you?" he inquired in an urgent tone.

"I can't think of it, don Juan," I muttered.

"Ah, you are back in your daily mind," he said and patted me forcefully on the back. "Your daily mind has taken over again. Let's relax it by talking about your collection of memorable events. I should tell you that the selection of what to put in your album is not an easy matter. This is the reason I say that making this album is an act of war. You have to remake yourself ten times over in order to know what to select."

I clearly understood then, if only for a second, that I had two minds; however, the thought was so vague that I lost it instantly. What remained was just the sensation of an incapacity to fulfill don Juan's requirement. Instead of graciously accepting my incapacity, though, I allowed it to become a threatening affair. The driving force of my life, in those days, was to appear always in a good light. To be incompetent was the equivalent of being a loser, something that was thoroughly intolerable to me. Since I didn't know how to respond to the challenge don Juan was posing, I did the only thing I knew how to do: I got angry.

"I've got to think a great deal more about this, don Juan," I said. "I've got to give my mind some time to settle on the idea."

"Of course, of course," don Juan assured me. "Take all the time in the world, but hurry."

Nothing else was said about the subject at that time. At home, I forgot about it completely until one day when, quite abruptly, in the middle of a lecture I was attending, the imperious command to search for the memorable events of my life hit me like a bodily jolt, a nervous spasm that shook my entire body from head to toe.

I began to work in earnest. It took me months to rehash experiences in my life that I believed were meaningful to me. However, upon examining my collection, I realized that I was dealing only with ideas that had no substance whatsoever. The events I remembered were just vague points of reference that I remembered abstractly. Once again, I had the most unsettling suspicion that I had been reared just to act without ever stopping to feel anything.

One of the vaguest events I recalled, which I wanted to make memorable at any cost, was the day I found out I had been admitted to graduate school at UCLA. No matter how hard I tried, I couldn't remember what I had been doing that day. There was nothing interesting or unique about that day, except for the idea that it had to be memorable. Entering graduate school should have made me happy or proud of myself, but it didn't.

Another sample in my collection was the day I almost got married to Kay Condor. Her last name wasn't really Condor, but she had changed it because she wanted to be an actress. Her ticket to fame was that she actually looked like Carole Lombard. That day was memorable in my mind, not so much because of the events that took place but because she was beautiful and wanted to marry me. She was a head taller than I was, which made her all the more interesting to me.

I was thrilled with the idea of marrying a tall woman, in a church ceremony. I rented a gray tuxedo. The pants were quite

12

wide for my height. They were not bell-bottoms; they were just wide, and that bothered me no end. Another thing that annoyed me immensely was that the sleeves of the pink shirt I had bought for the occasion were about three inches too long; I had to use rubber bands to hold them up. Outside of that, everything was perfect until the moment when the guests and I found out that Kay Condor had gotten cold feet and wasn't going to show up.

Being a very proper young lady, she had sent me a note of apology by motorcycle messenger. She wrote that she didn't believe in divorce, and couldn't commit herself for the rest of her days to someone who didn't quite share her views on life. She reminded me that I snickered every time I said the name "Condor," something that showed a total lack of respect for her person. She said that she had discussed the matter with her mother. Both of them loved me dearly, but not enough to make me part of their family. She added that, bravely and wisely, we all had to cut our losses.

My state of mind was one of total numbness. When I tried to recollect that day, I couldn't remember whether I felt horribly humiliated at being left standing in front of a lot of people in my gray, rented tuxedo with the wide-legged pants, or whether I was crushed because Kay Condor didn't marry me.

These were the only two events I was capable of isolating with clarity. They were meager examples, but after rehashing them, I had succeeded in re-dressing them as tales of philosophical acceptance. I thought of myself as a being who goes through life with no real feelings, who has only intellectual views of every-thing. Taking don Juan's metaphors as models, I even con-structed one of my own: a being who lives his life vicariously in terms of what it should be.

I believed, for instance, that the day I was admitted to gradu-ate school at UCLA should have been a memorable day. Since it wasn't, I tried my best to imbue it with an importance I was far from feeling. A similar thing happened with the day I nearly married Kay Condor. It should have been a devastating day for me, but it wasn't. At the moment of recollecting it, I knew that there was nothing there and began to work as hard as I could to construct what I should have felt.

The next time I went to don Juan's house I presented to him my two samples of memorable events as soon as I arrived.

"This is a pile of nonsense," he declared. "None of it will do. The stories are related exclusively to you as a person who thinks, feels, cries, or doesn't feel anything at all. The memorable events of a shaman's album are affairs that will stand the test of time because they have nothing to do with him, and yet he is in the thick of them. He'll always be in the thick of them, for the duration of his life, and perhaps beyond, but not quite personally."

His words left me feeling dejected, totally defeated. I sincerely believed in those days that don Juan was an intransigent old man who found special delight in making me feel stupid. He reminded me of a master craftsman I had met at a sculptor's foundry where I worked while going to art school. The master artisan used to criticize and find flaws with everything his advanced apprentices did, and would demand that they correct their work according to his recommendations. His apprentices would turn around and pretend to correct their work. I remembered the glee of the master when he would say, upon being presented with the same work, "Now you have a real thing!"

"Don't feel bad," don Juan said, shaking me out of my recollection. "In my time, I was in the same spot. For years, not only did I not know what to choose, I thought I had no experiences to choose from. It seemed that nothing had ever happened to me. Of course, everything had happened to me, but in my effort to defend the idea of myself, I had no time or inclination to notice anything."

"Can you tell me, don Juan, specifically, what is wrong with my stories? I know that they are nothing, but the rest of my life is just like that."

"I will repeat this to you," he said. "The stories of a warrior's album are not personal. Your story of the day you were admitted to school is nothing but your assertion about you as the center of everything. You feel, you don't feel; you realize, you don't realize. Do you see what I mean? All of the story is just you."

"But how can it be otherwise, don Juan?" I asked.

"In your other story, you almost touch on what I want, but you turn it again into something extremely personal. I know that you could add more details, but all those details would be an extension of your person and nothing else."

"I sincerely cannot see your point, don Juan," I protested. "Every story seen through the eyes of the witness has to be, perforce, personal."

"Yes, yes, of course," he said, smiling, delighted as usual by my confusion. "But then they are not stories for a warrior's album. They are stories for other purposes. The memorable events we are after have the dark touch of the impersonal. That touch permeates them. I don't know how else to explain this."

I believed then that I had a moment of inspiration and that I understood what he meant by the dark touch of the impersonal. I thought that he meant something a bit morbid. Darkness meant that for me. And I related to him a story from my childhood.

One of my older cousins was in medical school. He was an intern, and one day he took me to the morgue. He assured me that a young man owed it to himself to see dead people because that sight was very educational; it demonstrated the transitoriness of life. He harangued me, on and on, in order to convince me to go. The more he talked about how unimportant we were in death, the more curious I became. I had never seen a corpse. My curiosity, in the end, to see one overwhelmed me and I went with him.

He showed me various corpses and succeeded in scaring me stiff. I found nothing educational or illuminating about them. They were, outright, the most frightening things I had ever seen. As he talked to me, he kept looking at his watch as if he were waiting for someone who was going to show up at any moment. He obviously wanted to keep me in the morgue longer than my strength permitted. Being the competitive creature that I was, I believed that he was testing my endurance, my manhood. I clenched my teeth and made up my mind to·stay until the bitter end.

The bitter end came in ways that I had not dreamed of. A corpse that was covered with a sheet actually moved up with a rattle on the marble table where all the corpses were lying, as if it were getting ready to sit up. It made a burping sound that was so awful it burned through me and will remain in my memory for the rest of my life. My cousin, the doctor, the scientist, explained that it was the corpse of a man who had died of tuberculosis, and that his lungs had been eaten away by bacilli that had left enormous holes filled with air, and that in cases like this, when the air changed temperature, it sometimes forced the body to sit up or at least convulse.

"No, you haven't gotten it yet," don Juan said, shaking his head from side to side. "It is merely a story about your fear. I would have been scared to death myself; however, being scared like that doesn't illuminate anyone's path. But I'm curious to know what happened to you."

"I yelled like a banshee," I said. "My cousin called me a coward, a yellow-belly, for hiding my face against his chest and for getting sick to my stomach all over him."

I had definitely hooked on to a morbid strand in my life. I came up with another story about a sixteen-year-old boy I knew in high school who had a glandular disease and grew to a gigantic height. His heart did not grow at the same rate as the rest of his body and one day he died of heart failure. I went with another boy to the mortuary out of morbid curiosity. The mortician, who was perhaps more morbid than the two of us, opened the back door and let us in. He showed us his masterpiece. He had put the gigantic boy, who had been over seven feet, seven inches tall, into a coffin for a normal person by sawing off his legs. He showed us how he had arranged his legs as if the dead boy were holding them with his arms like two trophies.

The fright I experienced was comparable to the fright I had experienced in the morgue as a child, but this new fright was not a physical reaction; it was a reaction of psychological revulsion.

"You're almost there," don Juan said. "However, your story is still too personal. It's revolting. It makes me sick, but I see great potential."

Don Juan and I laughed at the horror found in situations of everyday life. By then I was hopelessly lost in the morbid strands I had caught and released. I told him then the story of my best friend, Roy Goldpiss. He actually had a Polish surname, but his friends called him Goldpiss because whatever he touched, he turned to gold; he was a great businessman.

His talent for business made him a super-ambitious being. He wanted to be the richest man in the world. However, he found that the competition was too tough. According to him, doing business alone he couldn't possibly compete, for instance, with the head of an Islamic sect who, at that time, got paid his weight in gold every year. The head of the sect would fatten himself as much as his body allowed him before he was weighed.

Then my friend Roy lowered his sights to being the richest man in the United States. The competition in this sector was ferocious. He went down a notch: Perhaps he could be the richest man in California. He was too late for that, too. He gave up hope that, with his chains of pizza and ice cream parlors, he could ever rise in the business world to compete with the established families who owned California. He settled for being the richest man in Woodland Hills, the suburb of Los Angeles where he lived. Unfortunately for him, down the street from his house lived Mr. Marsh, who owned factories that produced A-one quality mattresses all over the United States, and he was rich beyond belief. Roy's frustration knew no limits. His drive to accomplish was so intense that it finally impaired his health. One day he died from an aneurysm in his brain.

His death brought, as a consequence, my third visit to a morgue or a mortuary. Roy's wife begged me, as his best friend, to make sure that the corpse was properly dressed. I went to the funeral parlor, where I was led by a male secretary to the inner chambers. At the precise moment I arrived, the mortician, working on a high marble-topped table, was forcefully pushing up the corners of the upper lip of the corpse, which had already entered rigor mortis, with the index and little finger of his right hand while he held his middle finger against his palm. As a grotesque smile appeared on Roy's dead face, the mortician half-turned to me and said in a servile tone, "I hope all this is to your satisfaction, sir."

Roy's wife—it will never be known whether she liked him or not—decided to bury him with all the garishness that, in her opinion, his life deserved. She had bought a very expensive coffin, a custom-made affair that looked like a telephone booth; she had gotten the idea from a movie. Roy was going to be buried sitting, as if he were making a business call on the telephone.

I didn't stay for the ceremony. I left in the midst of a most violent reaction, a mixture of impotence and anger, the kind of anger that couldn't be vented on anyone.

"You certainly are morbid today," don Juan commented, laughing. "But in spite of that, or perhaps because of that, you're almost there. You're touching it."

I never ceased to marvel at the way in which my mood changed every time I went to see don Juan. I always arrived moody, grouchy, filled with self-assertions and doubts. After a while, my mood would mysteriously change and I would become more expansive, by degrees, until I was as calm as I had ever been. However, my new mood was couched in my old vocabulary. My usual way of talking was that of a totally dissatisfied person who is containing himself from complaining out loud, but whose endless complaints are implied at every turn of the conversation.

"Can you give me an example of a memorable event from your album, don Juan?" I asked in my habitual tone of veiled complaint. "If I knew the pattern you were after, I might be able to come up with something. As it is, I am whistling hopelessly in the dark."

"Don't explain yourself so much," don Juan said with a stern look in his eyes. "Sorcerers say that in every explanation there is a hidden apology. So, when you are explaining why you cannot do this or that, you're really apologizing for your shortcomings, hoping that whoever is listening to you will have the kindness to understand them."

My most useful maneuver, when I was attacked, had always been to turn my attackers off by not listening to them. Don Juan, however, had the disgusting ability to trap every bit of my attention. No matter how he attacked me, no matter what he said, he always managed to have me riveted to his every word. On this occasion, what he was saying about me didn't please me at all because it was the naked truth.

I avoided his eyes. I felt, as usual, defeated, but it was a peculiar defeat this time. It didn't bother me as it would have if it had happened in the world of everyday life, or right after I had arrived at his house.

After a very long silence, don Juan spoke to me again.

"I'll do better than give you an example of a memorable event from my album," he said. "I'll give you a memorable event from your own life, one that should go for sure in your collection. Or, I should say, if I were you, I would certainly put it in my collection of memorable events."

I thought don Juan was joking and I laughed stupidly.

"This is not a laughing matter," he said cuttingly. "I am serious. You once told me a story that fits the bill."

"What story is that, don Juan?"

"The story of 'figures in front of a mirror,'" he said. "Tell me that story again. But tell it to me in all the detail you can remember."

I began to retell the story in a cursory fashion. He stopped me and demanded a careful, detailed narration, starting at the beginning. I tried again, but my rendition didn't satisfy him.

"Let's go for a walk," he proposed. "When you walk, you are much more accurate than when you're sitting down. It is not an idle idea that you should pace back and forth when you try to relate something."

We had been sitting, as we usually did during the day, under the house ramada. I had developed a pattern: Whenever I sat there, I always did it on the same spot, with my back against the wall. Don Juan sat in various places under the ramada, but never on the same spot.

We went for a hike at the worst time of the day, noon. He outfitted me with an old straw hat, as he always did whenever we went out in the heat of the sun. We walked for a long time in complete silence. I tried to the best of my ability to force myself to remember all the details of the story. It was mid afternoon when we sat down under the shade of some tall bushes, and I retold the full story.

Years before, while I was studying sculpture in a fine arts school in Italy, I had a close friend, a Scotsman who was studying art in order to become an art critic. What stood out most vividly in my mind about him, and had to do with the story I was telling don Juan, was the bombastic idea he had of himself; he thought he was the most licentious, lusty, all-around scholar and craftsman, a man of the Renaissance. Licentious he was, but lustiness was something in complete contradiction to his bony, dry, serious person. He was a vicarious follower of the English philosopher Bertrand Russell and dreamed of applying the principles of logical positivism to art criticism. To be an all-around scholar and craftsman was perhaps his wildest fantasy because he was a procrastinator; work was his nemesis.

His dubious specialty wasn't art criticism, but his personal knowledge of all the prostitutes of the local bordellos, of which there were plenty. The colorful and lengthy accounts he used to give me—in order to keep me, according to him, up to date about all the marvelous things he did in the world of his specialty—were delightful. It was not surprising to me, therefore, that one day he came to my apartment, all excited, nearly out of breath, and told me that something extraordinary had happened to him and that he wanted to share it with me.

"I say, old man, you must see this for yourself!" he said excitedly in the Oxford accent he affected every time he talked to
me. He paced the room nervously. "It's hard to describe, but I
know it's something you will appreciate. Something, the impression of which will last you for a lifetime. I am going to give you a
marvelous gift for life. Do you understand?"

I understood that he was a hysterical Scotsman. It was always
my pleasure to humor him and tag along. I had never regretted
it.

"Calm down, calm down, Eddie," I said. "What are you trying
to tell me?"

He related to me that he had been in a bordello, where he had
found an unbelievable woman who did an incredible thing she
called "figures in front of a mirror." He assured me repeatedly,
almost stuttering, that I owed it to myself to experience this
unbelievable event personally.

"I say, don't worry about money!" he said, since he knew I didn't
have any. "I've already paid the price. All you have to do is go
with me. Madame Ludmilla will show you her 'figures in front of
a mirror.' It's a blast!"

In a fit of uncontrollable glee, Eddie laughed uproariously,
oblivious to his bad teeth, which he normally hid behind a tight-
lipped smile or laugh. "I say, it's absolutely great!"

My curiosity mounted by the minute. I was more than willing
to participate in his new delight. Eddie drove me to the outskirts
of the city. We stopped in front of a dusty, badly kept building;
the paint was peeling off the walls. It had the air of having been
a hotel at one time, a hotel that had been turned into an apartment building. I could see the remnants of a hotel sign that
seemed to have been ripped to pieces. On the front of the building there were rows of dirty single balconies filled with flowerpots or draped with carpets put out to dry.

At the entrance to the building were two dark, shady-looking
men wearing pointed black shoes that seemed too tight on their
feet; they greeted Eddie effusively. They had black, shifty, men-

acing eyes. Both of them were wearing shiny light-blue suits, also too tight for their bulky bodies. One of them opened the door for Eddie. They didn't even look at me.

We went up two flights of stairs on a dilapidated staircase that at one time must have been luxurious. Eddie led the way and walked the length of an empty, hotellike corridor with doors on both sides. All the doors were painted in the same drab, dark, olive green. Every door had a brass number, tarnished with age, barely visible against the painted wood.

Eddie stopped in front of a door. I noticed the number 112 on it. He rapped repeatedly. The door opened, and a round, short woman with bleached-blonde hair beckoned us in without saying a word. She was wearing a red silk robe with feathery, flouncy sleeves and red slippers with furry balls on top. Once we were inside a small hall and she had closed the door behind us, she greeted Eddie in terribly accented English.

"Hallo, Eddie. You brought friend, eh?"

Eddie shook her hand, and then kissed it, gallantly. He acted as if he were most calm, yet I noticed his unconscious gestures of being ill at ease.

"How are you today, Madame Ludmilla?" he said, trying to sound like an American and flubbing it.

I never discovered why Eddie always wanted to sound like an American whenever he was transacting business in those houses of ill repute. I had the suspicion that he did it because Americans were known to be wealthy, and he wanted to establish his rich man's bona fides with them.

Eddie turned to me and said in his phony American accent, "I leave you in good hands, kiddo."

He sounded so awful, so foreign to my ears, that I laughed out loud. Madame Ludmilla didn't seem perturbed at all by my explosion of mirth. Eddie kissed Madame Ludmilla's hand again and left.

"You speak English, my boy?" she shouted as if I were deaf. "You look Eyipcian, or perhaps Torkish."

I assured Madame Ludmilla that I was neither, and that I did speak English. She asked me then if I fancied her "figures in front of a mirror." I didn't know what to say. I just shook my head affirmatively.

"I give you good show," she assured me. "Figures in front of a mirror is only foreplay. When you are hot and ready, tell me to stop."

From the small hall where we were standing we walked into a dark and eerie room. The windows were heavily curtained. There were some low-voltage light bulbs on fixtures attached to the wall. The bulbs were shaped like tubes and protruded straight out at right angles from the wall. There was a profusion of objects around the room: pieces of furniture like small chests of drawers, antique tables and chairs; a roll-top desk set against the wall and crammed with papers, pencils, rulers, and at least a dozen pairs of scissors. Madame Ludmilla made me sit down on an old stuffed chair.

"The bed is in the other room, darling," she said, pointing to the other side of the room. "This is my *antisala*. Here I give show to get you hot and ready."

She dropped her red robe, kicked off her slippers, and opened the double doors of two armoires standing side by side against the wall. Attached to the inside of each door was a full-length mirror.

"And now the music, my boy," Madame Ludmilla said, then cranked a Victrola that appeared to be in mint condition, shiny, like new. She put on a record. The music was a haunting melody that reminded me of a circus march.

"And now my show," she said, and began to twirl around to the accompaniment of the haunting melody. The skin of Madame Ludmilla's body was tight, for the most part, and extraordinarily white, though she was not young. She must have been in her well-lived late forties. Her belly sagged, not a great deal, but a bit, and so did her voluminous breasts. The skin of her face also sagged into noticeable jowls. She had a small nose and heavily painted red lips. She wore thick black mascara. She brought to mind the prototype of an aging prostitute. Yet there was something childlike about her, a girlish abandon and trust, a sweetness that jolted me.

"And now, figures in front of a mirror," Madame Ludmilla announced while the music continued.

"Leg, leg, leg!" she said, kicking one leg up in the air, and then the other, in time with the music. She had her right hand on top of her head, like a little girl who is not sure that she can perform the movements.

"Turn, turn, turn!" she said, turning like a top.

"Butt, butt, butt!" she said then, showing me her bare behind like a cancan dancer.

She repeated the sequence over and over until the music began to fade when the Victrola's spring wound down. I had the feeling that Madame Ludmilla was twirling away into the distance, becoming smaller and smaller as the music faded. Some despair and loneliness that I didn't know existed in me came to the surface, from the depths of my very being, and made me get up and run out of the room, down the stairs like a madman, out of the building, into the street.

Eddie was standing outside the door talking to the two men in light-blue shiny suits. Seeing me running like that, he began to laugh uproariously.

"Wasn't it a blast?" he said, still trying to sound like an American. "'Figures in front of a mirror is only the foreplay.' What a thing! What a thing!"

The first time I had mentioned the story to don Juan, I had told him that I had been deeply affected by the haunting melody and the old prostitute clumsily twirling to the music. And I had been deeply affected also by the realization of how callous my friend was.

When I had finished retelling my story to don Juan, as we sat in the hills of a range of mountains in Sonora I was shaking, mysteriously affected by something quite undefined.

"That story," don Juan said, "should go in your album of memorable events. Your friend, without having any idea of what he was doing, gave you, as he himself said, something that will indeed last you for a lifetime."

"I see this as a sad story, don Juan, but that's all," I declared.

"It's indeed a sad story, just like your other stories," don Juan replied, "but what makes it different and memorable to me is that it touches every one of us human beings, not just you, like your other tales. You see, like Madame Ludmilla, every one of us, young and old alike, is making figures in front of a mirror in one way or another. Tally what you know about people. Think of any human being on this earth, and you will know, without the shadow of a doubt, that no matter who they are, or what they think of themselves, or what they do, the result of their actions is always the same: senseless figures in front of a mirror."

# A Tremor in the Air

# A Journey of Power

AT THE TIME I met don Juan I was a fairly studious anthro-pology student, and I wanted to begin my career as a professional anthropologist by publishing as much as possible. I was bent on climbing the academic ladder, and in my calculations, I had determined that the first step was to collect data on the uses of medicinal plants by the Indians of the southwestern United States.

I first asked a professor of anthropology who had worked in that area for advice about my project. He was a prominent ethnologist who had published extensively in the late thirties and early for-ties on the California Indians and the Indians of the Southwest and Sonora, Mexico. He patiently listened to my exposition. My idea was to write a paper, call it "Ethnobotanical Data," and pub-lish it in a journal that dealt exclusively with anthropological issues of the southwestern United States.

I proposed to collect medicinal plants, take the samples to the Botanical Garden at UCLA to be properly identified, and then describe why and how the Indians of the Southwest used them. I envisioned collecting thousands of entries. I even envisioned publishing a small encyclopedia on the subject.

The professor smiled forgivingly at me. "I don't want to dampen your enthusiasm," he said in a tired voice, "but I can't help commenting negatively on your eagerness. Eagerness is welcome in anthropology, but it must be properly channeled. We are still in the golden age of anthropology. It was my luck to study with Alfred Kröber and Robert Lowie, two pillars of social science. I haven't betrayed their trust. Anthropology is still the master discipline. Every other discipline should stem from anthropology. The entire field of history, for example, should be called 'historical anthropology,' and the field of philosophy should be called 'philosophical anthropology.' Man should be the measure of everything. Therefore, anthropology, the study of man, should be the core of every other discipline. Someday, it will."

I looked at him, bewildered. He was, in my estimation, a totally passive, benevolent old professor who had recently had a heart attack. I seemed to have struck a chord of passion in him.

"Don't you think that you should pay more attention to your formal studies?" he continued. "Rather than doing fieldwork, wouldn't it be better for you to study linguistics? We have in the department here one of the most prominent linguists in the world. If I were you, I'd be sitting at his feet, catching any drift emanating from him.

"We also have a superb authority in comparative religions. And there are some exceptionally competent anthropologists here who have done work on kinship systems in cultures all over the world, from the point of view of linguistics and from the point of view of cognition. You need a lot of preparation. To think that you could do fieldwork now is a travesty. Plunge into your books, young man. That's my advice."

Stubbornly, I took my proposition to another professor, a younger one. He wasn't in any way more helpful. He laughed at me openly. He told me that the paper I wanted to write was a Mickey Mouse paper, and that it wasn't anthropology by any stretch of the imagination.

"Anthropologists nowadays," he said professorially, "are concerned with issues that have relevance. Medical and pharmaceutical scientists have done endless research on every possible medicinal plant in the world. There's no longer any bone to chew on there. Your kind of data collecting belongs to the turn of the nineteenth century. Now it's nearly two hundred years later. There is such a thing as progress, you know."

He proceeded to give me, then, a definition and a justification of progress and perfectibility as two issues of philosophical discourse, which he said were most relevant to anthropology.

"Anthropology is the only discipline in existence," he continued, "which can clearly substantiate the concept of perfectibility and progress. Thank God that there's still a ray of hope in the midst of the cynicism of our times. Only anthropology can show the actual development of culture and social organization. Only anthropologists can prove to mankind beyond the shadow of a doubt the progress of human knowledge. Culture evolves, and only anthropologists can present samples of societies that fit definite cubbyholes in a line of progress and perfectibility. That's anthropology for you! Not some puny fieldwork, which is not fieldwork at all, but mere masturbation."

It was a blow on the head to me. As a last resort, I went to Arizona to talk to anthropologists who were actually doing fieldwork there. By then, I was ready to give up on the whole idea. I understood what the two professors were trying to tell me. I couldn't have agreed with them more. My attempts at doing fieldwork were definitely simpleminded. Yet I wanted to get my feet wet in the field; I didn't want to do only library research.

In Arizona, I met with an extremely seasoned anthropologist who had written copiously on the Yaqui Indians of Arizona as well as those of Sonora, Mexico. He was extremely kind. He didn't run me down, nor did he give me any advice. He only commented that the Indian societies of the Southwest were extremely isolationist, and that foreigners, especially those of Hispanic origin, were distrusted, even abhorred, by those Indians.

A younger colleague of his, however, was more outspoken. He said that I was better off reading herbalists' books. He was an authority in the field and his opinion was that anything to be known about medicinal plants from the Southwest had already been classified and talked about in various publications. He went as far as to say that the sources of any Indian curer of the day were precisely those publications rather than any traditional knowledge. He finished me off with the assertion that if there still were any traditional curing practices, the Indians would not divulge them to a stranger.

"Do something worthwhile," he advised me. "Look into urban anthropology. There's a lot of money for studies on alcoholism among Indians in the big city, for example. Now that's something that any anthropologist can do easily. Go and get drunk with local Indians in a bar. Then arrange whatever you find out about them in terms of statistics. Turn everything into numbers. Urban anthropology is a real field."

There was nothing else for me to do except to take the advice of those experienced social scientists. I decided to fly back to Los Angeles, but another anthropologist friend of mine let me know then that he was going to drive throughout Arizona and New Mexico, visiting all the places where he had done work in the past, renewing in this fashion his relationships with the people who had been his anthropological informants.

"You're welcome to come with me," he said. "I'm not going to do any work. I'm just going to visit with them, have a few drinks with them, bullshit with them. I bought gifts for them—blankets, booze, jackets, ammunition for twenty-two-caliber rifles. My car is loaded with goodies. I usually drive alone whenever I go to see them, but by myself I always run the risk of falling asleep. You could keep me company, keep me from dozing off, or drive a little bit if I'm too drunk."

I felt so despondent that I turned him down.

"I'm very sorry, Bill," I said. "The trip won't do for me. I see no point in pursuing this idea of fieldwork any longer."

"Don't give up without a fight," Bill said in a tone of paternal concern. "Give all you have to the fight, and if it licks you, then it's okay to give up, but not before. Come with me and see how you like the Southwest."

He put his arm around my shoulders. I couldn't help noticing how immensely heavy his arm was. He was tall and husky, but in recent years his body had acquired a strange rigidity. He had lost his boyish quality. His round face was no longer filled, youthful, the way it had been. Now it was a worried face. I believed that he worried because he was losing his hair, but at times it seemed to me that it was something more than that. And it wasn't that he was fatter; his body was heavy in ways that were impossible to explain. I noticed it in the way that he walked, and got up, and sat down. Bill seemed to me to be fighting gravity with every fiber of his being, in everything he did.

Disregarding my feelings of defeat, I started on a journey with him. We visited every place in Arizona and New Mexico where there were Indians. One of the end results of this trip was that I found out that my anthropologist friend had two definite facets to his person. He explained to me that his opinions as a professional anthropologist were very measured, and congruous with the anthropological thought of the day, but that as a private person, his anthropological fieldwork had given him a wealth of experiences that he never talked about. These experiences were not congruous with the anthropological thought of the day because they were events that were impossible to catalog.

During the course of our trip, he would invariably have some drinks with his ex-informants, and feel very relaxed afterward. I would take the wheel then and drive as he sat in the passenger seat taking sips from his bottle of thirty-year-old Ballantine's. It was then that Bill would talk about his uncataloged experiences.

"I have never believed in ghosts," he said abruptly one day. "I never went in for apparitions and floating essences, voices in the dark, you know. I had a very pragmatic, serious upbringing. Science had always been my compass. But then, working in the field, all kinds of weird crap began to filter through to me. For instance, I went with some Indians one night on a vision quest. They were going to actually initiate me by some painful business of piercing the muscles of my chest. They were preparing a sweat lodge in the woods. I had resigned myself to withstand the pain. I took a couple of drinks to give me strength. And then the man who was going to intercede for me with the people who actually performed the ceremony yelled in horror and pointed at a dark, shadowy figure walking toward us.

"When the shadowy figure came closer to me," Bill went on, "I noticed that what I had in front of me was an old Indian dressed in the weirdest getup you could imagine. He had the paraphernalia of shamans. The man I was with that night fainted shamelessly at the sight of the old man. The old man came to me and pointed a finger at my chest. His finger was just skin and bone. He babbled incomprehensible things to me. By then, the rest of the people had seen the old man, and started to rush silently toward me. The old man turned to look at them, and every one of them froze. He harangued them for a moment. His voice was something unforgettable. It was as if he were talking from a tube, or as if he had something attached to his mouth that carried the words out of him. I swear to you that I saw the man talking inside his body, and his mouth broadcasting the words as a mechanical apparatus. After haranguing the men, the old man continued walking, past me, past them, and disappeared, swallowed by the darkness."

Bill said that the plan to have an initiation ceremony went to pot; it was never performed; and the men, including the shamans in charge, were shaking in their boots. He stated that they were so frightened that they disbanded and left.

"People who had been friends for years," he went on, "never spoke to each other again. They claimed that what they had seen was the apparition of an incredibly old shaman, and that it would bring bad luck to talk about it among themselves. In fact, they said that the mere act of setting eyes on one another would bring them bad luck. Most of them moved away from the area."

"Why did they feel that talking to each other or seeing each other would bring them bad luck?" I asked him.

"Those are their beliefs," he replied. "A vision of that nature means to them that the apparition spoke to each of them individually. To have a vision of that nature is, for them, the luck of a lifetime."

"And what was the individual thing that the vision told each of them?" I asked.

"Beats me," he replied. "They never explained anything to me. Every time I asked them, they entered into a profound state of numbness. They hadn't seen anything, they hadn't heard anything. Years after the event, the man who had fainted next to me swore to me that he had just faked the faint because he was so frightened that he didn't want to face the old man, and that what he had to say was understood by everybody at a level other than language comprehension."

Bill said that in his case, what the apparition voiced to him he understood as having to do with his health and his expectations in life.

"What do you mean by that?" I asked him.

"Things are not that good for me," he confessed. "My body doesn't feel well."

"But do you know what is really the matter with you?" I asked.

"Oh, yes," he said nonchalantly. "Doctors have told me. But I'm not gonna worry about it, or even think about it."

Bill's revelations left me feeling thoroughly uneasy. This was a facet of his person that I didn't know. I had always thought that he was a tough old cookie. I could never conceive of him as vulnerable. I didn't like our exchange. It was, however, too late for me to retreat. Our trip continued.

On another occasion, he confided that the shamans of the Southwest were capable of transforming themselves into different entities, and that the categorization schemes of "bear shaman" or "mountain lion shaman," etc., should not be taken as euphemisms or metaphors because they were not.

"Would you believe it," he said in a tone of great admiration, "that there are some shamans who actually become bears, or mountain lions, or eagles? I'm not exaggerating, nor am I fabricating anything when I say that once I witnessed the transformation of a shaman who called himself 'River Man,' or 'River Shaman,' or 'Proceeding from River, Returning to River.' I was out in the mountains of New Mexico with this shaman. I was driving for him; he trusted me, and he was going in search of his origin, or so he said. We were walking along a river when he suddenly got very excited. He told me to move away from the shore to some high rocks, and hide there, put a blanket over my head and shoulders, and peek through it so I would not miss what he was about to do."

"What was he going to do?" I asked him, incapable of containing myself.

"I didn't know," he said. "Your guess would have been as good as mine. I had no way of conceiving of what he was going to do. He just walked into the water, fully dressed. When the water reached him at mid-calf, because it was a wide but shallow river, the shaman simply vanished, disappeared. Prior to entering the water, he had whispered in my ear that I should go downstream and wait for him. He told me the exact spot to wait. I, of course, didn't believe a word of what he was saying, so at first I couldn't remember where he had said I had to wait for him, but then I found the spot and I saw the shaman coming out of the water. It sounds stupid to say 'coming out of the water.' I saw the shaman turning into water and then being remade out of the water. Can you believe that?"

I had no comments on his stories. It was impossible for me to believe him, but I could not disbelieve him either. He was a very serious man. The only possible explanation that I could think of was that as we continued our trip he drank more and more every day. He had in the trunk of the car a box of twenty-four bottles of Scotch for only himself. He actually drank like a fish.

"I have always been partial to the esoteric mutations of

shamans," he said to me another day. "It's not that I can explain the mutations, or even believe that they take place, but as an intellectual exercise I am very interested in considering that mutations into snakes and mountain lions are not as difficult as what the water shaman did. It is at moments like this, when I engage my intellect in such a fashion, that I cease to be an anthropologist and I begin to react, following a gut feeling. My gut feeling is that those shamans certainly do something that can't be measured scientifically or even talked about intelligently.

"For instance, there are cloud shamans who turn into clouds, into mist. I have never seen this happen, but I knew a cloud shaman. I never saw him disappearing or turning into mist in front of my eyes as I saw that other shaman turning into water right in front of me. But I chased that cloud shaman once, and he simply vanished in an area where there was no place for him to hide. Although I didn't see him turning into a cloud, he disappeared. I couldn't explain where he went. There were no rocks or vegetation around the place where he ended up. I was there half a minute after he was, but the shaman was gone.

"I chased that man all over the place for information," Bill went on. "He wouldn't give me the time of day. He was very friendly to me, but that was all."

Bill told me endless other stories about strife and political factions among Indians in different Indian reservations, or stories about personal vendettas, animosities, friendships, etc., etc., which did not interest me in the least. On the other hand, his stories about shamans' mutations and apparitions had caused a true emotional upheaval in me. I was at once both fascinated and appalled by them. However, when I tried to think about why I was fascinated or appalled, I couldn't tell. All I could have said was that his stories about shamans hit me at an unknown, visceral level.

Another realization brought by this trip was that I verified for myself that the Indian societies of the Southwest were indeed closed to outsiders. I finally came to accept that I did need a great deal of preparation in the science of anthropology, and that it was more functional to do anthropological fieldwork in an area with which I was familiar or one in which I had an entree.

When the journey ended, Bill drove me to the Greyhound bus depot in Nogales, Arizona, for my return trip to Los Angeles. As we were sitting in the waiting area before the bus came, he consoled me in a paternal manner, reminding me that failures were a matter of course in anthropological fieldwork, and that they meant only the hardening of one's purpose or the coming to maturity of an anthropologist.

Abruptly, he leaned over and pointed with a slight movement of his chin to the other side of the room. "I think that old man sitting on the bench by the corner over there is the man I told you about," he whispered in my ear. "I am not quite sure because I've had him in front of me, face-to-face, only once."

"What man is that? What did you tell me about him?" I asked.

"When we were talking about shamans and shamans' transformations, I told you that I had once met a cloud shaman."

"Yes, yes, I remember that," I said. "Is that man the cloud shaman?"

"No," he said emphatically. "But I think he is a companion or a teacher of the cloud shaman. I saw both of them together in the distance various times, many years ago."

I did remember Bill mentioning, in a very casual manner, but not in relation to the cloud shaman, that he knew about the existence of a mysterious old man who was a retired shaman, an old Indian misanthrope from Yuma who had once been a terrifying sorcerer. The relationship of the old man to the cloud shaman was never voiced by my friend, but obviously it was foremost in Bill's mind, to the point where he believed that he had told me about him.

A strange anxiety suddenly possessed me and made me jump out of my seat. As if I had no volition of my own, I approached the old man and immediately began a long tirade on how much I knew about medicinal plants and shamanism among the

American Indians of the plains and their Siberian ancestors. As a secondary theme, I mentioned to the old man that I knew that he was a shaman. I concluded by assuring him that it would be thoroughly beneficial for him to talk to me at length.

"If nothing else," I said petulantly, "we could swap stories. You tell me yours and I'll tell you mine."

The old man kept his eyes lowered until the last moment. Then he peered at me. "I am Juan Matus," he said, looking me squarely in the eyes.

My tirade shouldn't have ended by any means, but for no reason that I could discern I felt that there was nothing more I could have said. I wanted to tell him my name. He raised his hand to the height of my lips as if to prevent me from saying it.

At that instant, a bus pulled up to the bus stop. The old man muttered that it was the bus he had to take, then he earnestly asked me to look him up so we could talk with more ease and swap stories. There was an ironic smirk on the corner of his mouth when he said that. With an incredible agility for a man his age—I figured he must have been in his eighties—he covered, in a few leaps, the fifty yards between the bench where he was sitting and the door of the bus. As if the bus had stopped just to pick him up, it moved away as soon as he had jumped in and the door had closed.

After the old man left, I went back to the bench where Bill was sitting.

"What did he say, what did he say?" he asked excitedly.

"He told me to look him up and come to his house to visit," I said. "He even said that we could talk there."

"But what did you say to him to get him to invite you to his house?" he demanded.

I told Bill that I had used my best sales pitch, and that I had promised the old man to reveal to him everything I knew, from the point of view of my reading, about medicinal plants.

Bill obviously didn't believe me. He accused me of holding out on him. "I know the people around this area," he said belligerently, "and that old man is a very strange fart. He doesn't talk to anybody, Indians included. Why would he talk to you, a perfect stranger? You're not even cute!"

It was obvious that Bill was annoyed with me. I couldn't figure out why though. I didn't dare ask him for an explanation. He gave me the impression of being a bit jealous. Perhaps he felt that I had succeeded where he had failed. However, my success had been so inadvertent that it didn't mean anything to me. Except for Bill's casual remarks, I didn't have any conception of how difficult it was to approach that old man, and I couldn't have cared less. At the time, I found nothing remarkable in the exchange. It baffled me that Bill was so upset about it.

"Do you know where his house is?" I asked him.

"I haven't the foggiest idea," he answered curtly. "I have heard people from this area say that he doesn't live anywhere, that he just appears here and there unexpectedly, but that's a lot of horse-shit. He probably lives in some shack in Nogales, Mexico."

"Why is he so important?" I asked him. My question made me gather enough courage to add, "You seem to be upset because he talked to me. Why?"

Without any ado, he admitted that he was chagrined because he knew how useless it was to try to talk to that man. "That old man is as rude as anyone can be," he added. "At best, he stares at you without saying a word when you talk to him. At other times, he doesn't even look at you; he treats you as if you didn't exist. The one time I tried to talk to him he brutally turned me down. Do you know what he said to me? He said, 'If I were you, I wouldn't waste my energy opening my mouth. Save it. You need it.' If he weren't such an old fart, I would have punched him in the nose."

I pointed out to Bill that to call him an "old" man was more a figure of speech than an actual description. He didn't really appear to be that old, although he was definitely old. He possessed a tremendous vigor and agility. I felt that Bill would have failed miserably if he had tried to punch him in the nose. That old Indian was powerful. In fact, he was downright scary.

I didn't voice my thoughts. I let Bill go on telling me how disgusted he was at the nastiness of that old man, and how he would have dealt with him had it not been for the fact that the old man was so feeble.

"Who do you think could give me some information about where he might live?" I asked him.

"Perhaps some people in Yuma," he replied, a bit more relaxed. "Maybe the people I introduced you to at the beginning of our trip. You wouldn't lose anything by asking them. Tell them that I sent you to them."

I changed my plans right then and instead of going back to Los Angeles went directly to Yuma, Arizona. I saw the people to whom Bill had introduced me. They didn't know where the old Indian lived, but their comments about him inflamed my curiosity even more. They said that he was not from Yuma, but from Sonora, Mexico, and that in his youth he had been a fearsome sorcerer who did incantations and put spells on people, but that he had mellowed with age, turning into an ascetic hermit. They remarked that although he was a Yaqui Indian, he had once run around with a group of Mexican men who seemed to be extremely knowledgeable about bewitching practices. They all agreed that they hadn't seen those men in the area for ages.

One of the men added that the old man was contemporaneous with his grandfather, but that while his grandfather was senile and bedridden, the sorcerer seemed to be more vigorous than ever. The same man referred me to some people in Hermosillo, the capital of Sonora, who might know the old man and be able to tell me more about him. The prospect of going to Mexico was not at all appealing to me. Sonora was too far away from my area of interest. Besides, I reasoned that I was better off doing urban anthropology after all and I went back to Los Angeles. But before leaving for Los Angeles, I canvassed the area of Yuma, searching for information about the old man. No one knew anything about him.

As the bus drove to Los Angeles, I experienced a unique sensation. On the one hand, I felt totally cured of my obsession with fieldwork or my interest in the old man. On the other hand, I felt a strange nostalgia. It was, truthfully, something I had never felt before. Its newness struck me profoundly. It was a mixture of anxiety and longing, as if I were missing something of tremendous importance. I had the clear sensation as I approached Los Angeles that whatever had been acting on me around Yuma had begun to fade with distance; but its fading only increased my unwarranted longing.

# The Intent of Infinity

"I WANT YOU to think deliberately about every detail of what transpired between you and those two men, Jorge Campos and Lucas Coronado," don Juan said to me, "who are the ones who really delivered you to me, and then tell me all about it."

I found his request very difficult to fulfill, and yet I actually enjoyed remembering everything those two had said to me. He wanted every detail possible, something that forced me to push my memory to its limits.

The story don Juan wanted me to recollect began in the city of Guaymas, in Sonora, Mexico. In Yuma, Arizona, I had been given the names and addresses of some people who, I was told, might be able to shed light on the mystery of the old man I had met in the bus depot. The people I went to see not only didn't know any retired old shaman, they even doubted that such a man had ever existed. They were all filled to the brim, however, with scary stories about Yaqui shamans, and about the belligerent general mood of the Yaqui Indians. They insinuated that perhaps in

Vicam, a railroad-station town between the cities of Guaymas and Ciudad Obregon, I might find someone who could perhaps steer me in the proper direction.

"Is there anyone in particular I could look up?" I asked.

"Your best bet would be to talk to a field inspector of the official government bank," one of the men suggested. "The bank has a lot of field inspectors. They know all the Indians of the area because the bank is the government institution that buys their crops, and every Yaqui is a farmer, the proprietor of a parcel of land that he can call his own as long as he cultivates it."

"Do you know any field inspectors?" I asked.

They looked at each other and smiled apologetically at me. They didn't know any, but strongly recommended that I should approach one of those men on my own and put my case to him.

In Vicam Station, my attempts at making contact with the field inspectors of the government bank were a total disaster. I met three of them, and when I told them what I wanted, every one of them looked at me with utter distrust. They immediately suspected that I was a spy sent there by the Yankees to cause problems that they could not clearly define, but about which they made wild speculations ranging from political agitation to industrial espionage. It was the unsubstantiated belief of everyone around that there were copper deposits in the lands of the Yaqui Indians and that the Yankees coveted them.

After this resounding failure, I retreated to the city of Guaymas and stayed at a hotel that was very close to a fabulous restaurant. I went there three times a day. The food was superb. I liked it so much that I stayed in Guaymas for over a week. I practically lived in the restaurant, and became, in this manner, acquainted with the owner, Mr. Reyes.

One afternoon while I was eating, Mr. Reyes came to my table with another man, whom he introduced to me as Jorge Campos, a full-blooded Yaqui Indian entrepreneur who had lived in Arizona in his youth, who spoke English perfectly, and who was more American than any American. Mr. Reyes praised him as a true example of how hard work and dedication could develop a person into an exceptional man.

Mr. Reyes left and Jorge Campos sat down next to me and immediately took over. He pretended to be modest and denied all praise but it was obvious that he was as pleased as punch with what Mr. Reyes had said about him. At first sight, I had the clear impression that Jorge Campos was an entrepreneur of the particular kind that one finds in bars or on crowded corners of main streets trying to sell an idea or simply trying to find a way to con people out of their savings.

Mr. Campos was very pleasant looking, around six feet tall and lean, but with a high pot belly like a habitual drinker of hard liquor. He had a very dark complexion, with a touch of green to it, and wore expensive blue jeans and shiny cowboy boots with pointed toes and angular heels, as if he needed to dig them into the ground to stop being dragged by a lassoed steer.

He was wearing an impeccably ironed gray plaid shirt; in its right pocket was a plastic pocket guard into which he had inserted a row of pens. I had seen the same pocket guard among office workers who didn't want to stain their shirt pockets with ink. His attire also included an expensive-looking fringed reddish-brown suede jacket and a tall Texas-style cowboy hat. His round face was expressionless. He had no wrinkles even though he seemed to be in his early fifties. For some unknown reason, I believed that he was dangerous.

"Very pleased to meet you, Mr. Campos," I said in Spanish, extending my hand to him.

"Let's dispense with the formalities," he responded, also in Spanish, shaking my hand vigorously. "I like to treat young people as equals, regardless of age differences. Call me Jorge."

He was quiet for a moment, no doubt assessing my reaction. I didn't know what to say. I certainly didn't want to humor him, nor did I want to take him seriously.

"I'm curious to know what you're doing in Guaymas," he went on casually. "You don't seem to be a tourist, nor do you seem to be interested in deep-sea fishing."

"I am an anthropology student," I said, "and I am trying to establish my credentials with the local Indians in order to do some field research."

"And I am a businessman," he said. "My business is to supply information, to be the go-between. You have the need, I have the commodity. I charge for my services. However, my services are guaranteed. If you don't get satisfaction, you don't have to pay me."

"If your business is to supply information," I said, "I will gladly pay you whatever you charge."

"Ah!" he exclaimed. "You certainly need a guide, someone with more education than the average Indian here, to show you around. Do you have a grant from the United States government or from another big institution?"

"Yes," I lied. "I have a grant from the Esoterical Foundation of Los Angeles."

When I said that, I actually saw a glint of greed in his eyes.

"Ah!" he exclaimed again. "How big is that institution?"

"Fairly big," I said.

"My goodness! Is that so?" he said, as if my words were an explanation that he had wanted to hear. "And now, may I ask you, if you don't mind, how big is your grant? How much money did they give you?"

"A few thousand dollars to do preliminary fieldwork," I lied again, to see what he would say.

"Ah! I like people who are direct," he said, relishing his words. "I am sure that you and I are going to reach an agreement. I offer you my services as a guide and as a key that can open many secret doors among the Yaquis. As you can see by my general appearance, I am a man of taste and means."

"Oh, yes, definitely you are a man of good taste," I asserted.

"What I am saying to you," he said, "is that for a small fee, which you will find most reasonable, I will steer you to the right people, people to whom you could ask any question you want. And for some very little more, I will translate their words to you, verbatim, into Spanish or English. I can also speak French and German, but I have the feeling that those languages do not interest you."

"You are right, you are so very right," I said. "Those languages don't interest me at all. But how much would your fees be?"

"Ah! My fees!" he said, and took a leather-covered notebook out of his back pocket and flipped it open in front of my face; he scribbled quick notes on it, flipped it closed again, and put it in his pocket with precision and speed. I was sure that he wanted to give me the impression of being efficient and fast at calculating figures.

"I will charge you fifty dollars a day," he said, "with transportation, plus my meals. I mean, when you eat, I eat. What do you say?"

At that moment, he leaned over to me and, almost in a whisper, said that we should shift into English because he didn't want people to know the nature of our transactions. He began to speak to me then in something that wasn't English at all. I was at a loss. I didn't know how to respond. I began to fret nervously as the man kept on talking gibberish with the most natural air. He didn't bat an eyelash. He moved his hands in a very animated fashion and pointed around him as if he were instructing me. I didn't have the impression that he was speaking in tongues; I thought perhaps he was speaking the Yaqui language.

When people came around our table and looked at us, I nodded and said to Jorge Campos, "Yes, yes, indeed." At one point I said, "You could say that again," and this sounded so funny to me that I broke into a belly laugh. He also laughed heartily, as if I had said the funniest thing possible.

He must have noticed that I was finally at my wits' end, and before I could get up and tell him to get lost, he started to speak Spanish again.

"I don't want to tire you with my silly observations," he said. "But if I'm going to be your guide, as I think I am going to be, we will be spending long hours chatting. I was testing you just now, to see if you are a good conversationalist. If I'm going to spend time with you driving, I need someone by me who could be a good receptor and initiator. I'm glad to tell you that you are both."

Then he stood up, shook my hand, and left. As if on cue, the owner came to my table, smiling and shaking his head from side to side like a little bear.

"Isn't he a fabulous guy?" he asked me.

I didn't want to commit myself to a statement, and Mr. Reyes volunteered that Jorge Campos was at that moment a go-between in an extremely delicate and profitable transaction. He said that some mining companies in the United States were interested in the iron and copper deposits that belonged to the Yaqui Indians, and that Jorge Campos was there, in line to collect perhaps a five-million-dollar fee. I knew then that Jorge Campos was a con man. There were no iron or copper deposits on the lands owned by the Yaqui Indians. If there had been any, private enterprises would have already moved the Yaquis out of those lands and relocated them somewhere else.

"He's fabulous," I said. "Most wonderful guy I ever met. How can I get in touch with him again?"

"Don't worry about that," Mr. Reyes said. "Jorge asked me all about you. He has been watching you since you came. He'll probably come and knock on your door later today or tomorrow."

Mr. Reyes was right. A couple of hours later, somebody woke me from my afternoon nap. It was Jorge Campos. I had intended to leave Guaymas in the early evening and drive, all night, to California. I explained to him that I was leaving, but that I would come back in a month or so.

"Ah! But you must stay now that I have decided to be your guide," he said.

"I'm sorry, but we will have to wait for this because my time is very limited now," I replied.

I knew that Jorge Campos was a crook, yet I decided to reveal to him that I already had an informant who was waiting to work with me, and that I had met him in Arizona. I described the old man and said that his name was Juan Matus, and that other people had characterized him as a shaman. Jorge Campos smiled at me broadly. I asked him if he knew the old man.

"Ah, yes, I know him," he said jovially. "You may say that we are good friends." Without being invited, Jorge Campos came into the room and sat down at the table just inside the balcony.

"Does he live around here?" I asked.

"He certainly does," he assured me.

"Would you take me to him?"

"I don't see why not," he said. "I would need a couple of days to make my own inquiries, just to make sure that he is there, and then we will go and see him."

I knew that he was lying, yet I didn't want to believe it. I even thought that my initial distrust had perhaps been ill-founded. He seemed so convincing at that moment.

"However," he continued, "in order to take you to see the man, I will charge you a flat fee. My honorarium will be two hundred dollars."

That amount was more than I had at my disposal. I politely declined and said that I didn't have enough money with me.

"I don't want to appear mercenary," he said with his most winning smile, "but how much money can you afford? You must take into consideration that I have to do a little bribing. The Yaqui Indians are very private, but there are always ways; there are always doors that open with a magical key—money."

In spite of all my misgivings, I was convinced that Jorge Campos was my entry not only into the Yaqui world but to finding the old man who had intrigued me so much. I didn't want to haggle over money. I was almost embarrassed to offer him the fifty dollars I had in my pocket.

"I am at the end of my stay here," I said as a sort of apology, "so I have nearly run out of money. I have only fifty dollars left."

Jorge Campos stretched his long legs under the table and crossed his arms behind his head, tipping his hat over his face.

"I'll take your fifty dollars and your watch," he said shamelessly. "But for that money, I will take you to meet a minor shaman. Don't get impatient," he warned me, as if I were going to protest. "We must step carefully up the ladder, from the lower ranks to the man himself, who I assure you is at the very top."

"And when could I meet this minor shaman?" I asked, handing him the money and my watch.

"Right now!" he replied as he sat up straight and eagerly grabbed the money and the watch. "Let's go! There's not a minute to waste!"

We got into my car and he directed me to head off for the town of Potam, one of the traditional Yaqui towns along the Yaqui River. As we drove, he revealed to me that we were going to meet Lucas Coronado, a man who was known for his sorcery feats, his shamanistic trances, and for the magnificent masks that he made for the Yaqui festivities of Lent.

Then he shifted the conversation to the old man, and what he said was in total contradiction to what others had said to me about the man. While they had described him as a hermit and retired shaman, Jorge Campos portrayed him as the most prominent curer and sorcerer of the area, a man whose fame had turned him into a nearly inaccessible figure. He paused, like an actor, and then he delivered his blow: He said that to talk to the old man on a steady basis, the way anthropologists like to do, was going to cost me at least two thousand dollars.

I was going to protest such a drastic hike in price, but he anticipated me.

"For two hundred dollars, I could take you to him," he said. "Out of those two hundred dollars, I would clear about thirty. The rest would go for bribes. But to talk to him at length will cost more. You yourself could figure that out. He has actual body-guards, people who protect him. I have to sweet-talk them and come up with dough for them.

"In the end," he continued, "I will give you a total account with receipts and everything for your taxes. Then you will know that my commission for setting it all up is minimal."

I felt a wave of admiration for him. He was aware of everything, even receipts for income tax. He was quiet for a while, as if calculating his minimal profit. I had nothing to say. I was busy calculating myself, trying to figure out a way to get two thousand dollars. I even thought of really applying for a grant.

"But are you sure the old man would talk to me?" I asked.

"Of course," he assured me. "Not only would he talk to you, he's going to perform sorcery for you, for what you pay him. Then you could work out an agreement with him as to how much you could pay him for further lessons."

Jorge Campos kept silent again for a while, peering into my eyes.

"Do you think that you could pay me the two thousand dollars?" he asked in a tone so purposefully indifferent that I instantly knew it was a sham.

"Oh, yes, I can easily afford that," I lied reassuringly.

He could not disguise his glee.

"Good boy! Good boy!" he cheered. "We're going to have a ball!"

I tried to ask him some general questions about the old man; he forcefully cut me off. "Save all this for the man himself. He'll be all yours," he said, smiling.

He began to tell me then about his life in the United States and about his business aspirations, and to my utter bewilderment, since I had already classified him as a phony who didn't speak a word of English, he shifted into English.

"You *do* speak English!" I exclaimed without any attempt at hiding my surprise.

"Of course I do, my boy," he said, affecting a Texan accent, which he carried on for the duration of our conversation. "I told you, I wanted to test you, to see if you are resourceful. You are. In fact, you are quite clever, I may say."

His command of English was superb, and he delighted me with jokes and stories. In no time at all, we were in Potam. He directed me to a house on the outskirts of town. We got out of the car. He led the way, calling loudly in Spanish for Lucas Coronado.

We heard a voice from the back of the house that said, also in Spanish, "Come over here."

There was a man behind a small shack, sitting on the ground, on a goatskin. He was holding a piece of wood with his bare feet while he worked on it with a chisel and a mallet. By holding the piece of wood in place with the pressure of his feet, he had fashioned a stupendous potter's turning wheel, so to speak. His feet turned the piece as his hands worked the chisel. I had never seen anything like this in my life. He was making a mask, hollowing it with a curved chisel. His control of his feet in holding the wood and turning it around was remarkable.

The man was very thin; he had a thin face with angular features, high cheekbones, and a dark, copperish complexion. The skin of his face and neck seemed to be stretched to the maximum. He sported a thin, droopy mustache that gave his angular face a malevolent slant. He had an aquiline nose with a very thin bridge, and fierce black eyes. His extremely black eyebrows appeared as if they had been drawn on with a pencil, and so did his jet black hair, combed backward on his head. I had never seen a more hostile face. The image that came to mind looking at him was that of an Italian poisoner of the era of the Medicis. The words "truculent" and "saturnine" seemed to be the most apt descriptions when I focused my attention on Lucas Coronado's face.

I noticed that while he was sitting on the ground, holding the piece of wood with his feet, the bones of his legs were so long that his knees came to his shoulders. When we approached him, he stopped working and stood up. He was taller than Jorge Campos, and as thin as a rail. As a gesture of deference to us, I suppose, he put on his *guaraches*.

"Come in, come in," he said without smiling.

I had a strange feeling then that Lucas Coronado didn't know how to smile.

"To what do I owe the pleasure of this visit?" he asked Jorge Campos.

"I've brought this young man here because he wants to ask you some questions about your art," Jorge Campos said in a most patronizing tone. "I vouched that you would answer his questions truthfully."

"Oh, that's no problem, that's no problem," Lucas Coronado assured me, sizing me up with his cold stare.

He shifted into a different language then, which I presumed to be Yaqui. He and Jorge Campos got into an animated conversation that lasted for some time. Both of them acted as if I did not exist. Then Jorge Campos turned to me.

"We have a little problem here," he said. "Lucas has just informed me that this is a very busy season for him, since the festivities are approaching, so he won't be able to answer all the questions that you ask him, but he will at another time."

"Yes, yes, most certainly," Lucas Coronado said to me in Spanish. "At another time, indeed; at another time."

"We have to cut our visit short," Jorge Campos said, "but I'll bring you back again."

As we were leaving, I felt moved to express to Lucas Coronado my admiration for his stupendous technique of working with his hands and feet. He looked at me as if I were mad, his eyes widening with surprise.

"You've never seen anyone working on a mask?" he hissed through clenched teeth. "Where are you from? Mars?"

I felt stupid. I tried to explain that his technique was quite new to me. He seemed ready to hit me on the head. Jorge Campos said to me in English that I had offended Lucas Coronado with my comments. He had understood my praise as a veiled way of making fun of his poverty; my words had been to him an ironic statement of how poor and helpless he was.

"But it's the opposite," I said. "I think he's magnificent!"

"Don't try to tell him anything like that," Jorge Campos retorted. "These people are trained to receive and dispense insults in a most covert form. He thinks it's odd that you run him down when you don't even know him, and make fun of the fact that he cannot afford a vise to hold his sculpture."

I felt totally at a loss. The last thing I wanted was to foul up my only possible contact. Jorge Campos seemed to be utterly aware of my chagrin.

"Buy one of his masks," he advised me.

I told him that I intended to drive to Los Angeles in one lap, without stopping, and that I had just sufficient money to buy gasoline and food.

"Well, give him your leather jacket," he said matter-of-factly but in a confidential, helpful tone. "Otherwise, you're going to anger him, and all he'll remember about you will be your insults. But don't tell him that his masks are beautiful. Just buy one."

When I told Lucas Coronado that I wanted to trade my leather jacket for one of his masks, he grinned with satisfaction. He took the jacket and put it on. He walked to his house, but before he entered, he did some strange gyrations. He knelt in front of some sort of religious altar and moved his arms, as if to stretch them, and rubbed his hands on the sides of the jacket.

He went inside the house and brought out a bundle wrapped in newspapers, which he handed to me. I wanted to ask him some questions. He excused himself, saying that he had to work, but added that if I wanted I could come back at another time.

On the way back to the city of Guaymas, Jorge Campos asked me to open the bundle. He wanted to make sure that Lucas Coronado had not cheated me. I didn't care to open the bundle; my only concern was the possibility that I could come back by myself to talk to Lucas Coronado. I was elated.

"I must see what you have," Jorge Campos insisted. "Stop the car, please. Not under any conditions or for any reasons whatsoever would I endanger my clients. You paid me to render some services to you. That man is a genuine shaman, therefore very dangerous. Because you have offended him, he may have given you a witchcraft bundle. If that's the case, we have to bury it quickly in this area."

I felt a wave of nausea and stopped the car. With extreme care, I took out the bundle. Jorge Campos snatched it out of my hands and opened it. It contained three beautifully made traditional Yaqui masks. Jorge Campos mentioned, in a casual, disinterested tone, that it would be only proper that I give him one of them. I reasoned that since he had not yet taken me to see the old man, I had to preserve my connection with him. I gladly gave him one of the masks.

"If you allow me to choose, I would rather take that one," he said, pointing.

I told him to go ahead. The masks didn't mean anything to me; I had gotten what I was after. I would have given him the other two masks as well, but I wanted to show them to my anthropologist friends.

"These masks are nothing extraordinary," Jorge Campos declared. "You can buy them in any store in town. They sell them to tourists there."

I had seen the Yaqui masks that were sold in the stores in town. They were very rude masks in comparison to the ones I had, and Jorge Campos had indeed picked out the best.

I left him in the city and headed for Los Angeles. Before I said good-bye, he reminded me that I practically owed him two thousand dollars because he was going to start his bribing and working toward taking me to meet the big man.

"Do you think that you could give me my two thousand dollars the next time you come?" he asked daringly.

His question put me in a terrible position. I believed that to tell him the truth, that I doubted it, would have made him drop me. I was convinced then that in spite of his patent greed, he was my usher.

"I will do my best to have the money," I said in a noncommittal tone.

"You gotta do better than that, boy," he retorted forcefully, almost angrily. "I'm going to spend money on my own, setting up this meeting, and I must have some reassurance on your part. I know that you are a very serious young man. How much is your car worth? Do you have the pink slip?"

I told him what my car was worth, and that I did have the pink slip, but he seemed satisfied only when I gave him my word that I would bring him the money in cash on my next visit.

Five months later, I went back to Guaymas to see Jorge Campos. Two thousand dollars at that time was a considerable amount of money, especially for a student. I thought that if perhaps he were willing to take partial payments, I would be more than happy to commit myself to pay that amount in installments.

I couldn't find Jorge Campos anywhere in Guaymas. I asked the owner of the restaurant. He was as baffled as I was about his disappearance.

"He has just vanished," he said. "I'm sure he went back to Arizona, or to Texas, where he has business."

I took a chance and went to see Lucas Coronado by myself. I arrived at his house at midday. I couldn't find him either. I asked his neighbors if they knew where he might be. They looked at me belligerently and didn't dignify me with an answer. I left, but went by his house again in the late afternoon. I didn't expect anything at all. In fact, I was prepared to leave for Los Angeles immediately. To my surprise, Lucas Coronado was not only there but was extremely friendly to me. He frankly expressed his approval on seeing that I had come without Jorge Campos, who he said was an outright pain in the ass. He complained that Jorge Campos, to whom he referred as a renegade Yaqui Indian, took delight in exploiting his fellow Yaquis.

I gave Lucas Coronado some gifts that I had brought him and bought from him three masks, an exquisitely carved staff, and a pair of rattling leggings made out of the cocoons of some insects from the desert, leggings which the Yaquis used in their traditional dances. Then I took him to Guaymas for dinner.

I saw him every day for the five days that I remained in the area, and he gave me endless amounts of information about the

Yaquis—their history and social organization, and the meaning and nature of their festivities. I was having such fun as a field-worker that I even felt reluctant to ask him if he knew anything about the old shaman. Overcoming second thoughts, I finally asked Lucas Coronado if he knew the old man whom Jorge Campos had assured me was such a prominent shaman. Lucas Coronado seemed perplexed. He assured me that to his knowledge, no such man had ever existed in that part of the country and that Jorge Campos was a crook who only wanted to cheat me out of my money.

Hearing Lucas Coronado deny the existence of that old man had a terrible, unexpected impact on me. In one instant, it became evident to me that I really didn't give a damn about field-work. I only cared about finding that old man. I knew then that meeting the old shaman had indeed been the culmination of something that had nothing to do with my desires, aspirations, or even thoughts as an anthropologist.

I wondered more than ever who in the hell that old man was. Without any inhibitory checks, I began to rant and yell in frustration. I stomped on the floor. Lucas Coronado was quite taken aback by my display. He looked at me, bewildered, and then started to laugh. I had no idea that he could laugh. I apologized to him for my outburst of anger and frustration. I couldn't explain why I was so out of sorts. Lucas Coronado seemed to understand my quandary.

"Things like that happen in this area," he said.

I had no idea to what he was referring, nor did I want to ask him. I was deadly afraid of the easiness with which he took offense. A peculiarity of the Yaquis was the facility they had to feel offended. They seemed to be perennially on their toes, looking out for insults that were too subtle to be noticed by anyone else.

"There are magical beings living in the mountains around here," he continued, "and they can act on people. They make people go veritably mad. People rant and rave under their influence, and when they finally calm down, exhausted, they don't have any clue as to why they exploded."

"Do you think that's what happened to me?" I asked.

"Definitely," he replied with total conviction. "You already have a predisposition to going bonkers at the drop of a hat, but you are also very contained. Today, you weren't contained. You went bananas over nothing."

"It isn't over nothing," I assured him. "I didn't know it until now, but to me that old man is the driving force of all my efforts."

Lucas Coronado kept quiet, as if in deep thought. Then he began to pace up and down.

"Do you know any old man who lives around here but is not quite from this area?" I asked him.

He didn't understand my question. I had to explain to him that the old Indian I had met was perhaps like Jorge Campos, a Yaqui who had lived somewhere else. Lucas Coronado explained that the surname "Matus" was quite common in that area, but that he didn't know any Matus whose first name was Juan. He seemed despondent. Then he had a moment of insight and stated that because the man was old, he might have another name, and that perhaps he had given me a working name, not his real one.

"The only old man I know," he went on, "is Ignacio Flores's father. He comes to see his son from time to time, but he comes from Mexico City. Come to think of it, he's Ignacio's father, but he doesn't seem that old. But he's old. Ignacio's old, too. His father seems younger, though."

He laughed heartily at his realization. Apparently, he had never thought about the youth of the old man until that moment. He kept on shaking his head, as if in disbelief. I, on the other hand, was elated beyond measure.

"That's the man!" I yelled without knowing why.

Lucas Coronado didn't know where Ignacio Flores actually lived, but he was very accommodating and directed me to drive to a nearby Yaqui town, where he found the man for me.

Ignacio Flores was a big, corpulent man, perhaps in his mid-sixties. Lucas Coronado had warned me that the big man had been a career soldier in his youth, and that he still had the bearing of a military man. Ignacio Flores had an enormous mustache; that and the fierceness of his eyes made him for me the personification of a ferocious soldier. He had a dark complexion. His hair was still jet black in spite of his years. His forceful, gravelly voice seemed to be trained solely to give commands. I had the impression that he had been a cavalry man. He walked as if he were still wearing spurs, and for some strange reason, impossible to fathom, I heard the sound of spurs when he walked.

Lucas Coronado introduced me to him and said that I had come from Arizona to see his father, whom I had met in Nogales. Ignacio Flores didn't seem surprised at all.

"Oh yes," he said. "My father travels a great deal." Without any other preliminaries, he directed us to where we could find his father. He didn't come with us, I thought out of politeness. He excused himself and marched away, as if he were keeping step in a parade.

I prepared myself to go to the old man's house with Lucas Coronado. Instead, he politely declined; he wanted me to drive him back to his house.

"I think you found the man you were looking for, and I feel that you should be alone," he said.

I marveled at how extraordinarily polite these Yaqui Indians were, and yet, at the same time, so fierce. I had been told that the Yaquis were savages who had no qualms about killing anyone; as far as I was concerned, though, their most remarkable feature was their politeness and consideration.

I drove to the house of Ignacio Flores's father, and there I found the man I was looking for.

"I wonder why Jorge Campos lied and told me that he knew you," I said at the end of my account.

"He didn't lie to you," don Juan said with the conviction of someone who was condoning Jorge Campos's behavior. "He didn't even misrepresent himself. He thought you were an easy mark and was going to cheat you. He couldn't carry out his plan, though, because *infinity* overpowered him. Do you know that he disappeared soon after he met you, never to be found?

"Jorge Campos was a most meaningful personage for you," he continued. "You will find, in whatever transpired between the two of you, a sort of guiding blueprint, because he is the representation of your life."

"Why? I'm not a crook!" I protested.

He laughed, as if he knew something that I didn't. The next thing I knew, I found myself in the midst of an extensive explanation of my actions, my ideals, my expectations. However, a strange thought urged me to consider with the same fervor with which I was explaining myself that under certain circumstances, I might be like Jorge Campos. I found the thought inadmissible, and I used all my available energy to try to disprove it. However, down in the depths of myself, I didn't care to apologize if I were like Jorge Campos.

When I voiced my dilemma, don Juan laughed so hard that he choked, many times.

"If I were you," he commented, "I'd listen to my inner voice. What difference would it make if you were like Jorge Campos: a crook! He was a cheap crook. You are more elaborate. This is the power of the recounting. This is why sorcerers use it. It puts you into contact with something that you didn't even suspect existed in you."

I wanted to leave right then. Don Juan knew exactly how I felt.

"Don't listen to the superficial voice that makes you angry," he said commandingly. "Listen to that deeper voice that is going to guide you from now on, the voice that is laughing. Listen to it! And laugh with it. Laugh! Laugh!"

His words were like a hypnotic command to me. Against my will, I began to laugh. Never had I been so happy. I felt free, unmasked.

"Recount to yourself the story of Jorge Campos, over and over," don Juan said. "You will find endless wealth in it. Every detail is part of a map. It is the nature of *infinity*, once we cross a certain threshold, to put a blueprint in front of us."

He peered at me for a long time. He didn't merely glance as before, but he gazed intently at me. "One deed which Jorge Campos couldn't avoid performing," he finally said, "was to put you in contact with the other man: Lucas Coronado, who is as meaningful to you as Jorge Campos himself, maybe even more so."

In the course of recounting the story of those two men, I had realized that I had spent more time with Lucas Coronado than with Jorge Campos; however, our exchanges had not been as intense, and were marked by enormous lagoons of silence. Lucas Coronado was not by nature a talkative man, and by some strange twist, whenever he was silent he managed to drag me with him into that state.

"Lucas Coronado is the other part of your map," don Juan said. "Don't you find it strange that he is a sculptor, like yourself, a super-sensitive artist who was, like yourself at one time, in search of a sponsor for his art? He looked for a sponsor just like you looked for a woman, a lover of the arts, who would sponsor your creativity."

I entered into another terrifying struggle. This time my struggle was between my absolute certainty that I had not mentioned this aspect of my life to him, the fact that all of it was true, and the fact that I was unable to find an explanation for how he could have obtained this information. Again, I wanted to leave right away. But once more, the impulse was overpowered by a voice that came from a deep place. Without any coaxing, I began to laugh heartily. Some part of me, at a profound level, didn't give a hoot about finding out how don Juan had gotten that information. The fact that he had it, and had displayed it in such a delicate but conniving manner, was a delightful maneuver to witness. It was of no consequence that the superficial part of me got angry and wanted to leave.

"Very good," don Juan said to me, patting me forcefully on the back, "very good."

He was pensive for a moment, as if he were perhaps seeing things invisible to the average eye.

"Jorge Campos and Lucas Coronado are the two ends of an axis," he said. "That axis is you, at one end a ruthless, shameless, crass mercenary who takes care of himself; hideous, but indestructible. At the other end a super-sensitive, tormented artist, weak and vulnerable. That should have been the map of your life, were it not for the appearance of another possibility, the one that opened up when you crossed the threshold of *infinity*. You searched for me, and you found me; and so, you did cross the threshold. The *intent of infinity* told me to look for someone like you. I found you, thus crossing the threshold myself."

The conversation ended at that point. Don Juan went into one of his habitual long periods of total silence. It was only at the end of the day, when we had returned to his house and while we were sitting under his ramada, cooling off from the long hike we had taken, that he broke his silence.

"In your recounting of what happened between you and Jorge Campos, and you and Lucas Coronado," don Juan went on, "I found, and I hope you did, too, a very disturbing factor. For me, it's an omen. It points to the end of an era, meaning that whatever was standing there cannot remain. Very flimsy elements brought you to me. None of them could stand on their own. This is what I drew from your recounting."

I remembered that don Juan had revealed to me one day that Lucas Coronado was terminally ill. He had some health condition that was slowly consuming him.

"I have sent word to him through my son Ignacio about what he should do to cure himself," don Juan went on, "but he thinks it's nonsense and doesn't want to hear it. It isn't Lucas's fault. The entire human race doesn't want to hear anything. They hear only what they want to hear."

I remembered that I had prevailed upon don Juan to tell me

what I could say to Lucas Coronado to help him alleviate his physical pain and mental anguish. Don Juan not only told me what to tell him, but asserted that if Lucas Coronado wanted to, he could easily cure himself. Nevertheless, when I delivered don Juan's message, Lucas Coronado looked at me as if I had lost my mind. Then he shifted into a brilliant, and, had I been a Yaqui, deeply insulting, portrayal of a man who is bored to death by someone's unwarranted insistence. I thought that only a Yaqui Indian could be so subtle.

"Those things don't help me," he finally said defiantly, angered by my lack of sensibility. "It doesn't really matter. We all have to die. But don't you dare believe that I have lost hope. I'm going to get some money from the government bank. I'll get an advance on my crops, and then I'll get enough money to buy something that will cure me, ipso facto. It's name is Vi-ta-mi-nol."

"What is Vitaminol?" I had asked.

"It's something that's advertised on the radio," he said with the innocence of a child. "It cures everything. It's recommended for people who don't eat meat or fish or fowl every day. It's recommended for people like myself who can barely keep body and soul together."

In my eagerness to help Lucas Coronado, I committed right then the biggest blunder imaginable in a society of such hypersensitive beings as the Yaquis: I offered to give him the money to buy Vitaminol. His cold stare was the measure of how deeply I had hurt him. My stupidity was unforgivable. Very softly, Lucas Coronado said that he was capable of affording Vitaminol himself.

I went back to don Juan's house. I felt like weeping. My eagerness had betrayed me.

"Don't waste your energy worrying about things like that," don Juan said coldly. "Lucas Coronado is locked in a vicious cycle, but so are you. So is everyone. He has Vitaminol, which he trusts will cure everything, and resolve every one of his problems. At the moment, he can't afford it, but he has great hopes that he eventually will be able to."

Don Juan peered at me with his piercing eyes. "I told you that Lucas Coronado's acts are the map of your life," he said. "Believe you me, they are. Lucas Coronado pointed out Vitaminol to you, and he did it so powerfully and painfully that he hurt you and made you weep."

Don Juan stopped talking then. It was a long and most effective pause. "And don't tell me that you don't understand what I mean," he said. "One way or another, we all have our own version of Vitaminol."

# Who Was Juan Matus, Really?

THE PART OF my account of meeting don Juan that he didn't want to hear about was my feelings and impressions on that fateful day when I walked into his house: the contradictory clash between my expectations and the reality of the situation, and the effect that was caused in me by a cluster of the most extravagant ideas I had ever heard.

"That is more in the line of confession than in the line of events," he had said to me once when I tried to tell him about all this.

"You couldn't be more wrong, don Juan," I began, but I stopped. Something in the way he looked at me made me realize that he was right. Whatever I was going to say could have sounded only like lip service, flattery. What had taken place on our first real meeting, however, was of transcendental importance to me, an event of ultimate consequence.

During my first encounter with don Juan, in the bus depot in

Nogales, Arizona, something of an unusual nature had happened to me, but it had come to me cushioned in my concerns with the presentation of the self. I had wanted to impress don Juan, and in attempting to do so I had focused all my attention on the act of selling my wares, so to speak. It was only months later that a strange residue of forgotten events began to appear.

One day, out of nowhere, and with no coaxing or coaching on my part, I recollected with extraordinary clarity something that had completely bypassed me during my actual encounter with don Juan. When he had stopped me from telling him my name, he had peered into my eyes and had numbed me with his look. There was infinitely more that I could have said to him about myself. I could have expounded on my knowledge and worth for hours if his look hadn't completely cut me off.

In light of this new realization, I reconsidered everything that had happened to me on that occasion. My unavoidable conclusion was that I had experienced the interruption of some mysterious flow that kept me going, a flow that had never been interrupted before, at least not in the manner in which don Juan had done it. When I tried to describe to any of my friends what I had physically experienced, a strange perspiration began to cover my entire body, the same perspiration that I had experienced when don Juan had given me that look; I had been, at that moment, not only incapable of voicing a single word, but incapable of having a single thought.

For some time after, I dwelled on the physical sensation of this interruption, for which I found no rational explanation. I argued for a while that don Juan must have hypnotized me, but then my memory told me that he hadn't given any hypnotic commands, nor had he made any movements that could have trapped my attention. In fact, he had merely glanced at me. It was the intensity of that glance that had made it appear as if he had stared at me for a long time. It had obsessed me, and had rendered me discombobulated at a deep physical level.

When I finally had don Juan in front of me again, the first

thing I noticed about him was that he didn't look at all as I had imagined him during all the time I had tried to find him. I had fabricated an image of the man I had met at the bus depot, which I perfected every day by allegedly remembering more details. In my mind, he was an old man, still very strong and nimble, yet almost frail. The man facing me was muscular and decisive. He moved with agility, but not nimbleness. His steps were firm and, at the same time, light. He exuded vitality and purpose. My composite memory was not at all in harmony with the real thing. I thought he had short, white hair and an extremely dark complexion. His hair was longer, and not as white as I had imagined. His complexion was not that dark either. I could have sworn that his features were birdlike, because of his age. But that was not so either. His face was full, almost round. In one glance, the most outstanding feature of the man looking at me was his dark eyes, which shone with a peculiar, dancing glow.

Something that had bypassed me completely in my prior assessment of him was the fact that his total countenance was that of an athlete. His shoulders were broad, his stomach flat; he seemed to be planted firmly on the ground. There was no feebleness to his knees, no tremor in his upper limbs. I had imagined detecting a slight tremor in his head and arms, as if he were nervous and unsteady. I had also imagined him to be about five feet six inches tall, three inches shorter than his actual height.

Don Juan didn't seem surprised to see me. I wanted to tell him how difficult it had been for me to find him. I would have liked to be congratulated by him on my titanic efforts, but he just laughed at me, teasingly.

"Your efforts are not important," he said. "What's important is that you found my place. Sit down, sit down," he said, enticing me, pointing to one of the freight boxes under his ramada and patting me on my back; but it wasn't a friendly pat.

It felt like he had slapped me on the back although he never actually touched me. His quasi-slap created a strange, unstable sensation, which appeared abruptly and disappeared before I had time to grasp what it was. What was left in me instead was a strange peace. I felt at ease. My mind was crystal clear. I had no expectations, no desires. My usual nervousness and sweaty hands, the marks of my existence, were suddenly gone.

"Now you will understand everything I am going to say to you," don Juan said to me, looking into my eyes as he had done in the bus depot.

Ordinarily, I would have found his statement perfunctory, perhaps rhetorical, but when he said it, I could only assure him repeatedly and sincerely that I would understand anything he said to me. He looked me in the eyes again with a ferocious intensity.

"I am Juan Matus," he said, sitting down on another freight box, a few feet away, facing me. "This is my name, and I voice it because with it, I am making a bridge for you to cross over to where I am."

He stared at me for an instant before he started talking again.

"I am a sorcerer," he went on. "I belong to a lineage of sorcerers that has lasted for twenty-seven generations. I am the nagual of my generation."

He explained to me that the leader of a party of sorcerers like himself was called the "nagual," and that this was a generic term applied to a sorcerer in each generation who had some specific energetic configuration that set him apart from the others. Not in terms of superiority or inferiority, or anything of the like, but in terms of the capacity to be responsible.

"Only the nagual," he said, "has the energetic capacity to be responsible for the fate of his cohorts. Every one of his cohorts knows this, and they accede. The nagual can be a man or a woman. In the time of the sorcerers who were the founders of my lineage, women were, by rule, the naguals. Their natural pragmatism—the product of their femaleness—led my lineage into pits of practicalities from which they could barely emerge. Then, the males took over, and led my lineage into pits of imbecility from which we are barely emerging now.

"Since the time of the nagual Lujan, who lived about two hundred years ago," he went on, "there has been a joint nexus of effort, shared by a man and a woman. The nagual man brings sobriety; the nagual woman brings innovation."

I wanted to ask him at this point if there was a woman in his life who was the nagual, but the depth of my concentration didn't allow me to formulate the question. Instead, he himself formulated it for me.

"Is there a nagual woman in my life?" he asked. "No, there isn't any. I am a solitary sorcerer. I have my cohorts, though. At the moment, they are not around."

A thought came with uncontainable vigor into my mind. At that instant, I remembered what some people in Yuma had told me about don Juan running with a party of Mexican men who seemed to be very versed in sorcery maneuvers.

"To be a sorcerer," don Juan continued, "doesn't mean to practice witchcraft, or to work to affect people, or to be possessed by demons. To be a sorcerer means to reach a level of awareness that makes inconceivable things available. The term 'sorcery' is inadequate to express what sorcerers do, and so is the term 'shamanism.' The actions of sorcerers are exclusively in the realm of the abstract, the impersonal. Sorcerers struggle to reach a goal that has nothing to do with the quests of an average man. Sorcerers' aspirations are to reach *infinity*, and to be conscious of it."

Don Juan continued, saying that the task of sorcerers was to face *infinity*, and that they plunged into it daily, as a fisherman plunges into the sea. It was such an overwhelming task that sorcerers had to state their names before venturing into it. He reminded me that, in Nogales, he had stated his name before any interaction had taken place between us. He had, in this manner, asserted his individuality in front of the infinite.

I understood with unequaled clarity what he was explaining. I didn't have to ask him for clarifications. My keenness of thought should have surprised me, but it didn't at all. I knew at that moment that I had always been crystal clear, merely playing dumb for someone else's benefit.

"Without you knowing anything about it," he continued, "I started you on a traditional quest. You are the man I was looking for. My quest ended when I found you, and yours when you found me now."

Don Juan explained to me that, as the nagual of his generation, he was in search of an individual who had a specific energetic configuration, adequate to ensure the continuity of his lineage. He said that at a given moment, the nagual of each generation for twenty-seven successive generations had entered into the most nerve-racking experience of their lives: the search for succession.

Looking me straight in the eyes, he stated that what made human beings into sorcerers was their capacity to perceive energy directly as it flows in the universe, and that when sorcerers perceive a human being in this fashion, they *see* a luminous ball, or a luminous egg-shaped figure. His contention was that human beings are not only capable of *seeing* energy directly as it flows in the universe, but that they actually do *see* it, although they are not deliberately conscious of *seeing* it.

He made right then the most crucial distinction for sorcerers, the one between the general state of being aware and the particular state of being deliberately conscious of something. He categorized all human beings as possessing awareness, in a general sense, which permits them to *see* energy directly, and he categorized sorcerers as the only human beings who were deliberately conscious of *seeing* energy directly. He then defined "awareness" as energy and "energy" as constant flux, a luminous vibration that was never stationary, but always moving of its own accord. He asserted that when a human being was *seen*, he was perceived as a conglomerate of energy fields held together by the most mysterious force in the universe: a binding, agglutinating, vibratory force that holds energy fields together in a cohesive unit. He further explained that the nagual was a specific sorcerer in each generation whom the other sorcerers were able to *see*, not as a single luminous ball but as a set of two spheres of luminosity fused, one over the other.

"This feature of doubleness," he continued, "permits the nagual to perform maneuvers that are rather difficult for an average sorcerer. For example, the nagual is a connoisseur of the force that holds us together as a cohesive unit. The nagual could place his full attention, for a fraction of a second, on that force, and numb the other person. I did that to you at the bus depot because I wanted to stop your barrage of *me, me, me, me, me, me, me.* I wanted you to find me and cut the crap.

"The sorcerers of my lineage maintained," don Juan went on, "that the presence of a double being—a nagual—is sufficient to clarify things for us. What's odd about it is that the presence of the nagual clarifies things in a veiled fashion. It happened to me when I met the nagual Julian, my teacher. His presence baffled me for years, because every time I was around him, I could think clearly, but when he moved away, I became the same idiot that I had always been.

"I had the privilege," don Juan went on, "of actually meeting and dealing with two naguals. For six years, at the request of the nagual Elias, the teacher of the nagual Julian, I went to live with him. He is the one who reared me, so to speak. It was a rare privilege. I had a ringside seat for watching what a nagual really is. The nagual Elias and the nagual Julian were two men of tremendously different temperaments. The nagual Elias was quieter, and lost in the darkness of his silence. The nagual Julian was bombastic, a compulsive talker. It seemed that he lived to dazzle women. There were more women in his life than one would care to think about. Yet both of them were astoundingly alike in that there was nothing inside them. They were empty. The nagual Elias was a collection of astounding, haunting stories of regions unknown. The nagual Julian was a collection of stories that would have anybody in stitches, sprawled on the ground laughing. Whenever I tried to pin down the man in them, the real man, the way I could pinpoint the man in my father, the man in everybody I knew, I found nothing. Instead of a real person inside them, there was a bunch of stories about persons unknown. Each of the two men had his own flair, but the end result was just the same: emptiness, an emptiness that reflected not the world, but *infinity*."

Don Juan went on explaining that the moment one crosses a peculiar threshold in *infinity*, either deliberately or, as in my case, unwittingly, everything that happens to one from then on is no longer exclusively in one's own domain, but enters into the realm of *infinity*.

"When we met in Arizona, both of us crossed a peculiar threshold," he continued. "And this threshold was not decided by either one of us, but by *infinity* itself. *Infinity* is everything that surrounds us." He said this and made a broad gesture with his arms. "The sorcerers of my lineage call it *infinity*, the *spirit*, the *dark sea of awareness*, and say that it is something that exists out there and rules our lives."

I was truly capable of comprehending everything he was saying, and yet I didn't know what the hell he was talking about. I asked if crossing the threshold had been an accidental event, born of unpredictable circumstances ruled by chance. He answered that his steps and mine were guided by *infinity*, and that circumstances that seemed to be ruled by chance were in essence ruled by the *active side of infinity*. He called it *intent*.

"What put you and me together," he went on, "was the *intent of infinity*. It is impossible to determine what this *intent of infinity* is, yet it is there, as palpable as you and I are. Sorcerers say that it is a *tremor in the air*. The advantage of sorcerers is to know that the *tremor in the air* exists, and to acquiesce to it without any further ado. For sorcerers, there's no pondering, wondering, or speculating. They know that all they have is the possibility of merging with the *intent of infinity*, and they just do it."

Nothing could have been clearer to me than those statements. As far as I was concerned, the truth of what he was telling me was so self-evident that it didn't permit me to ponder how such absurd assertions could have sounded so rational. I knew that everything that don Juan was saying was not only a truism, but I could corroborate it by referring to my own being. I knew about everything that he was saying. I had the sensation that I had lived every twist of his description.

Our interchange ended then. Something seemed to deflate inside me. It was at that instant that the thought crossed my mind that I was losing my marbles. I had been blinded by weird statements and had lost every conceivable sense of objectivity. Accordingly, I left don Juan's house in a real hurry, feeling threatened to the core by an unseen enemy. Don Juan walked me to my car, fully cognizant of what was going on inside me.

"Don't worry," he said, putting his hand on my shoulder. You're not going crazy. What you felt was a gentle tap of *infinity*."

As time went by, I was able to corroborate what don Juan had said about his two teachers. Don Juan Matus was exactly as he had described those two men to be. I would go as far as saying that he was an extraordinary blend of both of them: on the one hand, extremely quiet and introspective; on the other, extremely open and funny. The most accurate statement about what a nagual is, which he voiced the day I found him, was that a nagual is empty, and that that emptiness doesn't reflect the world, but reflects *infinity*.

Nothing could have been more true than this in reference to don Juan Matus. His emptiness reflected *infinity*. There was no boisterousness on his part, or assertions about the self. There was not a speck of a need to have either grievances or remorse. His was the emptiness of a *warrior-traveler*, seasoned to the point where he doesn't take anything for granted. A *warrior-traveler* who doesn't underestimate or overestimate anything. A quiet, disciplined fighter whose elegance is so extreme that no one, no matter how hard they try to look, will ever find the seam where all that complexity has come together.

# The End of an Era

# The Deep Concerns
# of Everyday Life

I WENT TO Sonora to see don Juan. I had to discuss with him the most serious event of that moment in my life. I needed his advice. When I arrived at his house, I barely went through the formality of greeting him. I sat down and blurted out my turmoil.

"Calm down, calm down," don Juan said. "Nothing can be that bad!"

"What's happening to me, don Juan?" I asked. It was a rhetorical question on my part.

"It is the workings of *infinity*," he replied. "Something happened to your way of perceiving the day you met me. Your sensation of nervousness is due to the subliminal realization that your time is up. You are aware of it, but not deliberately conscious of it. You feel the absence of time, and that makes you impatient. I know this, for it happened to me and to all the sorcerers of my lineage. At a given time, a whole era in my life, or their lives, ended. Now it's your turn. You have simply run out of time."

He demanded then a total account of whatever had happened to me. He said that it had to be a full account, sparing no details. He wasn't after sketchy descriptions. He wanted me to air the full impact of what was troubling me.

"Let's have this talk, as they say in your world, by the book," he said. "Let us enter into the realm of *formal talks.*"

Don Juan explained that the shamans of ancient Mexico had developed the idea of *formal* versus *informal talks*, and used both of them as devices for teaching and guiding their disciples. *Formal talks* were, for them, summations that they made from time to time of everything that they had taught or said to their disciples. *Informal talks* were daily elucidations in which things were explained without reference to anything but the phenomenon itself under scrutiny.

"Sorcerers keep nothing to themselves," he continued. "To empty themselves in this fashion is a sorcerers' maneuver. It leads them to abandon the fortress of the self."

I began my story, telling don Juan that the circumstances of my life have never permitted me to be introspective. As far back in my past as I can remember, my daily life has been filled to the brim with pragmatic problems that have clamored for immediate resolution. I remember my favorite uncle telling me that he was appalled at having found out that I had never received a gift for Christmas or for my birthday. I had come to live in my father's family's home not too long before he made that statement. He commiserated with me about the unfairness of my situation. He even apologized, although it had nothing to do with him.

"It is disgusting, my boy," he said, shaking with feeling. "I want you to know that I am behind you one hundred percent whenever the moment comes to redress wrongdoings."

He insisted over and over that I had to forgive the people who had wronged me. From what he said, I formed the impression that he wanted me to confront my father with his finding and accuse him of indolence and neglect, and then, of course, forgive him. He failed to see that I didn't feel wronged at all. What he was asking me to do required an introspective nature that would make me respond to the barbs of psychological mistreatment once they were pointed out to me. I assured my uncle that I was going to think about it, but not at the moment, because at that very instant, my girlfriend, from the living room where she was waiting for me, was signaling me desperately to hurry up.

I never had the opportunity to think about it, but my uncle must have talked to my father, because I got a gift from him, a package neatly wrapped up, with ribbon and all, and a little card that said "Sorry." I curiously and eagerly ripped the wrappings. There was a cardboard box, and inside it there was a beautiful toy, a tiny boat with a winding key attached to the steam pipe. It could be used by children to play with while they took baths in the bathtub. My father had thoroughly forgotten that I was already fifteen years old and, for all practical purposes, a man.

Since I had reached my adult years still incapable of serious introspection, it was quite a novelty when one day years later I found myself in the throes of a strange emotional agitation, which seemed to increase as time went by. I discarded it, attributing it to natural processes of the mind or the body that enter into action periodically, for no reason at all, or are perhaps triggered by biochemical processes within the body itself. I thought nothing of it. However, the agitation increased and its pressure forced me to believe that I had arrived at a moment in life when what I needed was a drastic change. There was something in me that demanded a rearrangement of my life. This urge to rearrange everything was familiar. I had felt it in the past, but it had been dormant for a long time.

I was committed to studying anthropology, and this commitment was so strong that not to study anthropology was never part of my proposed drastic change. It didn't occur to me to drop out of school and do something else. The first thing that came to mind was that I needed to change schools and go somewhere else, far away from Los Angeles.

Before I undertook a change of that magnitude, I wanted to

test the waters, so to speak. I enrolled in a full summer load of classes at a school in another city. The most important course, for me, was a class in anthropology taught by a foremost authority on the Indians of the Andean region. It was my belief that if I focused my studies on an area that was emotionally accessible to me I would have a better opportunity to do anthropological field-work in a serious manner when the time came. I conceived of my knowledge of South America as giving me a better entree into any given Indian society there.

At the same time that I registered for school, I got a job as a research assistant to a psychiatrist who was the older brother of one of my friends. He wanted to do a content analysis of excerpts from some innocuous tapes of question-and-answer sessions with young men and women about their problems arising from overwork in school, unfulfilled expectations, not being understood at home, frustrating love affairs, etc. The tapes were over five years old and were going to be destroyed, but before they were, random numbers were allotted to each reel, and following a table of random numbers, reels were picked by the psychiatrist and his research assistants and scanned for excerpts that could be analyzed.

On the first day of class in the new school, the anthropology professor talked about his academic bona fides and dazzled his students with the scope of his knowledge and his publications. He was a tall, slender man in his mid-forties, with shifty blue eyes. What struck me the most about his physical appearance was that his eyes were rendered enormous behind glasses for correcting far-sightedness, and each of his eyes gave the impression that it was rotating in an opposite direction from the other when he moved his head as he spoke. I knew that that couldn't be true; it was, however, a very disconcerting image. He was extremely well dressed for an anthropologist, who in my day were famous for their super-casual attire. Archaeologists, for example, were described by their students as creatures lost in carbon-14 dating who never took a bath.

However, for reasons unbeknownst to me, what really set him

apart wasn't his physical appearance, or his erudition, but his speech pattern. He pronounced every word as clearly as anyone I had ever heard, and emphasized certain words by elongating them. He had a markedly foreign intonation, but I knew that it was an affectation. He pronounced certain phrases like an Englishman and others like a revivalist preacher.

He fascinated me from the start despite his enormous pomposity. His self-importance was so blatant that it ceased to be an issue after the first five minutes of his class, which were always bombastic displays of knowledge cushioned in wild assertions about himself. His command of the audience was sensational. None of the students I talked to felt anything but supreme admiration for this extraordinary man. I earnestly thought that everything was moving along nicely, and that this move to another school in another city was going to be easy and uneventful, but thoroughly positive. I liked my new surroundings.

At my job, I became completely engrossed in listening to the tapes, to the point where I would sneak into the office and listen not to excerpts, but to entire tapes. What fascinated me beyond measure, at first, was the fact that I heard myself speaking in every one of those tapes. As the weeks went by and I heard more tapes, my fascination turned to sheer horror. Every line that was spoken, including the psychiatrist's questions, was mine. Those people were speaking from the depths of my own being. The revulsion that I experienced was something unique for me. Never had I dreamed that I could be repeated endlessly in every man or woman I heard speaking on the tapes. My sense of individuality, which had been ingrained in me from birth, tumbled down hopelessly under the impact of this colossal discovery.

I began then an odious process of trying to restore myself. I unconsciously made a ludicrous attempt at introspection; I tried to wriggle out of my predicament by endlessly talking to myself. I rehashed in my mind all the possible rationales that would support my sense of uniqueness, and then talked out loud to myself about them. I even experienced something quite revolutionary to me: waking myself up many times by my loud talking in my sleep, discoursing about my value and distinctiveness.

Then, one horrifying day, I suffered another deadly blow. In the wee hours of the night, I was woken up by an insistent knocking on my door. It wasn't a mild, timid knock, but what my friends called a "Gestapo knock." The door was about to come off its hinges. I jumped out of bed and opened the peephole. The person who was knocking on the door was my boss, the psychiatrist. My being his younger brother's friend seemed to have created an avenue of communication with him. He had befriended me without any hesitation, and there he was on my doorstep. I turned on the light and opened the door.

"Please come in," I said. "What happened?"

It was three o'clock in the morning, and by his livid expression, and his sunken eyes, I knew that he was deeply upset. He came in and sat down. His pride and joy, his black mane of longish hair, was falling all over his face. He didn't make any effort to comb his hair back, the way he usually wore it. I liked him very much because he was an older version of my friend in Los Angeles, with black, heavy eyebrows, penetrating brown eyes, a square jaw, and thick lips. His upper lip seemed to have an extra fold inside, which at times, when he smiled in a certain way, gave the impression that he had a double upper lip. He always talked about the shape of his nose, which he described as an impertinent, pushy nose. I thought he was extremely sure of himself, and opinionated beyond belief. He claimed that in his profession those qualities were winning cards.

"What happened!" he repeated with a tone of mockery, his double upper lip trembling uncontrollably. "Anyone can tell that everything has happened to me tonight."

He sat down in a chair. He seemed dizzy, disoriented, looking for words. He got up and went to the couch, slumping down on it.

"It's not only that I have the responsibility of my patients," he went on, "but my research grant, my wife and kids, and now another fucking pressure has been added to it, and what burns me up is that it was my own fault, my own stupidity for putting my trust in a stupid cunt!

"I'll tell you, Carlos," he continued, "there's nothing more appalling, disgusting, fucking nauseating than the insensitivity of women. I'm not a woman hater, you know that! But at this moment it seems to me that every single cunt is just a cunt! Duplicitous and vile!"

I didn't know what to say. Whatever he was telling me didn't need affirmation or contradiction. I wouldn't have dared to contradict him anyway. I didn't have the ammunition for it. I was very tired. I wanted to go back to sleep, but he kept on talking as if his life depended on it.

"You know Theresa Manning, don't you?" he asked me in a forceful, accusatory manner.

For an instant, I believed that he was accusing me of having something to do with his young, beautiful student-secretary. Without giving me time to respond, he continued talking.

"Theresa Manning is an asshole. She's a schnook! A stupid, inconsiderate woman who has no incentive in life other than balling anyone with a bit of fame and notoriety. I thought she was intelligent and sensitive. I thought she had something, some understanding, some empathy, something that one would like to share, or hold as precious all to oneself. I don't know, but that's the picture that she painted for me, when in reality she's lewd and degenerate, and, I may add, incurably gross."

As he kept on talking, a strange picture began to emerge. Apparently, the psychiatrist had just had a bad experience involving his secretary.

"Since the day she came to work for me," he went on, "I knew that she was attracted to me sexually, but she never came around to saying it. It was all in the innuendos and the looks. Well, fuck it! This afternoon I got sick and tired of pussyfooting around and I came right to the point. I went up to her desk and said, 'I know what you want, and you know what I want.'"

He went into a great, elaborate rendition of how forcefully he had told her that he expected her in his apartment across the street from school at 11:30 P.M., and that he did not alter his routines for anybody, that he read and worked and drank wine until one o'clock, at which time he retired to the bedroom. He kept an apartment in town as well as the house he and his wife and children lived in in the suburbs.

"I was so confident that the affair was going to pan out, turn into something memorable," he said and sighed. His voice acquired the mellow tone of someone confiding something intimate. "I even gave her the key to my apartment," he said, and his voice cracked.

"Very dutifully, she came at eleven-thirty," he went on. "She let herself in with her own key, and sneaked into the bedroom like a shadow. That excited me terribly. I knew that she wasn't going to be any trouble for me. She knew her role. She probably fell asleep on the bed. Or maybe she watched TV. I became engrossed in my work, and I didn't care what the fuck she did. I knew that I had her in the bag.

"But the moment I came into the bedroom," he continued, his voice tense and constricted, as if he were morally offended, "Theresa jumped on me like an animal and went for my dick. She didn't even give me time to put down the bottle and the two glasses I was carrying. I had enough presence of mind to put my two Baccarat glasses on the floor without breaking them. The bottle flew across the room when she grabbed my balls as if they were made out of rocks. I wanted to hit her. I actually yelled in pain, but that didn't faze her. She giggled insanely, because she thought I was being cute and sexy. She said so, as if to placate me."

Shaking his head with contained rage, he said that the woman was so friggin' eager and utterly selfish that she didn't take into account that a man needs a moment's peace, he needs to feel at ease, at home, in friendly surroundings. Instead of showing consideration and understanding, as her role demanded, Theresa Manning pulled his sexual organs out of his pants with the expertise of someone who had done it hundreds of times.

"The result of all this shit," he said, "was that my sensuality retreated in horror. I was emotionally emasculated. My body abhorred that fucking woman, instantly. Yet my lust prevented me from throwing her out in the street."

He said that he decided then that instead of losing face by his impotence, miserably, the way he was bound to, he would have oral sex with her, and make her have an orgasm—put her at his mercy—but his body had rejected the woman so thoroughly that he couldn't do it.

"The woman was not even beautiful anymore," he said, "but plain. Whenever she's dressed up, the clothes that she wears hide the bulges of her hips. She actually looks okay. But when she's naked, she's a sack of bulging white flesh! The slenderness that she presents when she's clothed is fake. It doesn't exist."

Venom poured out of the psychiatrist in ways that I would never have imagined. He was shaking with rage. He wanted desperately to appear cool, and kept on smoking cigarette after cigarette.

He said that the oral sex was even more maddening and disgusting, and that he was just about to vomit when the friggin' woman actually kicked him in the belly, rolled him out of his own bed onto the floor, and called him an impotent faggot.

At this point in his narration, the psychiatrist's eyes were burning with hatred. His mouth was quivering. He was pale.

"I have to use your bathroom," he said. "I want to take a bath. I am reeking. Believe it or not, I have pussy breath."

He was actually weeping, and I would have given anything in the world not to be there. Perhaps it was my fatigue, or the mesmeric quality of his voice, or the inanity of the situation that created the illusion that I was listening not to the psychiatrist but to the voice of a male supplicant on one of his tapes complaining about minor problems turned into gigantic affairs by talking obsessively about them. My ordeal ended around nine o'clock in the morning. It was time for me to go to class and time for the psychiatrist to go and see his own shrink.

I went to class then, highly charged with a burning anxiety and a tremendous sensation of discomfort and uselessness. There, I received the final blow, the blow that caused my attempt at a drastic change to collapse. No volition of my own was involved in its collapse, which just happened not only as if it had been scheduled but as if its progression had been accelerated by some unknown hand.

The anthropology professor began his lecture about a group of Indians from the high plateaus of Bolivia and Peru, the *aymará*. He called them the "ey-MEH-ra," elongating the name as if his pronunciation of it was the only accurate one in existence. He said that the making of *chicha*, which is pronounced "CHEE-cha," but which he pronounced "CHAHI-cha," an alcoholic beverage made from fermented corn, was in the realm of a sect of priestesses who were considered semidivine by the *aymará*. He said, in a tone of revelation, that those women were in charge of making the cooked corn into a mush ready for fermentation by chewing and spitting it, adding in this manner an enzyme found in human saliva. The whole class shrieked with contained horror at the mention of human saliva.

The professor seemed to be tickled pink. He laughed in little spurts. It was the chuckle of a nasty child. He went on to say that the women were expert chewers, and he called them the "chahicha chewers." He looked at the front row of the classroom, where most of the young women were sitting, and he delivered his punch line.

"I was p-r-r-rivileged," he said with a strange quasi-foreign intonation, "to be asked to sleep with one of the chahi-cha chewers. The art of chewing the chahi-cha mush makes them develop the muscles around their throat and cheeks to the point that they can do wonders with them."

He looked at his bewildered audience and paused for a long time, punctuating the pause with his giggles. "I'm sure you get my drift," he said, and went into fits of hysterical laughter.

The class went wild with the professor's innuendo. The lecture was interrupted by at least five minutes of laughter and a barrage of questions that the professor declined to answer, emitting more silly giggles.

I felt so compressed by the pressure of the tapes, the psychiatrist's story, and the professor's "chahi-cha chewers" that in one instantaneous sweep I quit the job, quit school, and drove back to L.A.

"Whatever happened to me with the psychiatrist and the professor of anthropology," I said to don Juan, "has plunged me into an unknown emotional state. I can only call it introspection. I've been talking to myself without stop."

"Your malady is a very simple one," don Juan said, shaking with laughter.

Apparently my situation delighted him. It was a delight I could not share, because I failed to see the humor in it.

"Your world is coming to an end," he said. "It is the end of an era for you. Do you think that the world you have known all your life is going to leave you peacefully, without any fuss or muss? No! It will wriggle underneath you, and hit you with its tail."

# The View
# I Could Not Stand

LOS ANGELES HAD always been home for me. My choice of Los Angeles had not been volitional. To me, staying in Los Angeles has always been the equivalent of having been born there, perhaps even more than that. My emotional attachment to it has always been total. My love for the city of Los Angeles has always been so intense, so much a part of me, that I have never had to voice it. I have never had to review it or renew it, ever.

I had, in Los Angeles, my family of friends. They were to me part of my immediate milieu, meaning that I had accepted them totally, the way I had accepted the city. One of my friends made the statement once, half in fun, that all of us hated each other cordially. Doubtless, they could afford feelings like that themselves, for they had other emotional arrangements at their disposal, like parents and wives and husbands. I had only my friends in Los Angeles.

For whatever reason, I was each one's confidant. Every one of them poured out to me their problems and vicissitudes. My friends were so close to me that I had never acknowledged their problems or tribulations as anything but normal. I could talk for hours to them about the very same things that had horrified me in the psychiatrist and his tapes.

Furthermore, I had never realized that every one of my friends was astoundingly similar to the psychiatrist and the professor of anthropology. I had never noticed how tense my friends were. All of them smoked compulsively, like the psychiatrist, but it had never been obvious to me because I smoked just as much myself and was just as tense. Their affectation in speech was another thing that had never been apparent to me, although it was there. They always affected a twang of the western United States, but they were very aware of what they were doing. Nor had I ever noticed their blatant innuendos about a sensuality that they were incapable of feeling, except intellectually.

The real confrontation with myself began when I was faced with the dilemma of my friend Pete. He came to see me, all battered. He had a swollen mouth and a red and swollen left eye that had obviously been hit and was turning blue already. Before I had time to ask him what had happened to him, he blurted out that his wife, Patricia, had gone to a real estate brokers' convention over the weekend, in relation to her job, and that something terrible had happened to her. The way Pete looked, I thought that perhaps Patricia had been injured, or even killed, in an accident.

"Is she all right?" I asked, genuinely concerned.

"Of course she's all right," he barked. "She's a bitch and a whore, and nothing happens to bitch-whores except that they get fucked, and they *like* it!"

Pete was rabid. He was shaking, nearly convulsing. His bushy, curly hair was sticking out every which way. Usually, he combed it carefully and slicked his natural curls into place. Now, he looked as wild as a Tasmanian devil.

"Everything was normal until today," my friend continued. "Then, this morning, after I came out of the shower, she snapped a towel at my naked butt, and that's what made me aware of her shit! I knew instantly that she'd been fucking someone else."

I was puzzled by his line of reasoning. I questioned him further. I asked him how snapping a towel could reveal anything of this sort to anybody.

"It wouldn't reveal anything to assholes!" he said with pure venom in his voice. "But I know Patricia, and on Thursday, before she went to the brokers' convention, she could not snap a towel! In fact, she has *never* been able to snap a towel in all the time we've been married. Somebody must have taught her to do it, while they were naked! So I grabbed her by the throat and choked the truth out of her! Yes! She's fucking her boss!"

Pete said that he went to Patricia's office to have it out with her boss, but the man was heavily protected by bodyguards. They threw him out into the parking lot. He wanted to smash the windows of the office, throw rocks at them, but the bodyguards said that if he did that, he'd land in jail, or even worse, he'd get a bullet in his head.

"Are they the ones who beat you up, Pete?" I asked him.

"No," he said, dejected. "I walked down the street and went into the sales office of a used car lot. I punched the first salesman who came to talk to me. The man was shocked, but he didn't get angry. He said, 'Calm down, sir, calm down! There's room for negotiation.' When I punched him again in the mouth, he got pissed off. He was a big guy, and he hit me in the mouth and the eye and knocked me out. When I came to my senses," Pete continued, "I was lying on the couch in their office. I heard an ambulance approaching. I knew they were coming for me, so I got up and ran out. Then I came to see you."

He began to weep uncontrollably. He got sick to his stomach. He was a mess. I called his wife, and in less than ten minutes she was in the apartment. She kneeled in front of Pete and swore that she loved only him, that everything else she did was pure imbecility, and that theirs was a love that was a matter of life or death. The others were nothing. She didn't even remember them. Both of them wept to their hearts' content, and of course they forgave each other. Patricia was wearing sunglasses to hide the hematoma by her right eye where Pete had hit her—Pete was left-handed. Both of them were oblivious to my presence, and when they left, they didn't even know I was there. They just walked out, leaving the door open, hugging each other.

Life seemed to continue for me as it always had. My friends acted with me as they always did. We were, as usual, involved in going to parties, or the movies, or just simply "chewing the fat," or looking for restaurants where they offered "all you can eat" for the price of one meal. However, despite this pseudo-normality, a strange new factor seemed to have entered my life. As the subject who was experiencing it, it appeared to me that, all of a sudden, I had become extremely narrow-minded. I had begun to judge my friends in the same way I had judged the psychiatrist and the professor of anthropology. Who was I, anyway, to set myself up in judgment of anyone else?

I felt an immense sense of guilt. To judge my friends created a mood previously unknown to me. But what I considered to be even worse was that not only was I judging them, I was finding their problems and tribulations astoundingly banal. I was the same man; they were my same friends. I had heard their complaints and renditions of their situations hundreds of times, and I hadn't ever felt anything except a deep identification with whatever I was listening to. My horror at discovering this new mood in myself was staggering.

The aphorism that when it rains it pours couldn't have been more true for me at that moment in my life. The total disintegration of my way of life came when my friend Rodrigo Cummings asked me to take him to the Burbank airport; from there he was going to fly to New York. It was a very dramatic and desperate maneuver on his part. He considered it his damnation to be caught in Los Angeles. For the rest of his friends, it was a big joke, the fact that he had tried to drive across country to New York various times, and every time he had tried to do it, his car had broken down. Once, he had gone as far as Salt Lake City before his car collapsed; it needed a new motor. He had to junk it there. Most of the time, his cars petered out in the suburbs of Los Angeles.

"What happens to your cars, Rodrigo?" I asked him once, driven by truthful curiosity.

"I don't know," he replied with a veiled sense of guilt. And then, in a voice worthy of the professor of anthropology in his role of revivalist preacher, he said, "Perhaps it is because when I hit the road, I accelerate because I feel free. I usually open all my windows. I want the wind to blow on my face. I feel that I'm a kid in search of something new."

It was obvious to me that his cars, which were always jalopies, were no longer capable of speeding, and he just simply burned their motors out.

From Salt Lake City, Rodrigo had returned to Los Angeles, hitchhiking. Of course, he could have hitchhiked to New York, but it had never occurred to him. Rodrigo seemed to be afflicted by the same condition that afflicted me: an unconscious passion for Los Angeles, which he wanted to refuse at any cost.

Another time, his car was in excellent mechanical condition. It could have made the whole trip with ease, but Rodrigo was apparently not in any condition to leave Los Angeles. He drove as far as San Bernardino, where he went to see a movie—*The Ten Commandments.* This movie, for reasons known only to Rodrigo, created in him an unbeatable nostalgia for L.A. He came back, and wept, telling me how the fucking city of Los Angeles had built a fence around him that didn't let him go through. His wife was delighted that he hadn't gone, and his girlfriend, Melissa, was even more delighted, although also chagrined because she had to give back the dictionaries that he had given her.

His last desperate attempt to reach New York by plane was rendered even more dramatic because he borrowed money from his friends to pay for the ticket. He said that in this fashion, since he didn't intend to repay them, he was making sure that he wouldn't come back.

I put his suitcases in the trunk of my car and headed with him for the Burbank airport. He remarked that the plane didn't leave until seven o'clock. It was early afternoon, and we had plenty of time to go and see a movie. Besides, he wanted to take one last look at Hollywood Boulevard, the center of our lives and activities.

We went to see an epic in Technicolor and Cinerama. It was a long, excruciating movie that seemed to rivet Rodrigo's attention. When we got out of the movie, it was already getting dark. I rushed to Burbank in the midst of heavy traffic. He demanded that we go on surface streets rather than the freeway, which was jammed at that hour. The plane was just leaving when we reached the airport. That was the final straw. Meek and defeated, Rodrigo went to a cashier and presented his ticket to get his money back. The cashier wrote down his name and gave him a receipt and said that his money would be sent within six to twelve weeks from Tennessee, where the accounting offices of the airline were located.

We drove back to the apartment building where we both lived. Since he hadn't said good-bye to anybody this time, for fear of losing face, nobody had ever noticed that he had tried to leave one more time. The only drawback was that he had sold his car. He asked me to drive him to his parents' house, because his dad was going to give him the money he had spent on the ticket. His father had always been, as far back as I could remember, the man who had bailed Rodrigo out of every problematic situation that he had ever gotten into. The father's slogan was "Have no fear, Rodrigo Senior is here!" After he heard Rodrigo's request for a loan to pay his other loan, the father looked at my friend with the saddest expression that I had ever seen. He was having terrible financial difficulties himself.

Putting his arm around his son's shoulders, he said, "I can't help you this time, my boy. Now you should have fear, because Rodrigo Senior is no longer here."

I wanted desperately to identify with my friend, to feel his drama the way I always had, but I couldn't. I only focused on the

93

father's statement. It sounded to me so final that it galvanized me.

I sought don Juan's company avidly. I left everything pending in Los Angeles and made a trip to Sonora. I told him about the strange mood that I had entered into with my friends. Sobbing with remorse, I said to him that I had begun to judge them.

"Don't get so worked up over nothing," don Juan said calmly. "You already know that a whole era in your life is coming to an end, but an era doesn't really come to an end until the king dies."

"What do you mean by that, don Juan?"

"You are the king, and you are just like your friends. That is the truth that makes you shake in your boots. One thing you can do is to accept it at face value, which, of course, you can't do. The other thing you can do is to say, 'I am not like that, I am not like that,' and repeat to yourself that you are not like that. I promise you, however, that a moment will come when you will realize that you are like that."

# The Unavoidable
# Appointment

THERE WAS SOMETHING that kept nagging at me in
the back of my mind: I had to answer a most important letter I'd
received, and I had to do it at any cost. What had prevented me
from doing it was a mixture of indolence and a deep desire to
please. My anthropologist friend who was responsible for my
meeting don Juan Matus had written me a letter a couple of
months earlier. He wanted to know how I was doing in my studies
of anthropology, and urged me to pay him a visit. I composed
three long letters. On rereading each of them, I found them so
trite and obsequious that I tore them up. I couldn't express in
them the depth of my gratitude, the depth of my feelings for him.
I rationalized my delay in answering with a genuine resolve to go
to see him and tell him personally what I was doing with don
Juan Matus, but I kept postponing my imminent trip because I
wasn't sure what it was that I was doing with don Juan. I wanted
someday to show my friend real results. As it was, I had only

vague sketches of possibilities, which, in his demanding eyes, wouldn't have been anthropological fieldwork anyway.

One day I found out that he had died. His death brought to me one of those dangerous silent depressions. I had no way to express what I felt because what I was feeling was not fully formulated in my mind. It was a mixture of dejection, despondency, and abhorrence at myself for not having answered his letter, for not having gone to see him.

I paid a visit to don Juan Matus soon after that. On arriving at his house, I sat down on one of the crates under his ramada and tried to search for words that would not sound banal to express my sense of dejection over the death of my friend. For reasons incomprehensible to me, don Juan knew the origin of my turmoil and the overt reason for my visit to him.

"Yes," don Juan said dryly. "I know that your friend, the anthropologist who guided you to meet me, has died. For whatever reasons, I knew exactly the moment he died. I *saw* it."

His statements jolted me to my foundations.

"I saw it coming a long time ago. I even told you about it, but you disregarded what I said. I'm sure that you don't even remember it."

I remembered every word he had said, but it had no meaning for me at the time he had said it. Don Juan had stated that an event deeply related to our meeting, but not part of it, was the fact that he had *seen* my anthropologist friend as a dying man.

"I *saw* death as an outside force already opening your friend," he had said to me. "Every one of us has an energetic fissure, an energetic crack below the navel. That crack, which sorcerers call the *gap*, is closed when a man is in his prime."

He had said that, normally, all that is discernible to the sorcerer's eye is a tenuous discoloration in the otherwise whitish glow of the luminous sphere. But when a man is close to dying, that *gap* becomes quite apparent. He had assured me that my friend's *gap* was wide open.

"What is the significance of all this, don Juan?" I had asked perfunctorily.

"The significance is a deadly one," he had replied. "The spirit was signaling to me that something was coming to an end. I thought it was my life that was coming to an end, and I accepted it as gracefully as I could. It dawned on me much, much later that it wasn't my life that was coming to an end, but my entire lineage."

I didn't know what he was talking about. But how could I have taken all that seriously? As far as I was concerned, it was, at the time he said it, like everything else in my life: just talk.

"Your friend himself told you, though not in so many words, that he was dying," don Juan said. "You acknowledged what he was saying the way you acknowledged what I said, but in both cases, you chose to bypass it."

I had no comments to make. I was overwhelmed by what he was saying. I wanted to sink into the crate I was sitting on, to disappear, swallowed up by the earth.

"It's not your fault that you bypass things like this," he went on. "It's youth. You have so many things to do, so many people around you. You are not alert. You never learned to be alert, anyway."

In the vein of defending the last bastion of myself, my idea that I was watchful, I pointed out to don Juan that I had been in life-and-death situations that required my quick wit and vigilance. It wasn't that I lacked the capacity to be alert, but that I lacked the orientation for setting an appropriate list of priorities; therefore, everything was either important or unimportant to me.

"To be alert doesn't mean to be watchful," don Juan said. "For sorcerers, to be alert means to be aware of the fabric of the everyday world that seems extraneous to the interaction of the moment. On the trip that you took with your friend before you met me, you noticed only the details that were obvious. You didn't notice how his death was absorbing him, and yet something in you knew it."

I began to protest, to tell him that what he was saying wasn't true.

"Don't hide yourself behind banalities," he said in an accusing tone. "Stand up. If only for the moment you are with me, assume responsibility for what you know. Don't get lost in the extraneous fabric of the world around you, extraneous to what's going on. If you hadn't been so concerned with yourself and your problems, you would have known that that was his last trip. You would have noticed that he was closing his accounts, seeing the people who helped him, saying good-bye to them.

"Your anthropologist friend talked to me once," don Juan went on. "I remembered him so clearly that I wasn't surprised at all when he brought you to me at that bus depot. I couldn't help him when he talked to me. He wasn't the man I was looking for, but I wished him well from my sorcerer's emptiness, from my sorcerer's silence. For this reason, I know that on his last trip, he was saying thank you to the people who counted in his life."

I admitted to don Juan that he was so very right, that there had been so many details that I had been aware of, but that they hadn't meant a thing to me at the time, such as, for instance, my friend's ecstasy in watching the scenery around us. He would stop the car just to watch, for hours on end, the mountains in the distance, or the riverbed, or the desert. I discarded this as the idiotic sentimentality of a middle-aged man. I even made vague hints to him that perhaps he was drinking too much. He told me that in dire cases a drink would allow a man a moment of peace and detachment, a moment long enough to savor something unrepeatable.

"That was, for a fact, the trip for his eyes only," don Juan said. "Sorcerers take such a trip and, in it, nothing counts except what their eyes can absorb. Your friend was unburdening himself of everything superfluous."

I confessed to don Juan that I had disregarded what he had said to me about my dying friend because, at an unknown level, I had known that it was true.

"Sorcerers never say things idly," he said. "I am most careful about what I say to you or to anybody else. The difference between you and me is that I don't have any time at all, and I act accordingly. You, on the other hand, believe that you have all the time in the world, and you act accordingly. The end result of our individual behaviors is that I measure everything I do and say, and you don't."

I conceded that he was right, but I assured him that whatever he was saying did not alleviate my turmoil, or my sadness. I blurted out then, uncontrollably, every nuance of my confused feelings. I told him that I wasn't in search of advice. I wanted him to prescribe a sorcerer's way to end my anguish. I believed I was really interested in getting from him some natural relaxant, an organic Valium, and I said so to him. Don Juan shook his head in bewilderment.

"You are too much," he said. "Next you're going to ask for a sorcerer's medication to remove everything annoying from you, with no effort at all on your part—just the effort of swallowing whatever is given. The more awful the taste, the better the results. That's your Western man's motto. You want results—one potion and you're cured.

"Sorcerers face things in a different way," don Juan continued. "Since they don't have any time to spare, they give themselves fully to what's in front of them. Your turmoil is the result of your lack of sobriety. You didn't have the sobriety to thank your friend properly. That happens to every one of us. We never express what we feel, and when we want to, it's too late, because we have run out of time. It's not only your friend who ran out of time. You, too, ran out of it. You should have thanked him profusely in Arizona. He took the trouble to take you around, and whether you understand it or not, in the bus depot he gave you his best shot. But the moment when you should have thanked him, you were angry with him—you were judging him, he was nasty to you, whatever. And then you postponed seeing him. In reality, what you did was to postpone thanking him. Now you're stuck with a ghost on your tail. You'll never be able to pay what you owe him."

I understood the immensity of what he was saying. Never had I faced my actions in such a light. In fact, I had never thanked anyone, ever. Don Juan pushed his barb even deeper.

"Your friend knew that he was dying," he said. "He wrote you one final letter to find out about your doings. Perhaps unbeknownst to him, or to you, you were his last thought."

The weight of don Juan's words was too much for my shoulders. I collapsed. I felt that I had to lie down. My head was spinning. Maybe it was the setting. I had made the terrible mistake of arriving at don Juan's house in the late afternoon. The setting sun seemed astoundingly golden, and the reflections on the bare mountains to the east of don Juan's house were gold and purple. The sky didn't have a speck of a cloud. Nothing seemed to move. It was as if the whole world were hiding, but its presence was overpowering. The quietness of the Sonoran desert was like a dagger. It went to the marrow of my bones. I wanted to leave, to get in my car and drive away. I wanted to be in the city, get lost in its noise.

"You are having a taste of *infinity*," don Juan said with grave finality. "I know it, because I have been in your shoes. You want to run away, to plunge into something human, warm, contradictory, stupid, who cares? You want to forget the death of your friend. But *infinity* won't let you." His voice mellowed. "It has gripped you in its merciless clutches."

"What can I do now, don Juan?" I asked.

"The only thing you can do," don Juan said, "is to keep the memory of your friend fresh, to keep it alive for the rest of your life and perhaps even beyond. Sorcerers express, in this fashion, the thanks that they can no longer voice. You may think it is a silly way, but that's the best sorcerers can do."

It was my own sadness, doubtless, which made me believe that the ebullient don Juan was as sad as I was. I discarded the thought immediately. That couldn't be possible.

"Sadness, for sorcerers, is not personal," don Juan said, again erupting into my thoughts. "It is not quite sadness. It's a wave of energy that comes from the depths of the cosmos, and hits sorcerers when they are receptive, when they are like radios, capable of catching radio waves.

"The sorcerers of olden times, who gave us the entire format of sorcery, believed that there is sadness in the universe, as a force, a condition, like light, like *intent,* and that this perennial force acts especially on sorcerers because they no longer have any defensive shields. They cannot hide behind their friends or their studies. They cannot hide behind love, or hatred, or happiness, or misery. They can't hide behind anything.

"The condition of sorcerers," don Juan went on, "is that sadness, for them, is abstract. It doesn't come from coveting or lacking something, or from self-importance. It doesn't come from *me.* It comes from *infinity.* The sadness you feel for not thanking your friend is already leaning in that direction.

"My teacher, the nagual Julian," he went on, "was a fabulous actor. He actually worked professionally in the theater. He had a favorite story that he used to tell in his theater sessions. He used to push me into terrible outbursts of anguish with it. He said that it was a story for warriors who had everything and yet felt the sting of the universal sadness. I always thought he was telling it for me, personally."

Don Juan then paraphrased his teacher, telling me that the story referred to a man suffering from profound melancholy. He went to see the best doctors of his day and every one of those doctors failed to help him. He finally came to the office of a leading doctor, a healer of the soul. The doctor suggested to his patient that perhaps he could find solace, and the end of his melancholy, in love. The man responded that love was no problem for him, that he was loved perhaps like no one else in the world. The doctor's next suggestion was that maybe the patient should undertake a voyage and see other parts of the world. The man responded that, without exaggeration, he had been in every corner of the world. The doctor recommended hobbies like the arts, sports, etc. The man responded to every one of his recommendations in the same terms: He had done that and had had no relief. The doctor suspected that the man was possibly an incurable liar. He couldn't have done all those things, as he claimed. But being a good healer, the doctor had a final insight.

"Ah!" he exclaimed. "I have the perfect solution for you, sir. You must attend a performance of the greatest comedian of our day. He will delight you to the point where you will forget every twist of your melancholy. You must attend a performance of the Great Garrick!"

Don Juan said that the man looked at the doctor with the saddest look you can imagine, and said, "Doctor, if that's your recommendation, I am a lost man. I have no cure. I am the Great Garrick."

# The Breaking Point

DON JUAN DEFINED *inner silence* as a peculiar state of being in which thoughts were canceled out and one could function from a level other than that of daily awareness. He stressed that *inner silence* meant the suspension of the *internal dialogue*—the perennial companion of thoughts—and was therefore a state of profound quietude.

"The old sorcerers," don Juan said, "called it *inner silence* because it is a state in which perception doesn't depend on the senses. What is at work during *inner silence* is another faculty that man has, the faculty that makes him a magical being, the very faculty that has been curtailed, not by man himself but by some extraneous influence."

"What is this extraneous influence that curtails the magical faculty of man?" I asked.

"That is the topic for a future explanation," don Juan replied, "not the subject of our present discussion, even though it is indeed the most serious aspect of the sorcery of the shamans of ancient Mexico.

"*Inner silence,*" he continued, "is the stand from which everything stems in sorcery. In other words, everything we do leads to that stand, which, like everything else in the world of sorcerers, doesn't reveal itself unless something gigantic shakes us."

Don Juan said that the sorcerers of ancient Mexico devised endless ways to shake themselves or other sorcery practitioners at their foundations in order to reach that coveted state of *inner silence*. They considered the most far-fetched acts, which may seem totally unrelated to the pursuit of *inner silence*, such as, for instance, jumping into waterfalls or spending nights hanging upside down from the top branch of a tree, to be the key points that brought it into being.

Following the rationales of the sorcerers of ancient Mexico, don Juan stated categorically that *inner silence* was accrued, accumulated. In my case, he struggled to guide me to construct a core of *inner silence* in myself, and then add to it, second by second, on every occasion I practiced it. He explained that the sorcerers of ancient Mexico discovered that each individual had a different threshold of *inner silence* in terms of time, meaning that *inner silence* must be kept by each one of us for the length of time of our specific threshold before it can work.

"What did those sorcerers consider the sign that *inner silence* is working, don Juan?" I asked.

"*Inner silence* works from the moment you begin to accrue it," he replied. "What the old sorcerers were after was the final, dramatic, end result of reaching that individual threshold of silence. Some very talented practitioners need only a few minutes of silence to reach that coveted goal. Others, less talented, need long periods of silence, perhaps more than one hour of complete quietude, before they reach the desired result. The desired result is what the old sorcerers called *stopping the world*, the moment when everything around us ceases to be what it's always been.

"This is the moment when sorcerers return to the true nature of man," don Juan went on. "The old sorcerers also called it *total freedom*. It is the moment when man the slave becomes man the free being, capable of feats of perception that defy our linear imagination."

Don Juan assured me that *inner silence* is the avenue that leads to a true suspension of judgment—to a moment when sensory data emanating from the universe at large ceases to be interpreted by the senses; a moment when cognition ceases to be the force which, through usage and repetition, decides the nature of the world.

"Sorcerers need a *breaking point* for the workings of *inner silence* to set in," don Juan said. "The *breaking point* is like the mortar that a mason puts between bricks. It's only when the mortar hardens that the loose bricks become a structure."

From the beginning of our association, don Juan had drilled into me the value, the necessity, of *inner silence*. I did my best to follow his suggestions by accumulating *inner silence* second by second. I had no means to measure the effect of this accumulation, nor did I have any means to judge whether or not I had reached any threshold. I simply aimed doggedly at accruing it, not just to please don Juan but because the act of accumulating it had become a challenge in itself.

One day, don Juan and I were taking a leisurely stroll in the main plaza of Hermosillo. It was the early afternoon of a cloudy day. The heat was dry, and actually very pleasant. There were lots of people walking around. There were stores around the plaza. I had been to Hermosillo many times, and yet I had never noticed the stores. I knew that they were there, but their presence was not something I had been consciously aware of. I couldn't have made a map of that plaza if my life depended on it. That day, as I walked with don Juan, I was trying to locate and identify the stores. I searched for something to use as a mnemonic device that would stir my recollection for later use.

"As I have told you before, many times," don Juan said, jolting me out of my concentration, "every sorcerer I know, male or female, sooner or later arrives at a *breaking point* in their lives."

"Do you mean that they have a mental breakdown or something like that?" I asked.

"No, no," he said, laughing. "Mental breakdowns are for persons who indulge in themselves. Sorcerers are not persons. What I mean is that at a given moment the continuity of their lives has to break in order for *inner silence* to set in and become an active part of their structures.

"It's very, very important," don Juan went on, "that you yourself deliberately arrive at that *breaking point*, or that you create it artificially, and intelligently."

"What do you mean by that, don Juan?" I asked, caught in his intriguing reasoning.

"Your *breaking point*," he said, "is to discontinue your life as you know it. You have done everything I told you, dutifully and accurately. If you are talented, you never show it. That seems to be your style. You're not slow, but you act as if you were. You're very sure of yourself, but you act as if you were insecure. You're not timid, and yet you act as if you were afraid of people. Everything you do points at one single spot: your need to break all that, ruthlessly."

"But in what way, don Juan? What do you have in mind?" I asked, genuinely frantic.

"I think everything boils down to one act," he said. "You must leave your friends. You must say good-bye to them, for good. It's not possible for you to continue on the warriors' path carrying your personal history with you, and unless you discontinue your way of life, I won't be able to go ahead with my instruction."

"Now, now, now, don Juan," I said, "I have to put my foot down. You're asking too much of me. To be frank with you, I don't think I can do it. My friends are my family, my points of reference."

"Precisely, precisely," he remarked. "They are your points of reference. Therefore, they have to go. Sorcerers have only one point of reference: *infinity*."

"But how do you want me to proceed, don Juan?" I asked in a plaintive voice. His request was driving me up the wall.

"You must simply leave," he said matter-of-factly. "Leave any way you can."

"But where would I go?" I asked.

"My recommendation is that you rent a room in one of those chintzy hotels you know," he said. "The uglier the place, the better. If the room has drab green carpet, and drab green drapes, and drab green walls, so much the better—a place comparable to that hotel I showed you once in Los Angeles."

I laughed nervously at my recollection of a time when I was driving with don Juan through the industrial side of Los Angeles, where there were only warehouses and dilapidated hotels for transients. One hotel in particular attracted don Juan's attention because of its bombastic name: Edward the Seventh. We stopped across the street from it for a moment to look at it.

"That hotel over there," don Juan said, pointing at it, "is to me the true representation of life on Earth for the average person. If you are lucky, or ruthless, you will get a room with a view of the street, where you will see this endless parade of human misery. If you're not that lucky, or that ruthless, you will get a room on the inside, with windows to the wall of the next building. Think of spending a lifetime torn between those two views, envying the view of the street if you're inside, and envying the view of the wall if you're on the outside, tired of looking out."

Don Juan's metaphor bothered me no end, for I had taken it all in.

Now, faced with the possibility of having to rent a room in a hotel comparable to the Edward the Seventh, I didn't know what to say or which way to go.

"What do you want me to do there, don Juan?" I asked.

"A sorcerer uses a place like that to die," he said, looking at me with an unblinking stare. "You have never been alone in your life. This is the time to do it. You will stay in that room until you die."

His request scared me, but at the same time, it made me laugh.

"Not that I'm going to do it, don Juan," I said, "but what would be the criteria to know that I'm dead?—unless you want me to actually die physically."

"No," he said, "I don't want your body to die physically. I want your person to die. The two are very different affairs. In essence, your person has very little to do with your body. Your person is your mind, and believe you me, your mind is not yours."

"What is this nonsense, don Juan, that my mind is not mine?" I heard myself asking with a nervous twang in my voice.

"I'll tell you about that subject someday," he said, "but not while you're cushioned by your friends.

"The criteria that indicates that a sorcerer is dead," he went on, "is when it makes no difference to him whether he has company or whether he is alone. The day you don't covet the company of your friends, whom you use as shields, that's the day that your person has died. What do you say? Are you game?"

"I can't do it, don Juan," I said. "It's useless that I try to lie to you. I can't leave my friends."

"It's perfectly all right," he said, unperturbed. My statement didn't seem to affect him in the least. "I won't be able to talk to you anymore, but let's say that during our time together you have learned a great deal. You have learned things that will make you very strong, regardless of whether you come back or you stray away."

He patted me on the back and said good-bye to me. He turned around and simply disappeared among the people in the plaza, as if he had merged with them. For an instant, I had the strange sensation that the people in the plaza were like a curtain that he had opened and then disappeared behind. The end had come, as did everything else in don Juan's world: swiftly and unpredictably. Suddenly, it was on me, I was in the throes of it, and I didn't even know how I had gotten into it.

I should have been crushed. Yet I wasn't. I don't know why I was elated. I marveled at the facility with which everything had ended. Don Juan was indeed an elegant being. There were no recriminations or anger or anything of that sort, at all. I got in my car and drove, as happy as a lark. I was ebullient. How extraordinary that everything had ended so swiftly, I thought, so painlessly.

My trip home was uneventful. In Los Angeles, being in my familiar surroundings, I noticed that I had derived an enormous amount of energy from my last exchange with don Juan. I was actually very happy, very relaxed, and I resumed what I considered to be my normal life with renewed zest. All my tribulations with my friends, and my realizations about them, everything that I had said to don Juan in reference to this, were thoroughly forgotten. It was as if something had erased all that from my mind. I marveled a couple of times at the facility I had in forgetting something that had been so meaningful, and in forgetting it so thoroughly.

Everything was as expected. There was one single inconsistency in the otherwise neat paradigm of my new old life: I distinctly remembered don Juan saying to me that my departing from the sorcerers' world was purely academic, and that I would be back. I had remembered and written down every word of our exchange. According to my normal linear reasoning and memory, don Juan had never made those statements. How could I remember things that had never taken place? I pondered uselessly. My pseudorecollection was strange enough to make a case for it, but then I decided that there was no point to it. As far as I was concerned, I was out of don Juan's milieu.

Following don Juan's suggestions in reference to my behavior with those who had favored me in any way, I had come to an earthshaking decision for me: that of honoring and saying thank you to my friends before it was too late. One case in point was my friend Rodrigo Cummings. One incident involving my friend Rodrigo, however, toppled my new paradigm and sent it tumbling down to its total destruction.

My attitude toward him changed radically when I vanquished my competitiveness with him. I found out that it was the easiest thing in the world for me to project 100 percent into whatever Rodrigo did. In fact, I was exactly like him, but I didn't know it until I stopped competing with him. Then the truth emerged for

me with maddening vividness. One of Rodrigo's foremost wishes
was to finish college. Every semester, he registered for school and
took as many courses as was permitted. Then, as the semester progressed, he dropped them one by one. Sometimes he would with-
draw from school altogether. At other times he would keep one
three-unit course all the way through to the bitter end.

During his last semester, he kept a course in sociology because
he liked it. The final exam was approaching. He told me that he
had three weeks to study, to read the textbook for the course. He
thought that that was an exorbitant amount of time to read
merely six hundred pages. He considered himself something of a
speed reader, with a high level of retention; in his opinion, he
had a nearly 100 percent photographic memory.

He thought he had a great deal of time before the exam, so he
asked me if I would help him recondition his car for his paper
route. He wanted to take the right door off in order to throw the
paper through that opening with his right hand instead of over
the roof with his left. I pointed out to him that he was left-
handed, to which he retorted that among his many abilities,
which none of his friends noticed, was that of being ambidextrous. He was right about that; I had never noticed it myself.
After I helped him to take the door off, he decided to rip out the
roof lining, which was badly torn. He said that his car was in opti-
mum mechanical condition, and he would take it to Tijuana,
Mexico, which, as a good Angeleno of the day, he called "TJ," to
have it relined for a few bucks.

"We could use a trip," he said with glee. He even selected the
friends he would like to take. "In TJ, I'm sure that you'll go to
look for used books, because you're an asshole. The rest of us will
go to a bordello. I know quite a few."

It took us a week to rip out all the lining and sand the metal
surface to prepare it for its new lining. Rodrigo had two weeks left
to study then, and he still considered that to be too much time.
He engaged me then in helping him paint his apartment and redo
the floors. It took us over a week to paint it and sand the hard-

wood floors. He didn't want to paint over the wallpaper in one room. We had to rent a machine that removed wallpaper by applying steam to it. Naturally, neither Rodrigo nor I knew how to use the machine properly, and we botched the job horrendously. We ended up having to use Topping, a very fine mixture of plaster of paris and other substances that gives a wall a smooth surface.

After all these endeavors, Rodrigo ended up having only two days left to cram six hundred pages into his head. He went frantically into an all-day and all-night reading marathon, with the help of amphetamines. Rodrigo did go to school the day of the exam, and did sit down at his desk, and did get the multiple-choice exam sheet.

What he didn't do was stay awake to take the exam. His body slumped forward, and his head hit the desk with a terrifying thud. The exam had to be suspended for a while. The sociology teacher became hysterical, and so did the students sitting around Rodrigo. His body was stiff and icy cold. The whole class suspected the worst; they thought he had died of a heart attack. Paramedics were summoned to remove him. After a cursory examination, they pronounced Rodrigo profoundly asleep and took him to a hospital to sleep the effect of the amphetamines off.

My projection into Rodrigo Cummings was so total that it frightened me. I was exactly like him. The similarity became untenable to me. In an act of what I considered to be total, suicidal nihilism, I rented a room in a dilapidated hotel in Hollywood.

The carpets were green and had terrible cigarette burns that had obviously been snuffed out before they turned into full-fledged fires. It had green drapes and drab green walls. The blinking sign of the hotel shone all night through the window.

I ended up doing exactly what don Juan had requested, but in a roundabout way. I didn't do it to fulfill any of don Juan's requirements or with the intention of patching up our differences. I did stay in that hotel room for months on end, until my person, like don Juan had proposed, died, until it truthfully made no difference to me whether I had company or I was alone.

After leaving the hotel, I went to live alone, closer to school. I continued my studies of anthropology, which had never been interrupted, and I started a very profitable business with a lady partner. Everything seemed perfectly in order until one day when the realization hit me like a kick in the head that I was going to spend the rest of my life worrying about my business, or worrying about the phantom choice between being an academic or a businessman, or worrying about my partner's foibles and shenanigans. True desperation pierced the depths of my being. For the first time in my life, despite all the things that I had done and seen, I had no way out. I was completely lost. I seriously began to toy with the idea of the most pragmatic and painless way to end my days.

One morning, a loud and insistent knocking woke me up. I thought it was the landlady, and I was sure that if I didn't answer, she would enter with her passkey. I opened the door, and there was don Juan! I was so surprised that I was numb. I stammered and stuttered, incapable of saying a word. I wanted to kiss his hand, to kneel in front of him. Don Juan came in and sat down with great ease on the edge of my bed.

"I made the trip to Los Angeles," he said, "just to see you."

I wanted to take him to breakfast, but he said that he had other things to attend to, and that he had only a moment to talk to me. I hurriedly told him about my experience in the hotel. His presence had created such havoc that not for a second did it occur to me to ask him how he had found out where I lived. I told don Juan how intensely I regretted having said what I had in Hermosillo.

"You don't have to apologize," he assured me. "Every one of us does the same thing. Once, I ran away from the sorcerers' world myself, and I had to nearly die to realize my stupidity. The important issue is to arrive at a *breaking point*, in whatever way, and that's exactly what you have done. *Inner silence* is becoming real for you. This is the reason I am here in front of you, talking to you. Do you see what I mean?"

I thought I understood what he meant. I thought that he had intuited or read, the way he read things in the air, that I was at my wits' end and that he had come to bail me out.

"You have no time to lose," he said. "You must dissolve your business enterprise within an hour, because one hour is all I can afford to wait—not because I don't want to wait, but because *infinity* is pressing me mercilessly. Let's say that *infinity* is giving you one hour to cancel yourself out. For *infinity*, the only worthwhile enterprise of a warrior is freedom. Any other enterprise is fraudulent. Can you dissolve everything in one hour?"

I didn't have to assure him that I could. I knew that I had to do it. Don Juan told me then that once I had succeeded in dissolving everything, he was going to wait for me at the marketplace in a town in Mexico. In my effort to think about the dissolution of my business, I overlooked what he was saying. He repeated it and, of course, I thought he was joking.

"How can I reach that town, don Juan? Do you want me to drive, to take a plane?" I asked.

"Dissolve your business first," he commanded. "Then the solution will come. But remember, I'll be waiting for you only for an hour."

He left the apartment, and I feverishly endeavored to dissolve everything I had. Naturally, it took me more than an hour, but I didn't stop to consider this because once I had set the dissolution of the business in motion, its momentum carried me. It was only when I was through that the real dilemma faced me. I knew then that I had failed hopelessly. I was left with no business, and no possibilities of ever reaching don Juan.

I went to my bed and sought the only solace I could think of: quietude, silence. In order to facilitate the advent of *inner silence*, don Juan had taught me a way to sit down on my bed, with the knees bent and the soles of the feet touching, the hands pushing the feet together by holding the ankles. He had given me a thick dowel that I always kept at hand wherever I went. It was cut to a fourteen-inch length to support the weight of my head if I leaned over and put the dowel on the floor between my feet, and then placed the other end, which was cushioned, on the spot in the middle of my forehead. Every time I adopted this position, I fell sound asleep in a matter of seconds.

I must have fallen asleep with my usual facility, for I dreamed that I was in the Mexican town where don Juan had said he was going to meet me. I had always been intrigued by this town. The marketplace was open one day a week, and the farmers who lived in the area brought their products there to be sold. What fascinated me the most about that town was the paved road that led to it. At the very entrance to the town, it went over a steep hill. I had sat many times on a bench by a stand that sold cheese, and had looked at that hill. I would see people who were coming into town with their donkeys and their loads, but I would see their heads first; as they kept approaching I would see more of their bodies, until the moment they were on the very top of the hill, when I would see their entire bodies. It seemed to me always that they were emerging from the earth, either slowly or very fast, depending on their speed. In my dream, don Juan was waiting for me by the cheese stand. I approached him.

"You made it from your *inner silence*," he said, patting me on the back. "You did reach your *breaking point*. For a moment, I had begun to lose hope. But I stuck around, knowing that you would make it."

In that dream, we went for a stroll. I was happier than I had ever been. The dream was so vivid, so terrifyingly real, that it left me no doubts that I had resolved the problem, even if my resolving it was only a dream-fantasy.

Don Juan laughed, shaking his head. He had definitely read my thoughts. "You're not in a mere dream," he said, "but who am I to tell you that? You'll know it yourself someday—that there are no dreams from *inner silence*—because you'll choose to know it."

# The Measurements
# of Cognition

"THE END OF an era" was, for don Juan, an accurate description of a process that shamans go through in dismantling the structure of the world they know in order to replace it with another way of understanding the world around them. Don Juan Matus as a teacher endeavored, from the very instant we met, to introduce me to the *cognitive world* of the shamans of ancient Mexico. The term "cognition" was, for me at that time, a bone of tremendous contention. I understood it as the process by which we recognize the world around us. Certain things fall within the realm of that process and are easily recognized by us. Other things don't, and remain, therefore, as oddities, things for which we have no adequate comprehension.

Don Juan maintained, from the start of our association, that the world of the sorcerers of ancient Mexico was different from ours, not in a shallow way, but different in the way in which the process of cognition was arranged. He maintained that in our world our cognition requires the interpretation of sensory data. He said that the universe is composed of an infinite number of energy fields that exist in the universe at large as luminous filaments. Those luminous filaments act on man as an organism. The response of the organism is to turn those energy fields into sensory data. Sensory data is then interpreted, and that interpretation becomes our *cognitive system*. My understanding of cognition forced me to believe that it is a universal process, as language is a universal process. There is a different syntax for every language, as there must be a slightly different arrangement for every system of interpretation in the world.

Don Juan's assertion, however, that the shamans of ancient Mexico had a different *cognitive system*, was, for me, equivalent to saying that they had a different way of communicating that had nothing to do with language. What I desperately wanted him to say was that their different *cognitive system* was the equivalent of having a different language but that it was a language nonetheless. "The end of an era" meant, to don Juan, that the units of a foreign cognition were beginning to take hold. The units of my normal cognition, no matter how pleasant and rewarding they were for me, were beginning to fade. A grave moment in the life of a man!

Perhaps my most cherished unit was my academic life. Anything that threatened it was a threat to the very core of my being, especially if the attack was veiled, unnoticed. It happened with a professor in whom I had put all my trust, Professor Lorca.

I had enrolled in Professor Lorca's course on cognition because he was recommended to me as one of the most brilliant academics in existence. Professor Lorca was rather handsome, with blond hair neatly combed to the side. His forehead was smooth, wrinkle-free, giving the appearance of someone who had never worried in his life. His clothes were extremely well tailored. He didn't wear a tie, a feature that gave him a boyish look. He would put on a tie only to face important people.

On my memorable first class with Professor Lorca, I was bewildered and nervous at seeing how he paced back and forth for minutes that stretched themselves into an eternity for me. Professor Lorca kept on moving his thin, clenched lips up and down, adding immensities to the tension he was generating in that closed-window, stuffy room. Suddenly, he stopped walking. He stood in the center of the room, a few feet from where I was sitting, and, banging a carefully rolled newspaper on the podium, he began to talk.

"It'll never be known . . ." he began.

Everyone in the room at once started anxiously taking notes.

"It'll never be known," he repeated, "what a toad is feeling while he sits at the bottom of a pond and interprets the toad world around him." His voice carried a tremendous force and finality. "So, what do you think this thing is?" He waved the newspaper over his head.

He went on to read to the class an article in the newspaper in which the work of a biologist was reported. The scientist was quoted as describing what frogs felt when insects swam above their heads.

"This article shows the carelessness of the reporter, who has obviously misquoted the scientist," Professor Lorca asserted with the authority of a full professor. "A scientist, no matter how shoddy his work might be, would never allow himself to anthropomorphize the results of his research, unless, of course, he's a nincompoop."

With this as an introduction, he delivered a most brilliant lecture on the insular quality of our *cognitive system*, or the *cognitive system* of any organism, for that matter. He brought to me, in his initial lecture, a barrage of new ideas and made them extremely simple, ready for use. The most novel idea to me was that every individual of every species on this earth interprets the world around it, using data reported by its specialized senses. He asserted that human beings cannot even imagine what it must be like, for example, to be in a world ruled by echolocation, as in the world of bats, where any inferred point of reference could not even be conceived of by the human mind. He made it quite clear that, from that point of view, no two *cognitive systems* could be alike among species.

As I left the auditorium at the end of the hour-and-a-half lecture, I felt that I had been bowled over by the brilliance of Professor Lorca's mind. From then on, I was his confirmed admirer. I found his lectures more than stimulating and thought provoking. His were the only lectures I had ever looked forward to attending. All his eccentricities meant nothing to me in comparison with his excellence as a teacher and as an innovative thinker in the realm of psychology.

When I first attended the class of Professor Lorca, I had been working with don Juan Matus for almost two years. It was a well-established pattern of behavior with me, accustomed as I was to routines, to tell don Juan everything that happened to me in my everyday world. On the first opportunity I had, I related to him what was taking place with Professor Lorca. I praised Professor Lorca to the skies and told don Juan unabashedly that Professor Lorca was my role model. Don Juan seemed very impressed with my display of genuine admiration, yet he gave me a strange warning.

"Don't admire people from afar," he said. "That is the surest way to create mythological beings. Get close to your professor, talk to him, see what he's like as a man. Test him. If your professor's behavior is the result of his conviction that he is a being who is going to die, then everything he does, no matter how strange, must be premeditated and final. If what he says turns out to be just words, he's not worth a hoot."

I was insulted no end by what I considered to be don Juan's callousness. I thought he was a little bit jealous of my feelings for Professor Lorca. Once that thought was formulated in my mind I felt relieved; I understood everything.

"Tell me, don Juan," I said to end the conversation on a different note, "what is a being that is going to die, really? I have heard you talk about it so many times, but you haven't actually defined it for me."

"Human beings are beings that are going to die," he said.

"Sorcerers firmly maintain that the only way to have a grip on our world, and on what we do in it, is by fully accepting that we are beings on the way to dying. Without this basic acceptance, our lives, our doings, and the world in which we live are unmanageable affairs."

"But is the mere acceptance of this so far-reaching?" I asked in a tone of quasi-protest.

"You bet your life!" don Juan said, smiling. "However, it's not the mere acceptance that does the trick. We have to embody that acceptance and live it all the way through. Sorcerers throughout the ages have said that the view of our death is the most sobering view that exists. What is wrong with us human beings, and has been wrong since time immemorial, is that without ever stating it in so many words, we believe that we have entered the realm of immortality. We behave as if we were never going to die—an infantile arrogance. But even more injurious than this sense of immortality is what comes with it: the sense that we can engulf this inconceivable universe with our minds."

A most deadly juxtaposition of ideas had me mercilessly in its grip: don Juan's wisdom and Professor Lorca's knowledge. Both were difficult, obscure, all-encompassing, and most appealing. There was nothing for me to do except follow the course of events and go with them wherever they might take me.

I followed to the letter don Juan's suggestion about approaching Professor Lorca. I tried, for the whole semester, to get close to him, to talk to him. I went religiously to his office during his office hours, but he never seemed to have any time for me. But even though I couldn't speak to him, I admired him unbiasedly. I even accepted that he would never talk to me. It didn't matter to me; what mattered were the ideas that I gathered from his magnificent classes.

I reported to don Juan all my intellectual findings. I had done extensive reading on cognition. Don Juan Matus urged me, more than ever, to establish direct contact with the source of my intellectual revolution.

"It is imperative that you speak to him," he said with a note of urgency in his voice. "Sorcerers don't admire people in a vacuum. They talk to them; they get to know them. They establish points of reference. They compare. What you are doing is a little bit infantile. You are admiring from a distance. It is very much like what happens to a man who is afraid of women. Finally, his gonads overrule his fear and compel him to worship the first woman who says 'hello' to him."

I tried doubly hard to approach Professor Lorca, but he was like an impenetrable fortress. When I talked to don Juan about my difficulties, he explained that sorcerers viewed any kind of activity with people, no matter how minute or unimportant, as a battlefield. In that battlefield, sorcerers performed their best magic, their best effort. He assured me that the trick to being at ease in such situations, a thing that had never been my forte, was to face our opponents openly. He expressed his abhorrence of timid souls who shy away from interaction to the point where even though they interact, they merely infer or deduce, in terms of their own psychological states, what is going on without actually perceiving what is really going on. They interact without ever being part of the interaction.

"Always look at the man who is involved in a tug of war with you," he continued. "Don't just pull the rope; look up and see his eyes. You'll know then that he is a man, just like you. No matter what he's saying, no matter what he's doing, he's shaking in his boots, just like you. A look like that renders the opponent helpless, if only for an instant; deliver your blow then."

One day, luck was with me: I cornered Professor Lorca in the hall outside his office.

"Professor Lorca," I said, "do you have a free moment so I could talk to you?"

"Who in the hell are you?" he said with the most natural air, as if I were his best friend and he were merely asking me how I felt that day.

Professor Lorca was as rude as anyone could be, but his words didn't have the effect of rudeness on me. He grinned at me with tight lips, as if encouraging me to leave or to say something meaningful.

"I am an anthropology student, Professor Lorca," I said. "I am involved in a field situation where I have the opportunity to learn about the *cognitive system* of sorcerers."

Professor Lorca looked at me with suspicion and annoyance. His eyes seemed to be two blue points filled with spite. He combed his hair backward with his hand, as if it had fallen on his face.

"I work with a real sorcerer in Mexico," I continued, trying to encourage a response. "He's a real sorcerer, mind you. It has taken me over a year just to warm him up so he would consent to talk to me."

Professor Lorca's face relaxed; he opened his mouth and, waving a most delicate hand in front of my eyes, as if he were twirling pizza dough with it, he spoke to me. I couldn't help noticing his enameled gold cuff links, which matched his greenish blazer to perfection.

"And what do you want from me?" he said.

"I want you to hear me out for a moment," I said, "and see if whatever I'm doing may interest you."

He made a gesture of reluctance and resignation with his shoulders, opened the door of his office, and invited me to come in. I knew that I had no time at all to waste and I gave him a very direct description of my field situation. I told him that I was being taught procedures that had nothing to do with what I had found in the anthropological literature about shamanism.

He moved his lips for a moment without saying a word. When he spoke, he pointed out that the flaw of anthropologists in general is that they never allow themselves sufficient time to become fully cognizant of all the nuances of the particular *cognitive system* used by the people they are studying. He defined "cognition" as a system of interpretation, which through usage makes it possible for individuals to utilize, with the utmost expertise, all the nuances of meaning that make up the particular social milieu under consideration.

Professor Lorca's words illuminated the total scope of my field-work. Without gaining command of all the nuances of the *cognitive system* of the shamans of ancient Mexico, it would have been thoroughly superfluous for me to formulate any idea about that world. If Professor Lorca had not said another word to me, what he had just voiced would have been more than sufficient. What followed was a marvelous discourse on cognition.

"Your problem," Professor Lorca said, "is that the *cognitive system* of our everyday world with which we are all familiar, virtually from the day we are born, is not the same as the *cognitive system* of the sorcerers' world."

This statement created a state of euphoria in me. I thanked Professor Lorca profusely and assured him that there was only one course of action in my case: to follow his ideas through hell or high water.

"What I have told you, of course, is general knowledge," he said as he ushered me out of his office. "Anyone who reads is aware of what I have been telling you."

We parted almost friends. My account to don Juan of my success in approaching Professor Lorca was met with a strange reaction. Don Juan seemed, on the one hand, to be elated, and on the other, concerned.

"I have the feeling that your professor is not quite what he claims to be," he said. "That's, of course, from a sorcerer's point of view. Perhaps it would be wise to quit now, before all this becomes too involved and consuming. One of the high arts of sorcerers is to know when to stop. It appears to me that you've gotten from your professor all you can get from him."

I immediately reacted with a barrage of defenses on behalf of Professor Lorca. Don Juan calmed me down. He said that it wasn't his intention to criticize or judge anybody, but that to his knowledge, very few people knew when to quit and even fewer knew how to actually utilize their knowledge.

In spite of don Juan's warnings, I didn't quit; instead, I became Professor Lorca's faithful student, follower, admirer. He seemed to take a genuine interest in my work, although he felt frustrated no end with my reluctance and inability to formulate clear-cut concepts about the *cognitive system* of the sorcerers' world.

One day, Professor Lorca formulated for me the concept of the *scientist-visitor to another cognitive world*. He conceded that he was willing to be open-minded, and toy, as a social scientist, with the possibility of a different *cognitive system*. He envisioned an actual research in which protocols would be gathered and analyzed. Problems of cognition would be devised and given to the shamans I knew, to measure, for instance, their capacity to focus their cognition on two diverse aspects of behavior.

He thought that the test would begin with a simple paradigm in which they would try to comprehend and retain written text that they read while they played poker. The test would escalate, to measure, for instance, their capacity to focus their cognition on complex things that were being said to them while they slept, and so on. Professor Lorca wanted a linguistic analysis to be performed on the shamans' utterances. He wanted an actual measurement of their responses in terms of their speed and accuracy, and other variables that would become prevalent as the project progressed.

Don Juan veritably laughed his head off when I told him about Professor Lorca's proposed measurements of the cognition of shamans.

"Now, I truly like your professor," he said. "But you can't be serious about this idea of measuring our cognition. What could your professor get out of measuring our responses? He'll get the conviction that we are a bunch of morons, because that's what we are. We cannot possibly be more intelligent, faster than the average man. It's not his fault, though, to believe he can make measurements of cognition across worlds. The fault is yours. You have failed to express to your professor that when sorcerers talk about the *cognitive world* of the shamans of ancient Mexico they are talking about things for which we have no equivalent in the world of everyday life.

"For instance, perceiving energy directly as it flows in the universe is a unit of cognition that shamans live by. They *see* how energy flows, and they follow its flow. If its flow is obstructed, they move away to do something entirely different. Shamans *see* lines in the universe. Their art, or their job, is to choose the line that will take them, perception-wise, to regions that have no name. You can say that shamans react immediately to the lines of the universe. They *see* human beings as luminous balls, and they search in them for their flow of energy. Naturally, they react instantly to this sight. It's part of their cognition."

I told don Juan that I couldn't possibly talk about all this to Professor Lorca because I hadn't done any of the things that he was describing. My cognition remained the same.

"Ah!" he exclaimed. "It's simply that you haven't had the time yet to embody the units of cognition of the shamans' world."

I left don Juan's house more confused than ever. There was a voice inside me that virtually demanded that I end all endeavors with Professor Lorca. I understood how right don Juan was when he said to me once that the practicalities that scientists were interested in were conducive to building more and more complex machines. They were not the practicalities that changed an individual's life course from within. They were not geared to reaching the vastness of the universe as a personal, experiential affair. The stupendous machines in existence, or those in the making, were cultural affairs, the attainment of which had to be enjoyed vicariously, even by the creators of those machines themselves. The only reward for them was monetary.

In pointing out all of that to me, don Juan had succeeded in placing me in a more inquisitive frame of mind. I really began to question the ideas of Professor Lorca, something I had never done before. Meanwhile, Professor Lorca kept spouting astounding truths about cognition. Each declaration was more severe than the preceding one and, therefore, more incisive.

At the end of my second semester with Professor Lorca, I had reached an impasse. There was no way on earth for me to bridge the two lines of thought: don Juan's and Professor Lorca's. They were on parallel tracks. I understood Professor Lorca's drive to qualify and quantify the study of cognition. Cybernetics was just around the corner at that time, and the practical aspect of the studies of cognition was a reality. But so was don Juan's world, which could not be measured with the standard tools of cognition. I had been privileged to witness it, in don Juan's actions, but I hadn't experienced it myself. I felt that that was the drawback that made bridging those two worlds impossible.

I told all this to don Juan on one of my visits to him. He said that what I considered to be my drawback, and therefore the factor that made bridging these two worlds impossible, wasn't accurate. In his opinion, the flaw was something more encompassing than one man's individual circumstances.

"Perhaps you can recall what I said to you about one of our biggest flaws as average human beings," he said.

I couldn't recall anything in particular. He had pointed out so many flaws that plagued us as average human beings that my mind reeled.

"You want something specific," I said, "and I can't think of it."

"The big flaw I am talking about," he said, "is something you ought to bear in mind every second of your existence. For me, it's the issue of issues, which I will repeat to you over and over until it comes out of your ears."

After a long moment, I gave up any further attempt to remember.

"We are beings on our way to dying," he said. "We are not immortal, but we behave as if we were. This is the flaw that brings us down as individuals and will bring us down as a species someday."

Don Juan stated that the sorcerers' advantage over their average fellow men is that sorcerers know that they are beings on their way to dying and they don't let themselves deviate from

125

that knowledge. He emphasized that an enormous effort must be employed in order to elicit and maintain this knowledge as a total certainty.

"Why is it so hard for us to admit something that is so truthful?" I asked, bewildered by the magnitude of our internal contradiction.

"It's really not man's fault," he said in a conciliatory tone. "Someday, I'll tell you more about the forces that drive a man to act like an ass."

There wasn't anything else to say. The silence that followed was ominous. I didn't even want to know what the forces were that don Juan was referring to.

"It is no great feat for me to assess your professor at a distance," don Juan went on. "He is an immortal scientist. He is never going to die. And when it comes to any concerns about dying, I am sure that he has taken care of them already. He has a plot to be buried in, and a hefty life insurance policy that will take care of his family. Having fulfilled those two mandates, he doesn't think about death anymore. He thinks only about his work.

"Professor Lorca makes sense when he talks," don Juan continued, "because he is prepared to use words accurately. But he's not prepared to take himself seriously as a man who is going to die. Being immortal, he wouldn't know how to do that. It makes no difference what complex machines scientists can build. The machines can in no way help anyone face the unavoidable appointment: the appointment with *infinity*.

"The nagual Julian used to tell me," he went on, "about the conquering generals of ancient Rome. When they would return home victorious, gigantic parades were staged to honor them. Displaying the treasures that they had won, and the defeated people that they had turned into slaves, the conquerors paraded, riding in their war chariots. Riding with them was always a slave whose job was to whisper in their ear that all fame and glory is but transitory.

"If we are victorious in any way," don Juan went on, "we don't have anyone to whisper in our ear that our victories are fleeting. Sorcerers, however, do have the upper hand; as beings on their way to dying, they have someone whispering in their ear that everything is ephemeral. The whisperer is death, the infallible advisor, the only one who won't ever tell you a lie."

# Saying Thank You

"*WARRIOR-TRAVELERS* don't leave any debts unpaid," don Juan said.

"What are you talking about, don Juan?" I asked.

"It is time that you square certain indebtedness you have incurred in the course of your life," he said. "Not that you will ever pay in full, mind you, but you must make a gesture. You must make a token payment in order to atone, in order to appease *infinity*. You told me about your two friends who meant so much to you, Patricia Turner and Sandra Flanagan. It's time for you to go and find them and to make to each of them one gift in which you spend everything you have. You have to make two gifts that will leave you penniless. That's the gesture."

"I don't know where they are, don Juan," I said, almost in a mood of protest.

"To find them is your challenge. In your search for them, you will not leave any stone unturned. What you intend to do is something very simple, and yet nearly impossible. You want to cross over the threshold of personal indebtedness and in one sweep be free, in order to proceed. If you cannot cross that threshold, there won't be any point in trying to continue with me."

"But where did you get the idea of this task for me?" I asked. "Did you invent it yourself, because you think it is appropriate?"

"I don't invent anything," he said matter-of-factly. "I got this task from *infinity* itself. It's not easy for me to say all this to you. If you think that I'm enjoying myself pink with your tribulations, you're wrong. The success of your mission means more to me than it does to you. If you fail, you have very little to lose. What? Your visits to me. Big deal. But I would lose you, and that means to me losing either the continuity of my lineage or the possibility of your closing it with a golden key."

Don Juan stopped talking. He always knew when my mind became feverish with thoughts.

"I have told you over and over that *warrior-travelers* are pragmatists," he went on. "They are not involved in sentimentalism, or nostalgia, or melancholy. For *warrior-travelers*, there is only struggle, and it is a struggle with no end. If you think that you have come here to find peace, or that this is a lull in your life, you're wrong. This task of paying your debts is not guided by any feelings that you know about. It is guided by the purest sentiment, the sentiment of a *warrior-traveler* who is about to dive into *infinity*, and just before he does, he turns around to say thank you to those who favored him.

"You must face this task with all the gravity it deserves," he continued. "It is your last stop before *infinity* swallows you. In fact, unless a *warrior-traveler* is in a sublime state of being, *infinity* will not touch him with a ten-foot pole. So, don't spare yourself; don't spare any effort. Push it mercilessly, but elegantly, all the way through."

I had met the two people don Juan had referred to as my two friends who meant so much to me while going to junior college. I used to live in the garage apartment of the house belonging to Patricia Turner's parents. In exchange for room and board, I took care of vacuuming the pool, raking the leaves, putting the trash out, and making breakfast for Patricia and myself. I was also the handyman in the house as well as the family chauffeur; I drove Mrs. Turner to do her shopping and I bought liquor for Mr. Turner, which I had to sneak into the house and then into his studio.

He was an insurance executive who was a solitary drinker. He had promised his family that he was not going to touch the bottle ever again after some serious family altercations due to his excessive drinking. He confessed to me that he had tapered off enormously, but that he needed a swig from time to time. His studio was, of course, off limits to everybody except me. I was supposed to go in to clean it, but what I really did was hide his bottles inside a beam that appeared to support an arch in the ceiling in the studio but that was actually hollow. I had to sneak the bottles in and sneak the empties out and dump them at the market.

Patricia was a drama and music major in college and a fabulous singer. Her goal was to sing in musicals on Broadway. It goes without saying that I fell head over heels in love with Patricia Turner. She was very slim and athletic, a brunette with angular features and about a head taller than I am, my ultimate requisite for going bananas over any woman.

I seemed to fulfill a deep need in her, the need to nurture someone, especially after she realized that her daddy trusted me implicitly. She became my little mommy. I couldn't even open my mouth without her consent. She watched me like a hawk. She even wrote term papers for me, read textbooks and gave me synopses of them. And I liked it, but not because I wanted to be nurtured; I don't think that that need was ever part of my cognition. I relished the fact that *she* did it. I relished her company.

She used to take me to the movies daily. She had passes to all the big movie theaters in Los Angeles, given to her father courtesy of some movie moguls. Mr. Turner never used them himself; he felt that it was beneath his dignity to flash movie passes. The movie clerks always made the recipients of such passes sign a receipt. Patricia had no qualms about signing anything, but sometimes the nasty clerks wanted Mr. Turner to sign, and when I went to do that, they were not satisfied with only the signature of Mr. Turner. They demanded a driver's license. One of them, a sassy young guy, made a remark that cracked him up, and me, too, but which sent Patricia into a fit of fury.

"I think you're Mr. Turd," he said with the nastiest smile you could imagine, "not Mr. Turner."

I could have sloughed off the remark, but then he subjected us to the profound humiliation of refusing us entrance to see *Hercules* starring Steve Reeves.

Usually, we went everywhere with Patricia's best friend, Sandra Flanagan, who lived next door with her parents. Sandra was quite the opposite of Patricia. She was just as tall, but her face was round, with rosy cheeks and a sensuous mouth; she was healthier than a raccoon. She had no interest in singing. She was only interested in the sensual pleasures of the body. She could eat and drink anything and digest it, and—the feature that finished me off about her—after she had polished off her own plate, she managed to do the same with mine, a thing that, being a picky eater, I had never been able to do in all my life. She was also extremely athletic, but in a rough, wholesome way. She could punch like a man and kick like a mule.

As a courtesy to Patricia, I used to do the same chores for Sandra's parents that I did for hers: vacuuming their pool, raking the leaves from their lawn, taking the trash out on trash day, and incinerating papers and flammable trash. That was the time in Los Angeles when the air pollution was increased by the use of backyard incinerators.

Perhaps it was because of the proximity, or the ease of those young women, that I ended up madly in love with both of them.

I went to seek advice from a very strange young man who was my friend, Nicholas van Hooten. He had two girlfriends, and he lived with both of them, apparently in a state of bliss. He began by giving me, he said, the simplest advice: how to behave in a movie theater if you had two girlfriends. He said that whenever he went to a movie with his two girlfriends, all his attention was always centered on whoever sat to his left. After a while, the two girls would go to the bathroom and, on their return, he would have them change the seating arrangement. Anna would sit where Betty had been sitting, and nobody around them was the wiser. He assured me that this was the first step in a long process of breaking the girls into a matter-of-fact acceptance of the trio situation; Nicholas was rather corny, and he used that trite French expression: *ménage à trois*.

I followed his advice and went to a theater that showed silent movies on Fairfax Avenue in Los Angeles with Patricia and Sandy. I sat Patricia to my left and poured all my attention on her. They went to the bathroom, and when they returned I told them to switch places. I started then to do what Nicholas van Hooten had advised, but Patricia would not put up with any nonsense like that. She stood up and left the theater, offended, humiliated, and raving mad. I wanted to run after her and apologize, but Sandra stopped me.

"Let her go," she said with a poisonous smile. "She's a big girl. She has enough money to get a taxi and go home."

I fell for it and remained in the theater kissing Sandra, rather nervously, and filled with guilt. I was in the middle of a passionate kiss when I felt someone pulling me backward by the hair. It was Patricia. The row of seats was loose and tilted backward. Athletic Patricia jumped out of the way before the seats where we were sitting crashed on the row of seats behind. I heard the frightened screams of two movie watchers who were sitting at the end of the row, by the aisle.

Nicholas van Hooten's tip was miserable advice. Patricia, Sandra, and I returned home in absolute silence. We patched up our differences, in the midst of very weird promises, tears, the works. The outcome of our three-sided relationship was that, in the end, we nearly destroyed ourselves. We were not prepared for such an endeavor. We didn't know how to resolve the problems of affection, morality, duty, and social mores. I couldn't leave one of them for the other, and they couldn't leave me. One day, at the climax of a tremendous upheaval, and out of sheer desperation, all three of us fled in different directions, never to see one another again.

I felt devastated. Nothing of what I did could erase their impact on my life. I left Los Angeles and got busy with endless things in an effort to placate my longing. Without exaggerating in the least, I can sincerely say that I fell into the depths of hell, I believed, never to emerge again. If it hadn't been for the influence that don Juan had on my life and my person, I would never have survived my private demons. I told don Juan that I knew that whatever I had done was wrong, that I had no business engaging such wonderful people in such sordid, stupid shenanigans that I had no preparation to face.

"What was wrong," don Juan said, "was that the three of you were lost egomaniacs. Your self-importance nearly destroyed you. If you don't have self-importance, you have only feelings.

"Humor me," he went on, "and do the following simple and direct exercise that could mean the world to you: Remove from your memory of those two girls any statements that you make to yourself such as 'She said this or that to me, and she yelled, and the other one yelled, at ME!' and remain at the level of your feelings. If you hadn't been so self-important, what would you have had as the irreducible residue?"

"My unbiased love for them," I said, nearly choking.

"And is it less today than it was then?" don Juan asked.

"No, it isn't, don Juan," I said in truthfulness, and I felt the same pang of anguish that had chased me for years.

"This time, embrace them from your silence," he said. "Don't be a meager asshole. Embrace them totally for the last time. But *intend* that this is the last time on Earth. *Intend* it from your darkness. If you are worth your salt," he went on, "when you make your gift to them, you'll sum up your entire life twice. Acts of this nature make warriors airborne, almost vaporous."

Following don Juan's commands, I took the task to heart. I realized that if I didn't emerge victorious, don Juan was not the only one who was going to lose out. I would also lose something, and whatever I was going to lose was as important to me as what don Juan had described as being important to him. I was going to lose my chance to face *infinity* and be conscious of it.

The memory of Patricia Turner and Sandra Flanagan put me in a terrible frame of mind. The devastating sense of irreparable loss that had chased me all these years was as vivid as ever. When don Juan exacerbated that feeling, I knew for a fact that there are certain things that can remain with us, in don Juan's terms, for life and perhaps beyond. I had to find Patricia Turner and Sandra Flanagan. Don Juan's final recommendation was that if I did find them, I could not stay with them. I could have time only to atone, to envelop each of them with all the affection I felt, without the angry voices of recrimination, self-pity, or ego-mania.

I embarked on the colossal task of finding out what had become of them, where they were. I began by asking questions of the people who knew their parents. Their parents had moved out of Los Angeles, and nobody could give me a lead as to where to find them. There was no one to talk to. I thought of putting a personal ad in the paper. But then I thought that perhaps they had moved out of California. I finally had to hire a private investigator. Through his connections with official offices of records and whatnot, he located them within a couple of weeks.

They lived in New York, a short distance from one other, and their friendship was as close as it had ever been. I went to New York and tackled Patricia Turner first. She hadn't made it to stardom on Broadway the way she had wanted to, but she was part of a production. I didn't want to know whether it was in the capacity of a performer or as management. I visited her in her office. She didn't tell me what she did. She was shocked to see me. What we did was just sit together and hold hands and weep. I didn't tell her what I did either. I said that I had come to see her because I wanted to give her a gift that would express my gratitude, and that I was embarking on a journey from which I did not intend to come back.

"Why such ominous words?" she asked, apparently genuinely alarmed. "What are you planning to do? Are you ill? You don't look ill."

"It was a metaphorical statement," I assured her. "I'm going back to South America, and I intend to seek my fortune there. The competition is ferocious, and the circumstances are very harsh, that's all. If I want to succeed, I will have to give all I have to it."

She seemed relieved, and hugged me. She looked the same, except much bigger, much more powerful, more mature, very elegant. I kissed her hands and the most overwhelming affection enveloped me. Don Juan was right. Deprived of recriminations, all I had were feelings.

"I want to make you a gift, Patricia Turner," I said. "Ask me anything you want, and if it is within my means, I'll get it for you."

"Did you strike it rich?" she said and laughed. "What's great about you is that you never had anything, and you never will. Sandra and I talk about you nearly every day. We imagine you parking cars, living off women, et cetera, et cetera. I'm sorry, we can't help ourselves, but we still love you."

I insisted that she tell me what she wanted. She began to weep and laugh at the same time.

"Are you going to buy me a mink coat?" she asked me between sobs.

I ruffled her hair and said that I would.

"If you don't like it, you take it back to the store and get the money back," I said.

She laughed and punched me the way she used to. She had to go back to work, and we parted after I promised her that I would come back again to see her, but that if I didn't, I wanted her to understand that the force of my life was pulling me every which way, yet I would keep the memory of her in me for the rest of my life and perhaps beyond.

I did return, but only to see from a distance how they delivered the mink coat to her. I heard her screams of delight.

That part of my task was finished. I left, but I wasn't vaporous, the way don Juan had said I was going to be. I had opened up an old wound and it had started to bleed. It wasn't quite raining outside; it was a fine mist that seemed to penetrate all the way to the marrow of my bones.

Next, I went to see Sandra Flanagan. She lived in one of the suburbs of New York that is reached by train. I knocked on her door. Sandra opened it and looked at me as if I were a ghost. All the color drained out of her face. She was more beautiful than ever, perhaps because she had filled out and looked as big as a house.

"Why, you, you, you!" she stammered, not quite capable of articulating my name.

She sobbed, and she seemed indignant and reproachful for a moment. I didn't give her the chance to continue. My silence was total. In the end, it affected her. She let me in and we sat down in her living room.

"What are you doing here?" she said, quite a bit calmer. "You can't stay! I'm a married woman! I have three children! And I'm very happy in my marriage."

Shooting her words out rapidly, like a machine gun, she told me that her husband was very dependable, not too imaginative but a good man, that he was not sensual, that she had to be very careful because he tired very easily when they made love, that he got sick easily and sometimes couldn't go to work but that he had managed to produce three beautiful children, and that after her third child, her husband, whose name seemed to be Herbert, had just simply quit. He didn't have it anymore, but it didn't matter to her.

I tried to calm her down by assuring her over and over that I had come to visit her only for a moment, that it was not my intention to alter her life or to bother her in any way. I described to her how hard it had been to find her.

"I have come here to say good-bye to you," I said, "and to tell you that you are the love of my life. I want to make you a token gift, a symbol of my gratitude and my undying affection."

She seemed to be deeply affected. She smiled openly the way she used to. The separation between her teeth made her look childlike. I commented to her that she was more beautiful than ever, which was the truth to me.

She laughed and said that she was going on a strict diet, and if she had known that I was coming to see her, she would have started her diet a long time ago. But she would start now, and I would find her the next time as lean as she had always been. She reiterated the horror of our life together and how profoundly affected she had been. She had even thought, in spite of being a devout Catholic, of committing suicide, but she had found in her children the solace that she needed; whatever we had done were quirks of youth that would never be vacuumed away, but had to be swept under the rug.

When I asked if there was some gift that I could make to her as a token of my gratitude and affection for her, she laughed and said exactly what Patricia Turner had said: that I didn't have a pot to piss in, nor would I ever have one, because that's the way I was made. I insisted that she name something.

"Can you buy me a station wagon where all my children could fit?" she said, laughing. "I want a Pontiac, or an Oldsmobile, with all the trimmings."

She said that knowing in her heart of hearts that I could not possibly make her such a gift. But I did.

I drove the dealer's car, following him as he delivered the station wagon to her the next day, and from the parked car where I was hiding, I heard her surprise; but congruous with her sensual being, her surprise was not an expression of delight. It was a bodily reaction, a sob of anguish, of bewilderment. She cried, but I knew that she was not crying because she had received the gift. She was expressing a longing that had echoes in me. I crumpled in the seat of the car.

On my train ride to New York, and my flight to Los Angeles, the feeling that persisted was that my life was running out; it was running out of me like clutched sand. I didn't feel in any way liberated or changed by saying thank you and good-bye. Quite the contrary, I felt the burden of that weird affection more deeply than ever. I felt like weeping. What ran through my mind over and over were the titles that my friend Rodrigo Cummings had invented for books that were never to be written. He specialized in writing titles. His favorite was "We'll All Die in Hollywood"; another was "We'll Never Change"; and my favorite, the one that I bought for ten dollars, was "From the Life and Sins of Rodrigo Cummings." All those titles played in my mind. I was Rodrigo Cummings, and I was stuck in time and space, and I did love two women more than my life, and that would never change. And like the rest of my friends, I would die in Hollywood.

I told don Juan all of this in my report of what I considered to be my pseudo-success. He discarded it shamelessly. He said that what I felt was merely the result of indulging and self-pity, and that in order to say good-bye and thank you, and really mean it and sustain it, sorcerers had to remake themselves.

"Vanquish your self-pity right now," he demanded. "Vanquish the idea that you are hurt and what do you have as the irreducible residue?"

What I had as the irreducible residue was the feeling that I had made my ultimate gift to both of them. Not in the spirit of renewing anything, or harming anyone, including myself, but in the true spirit that don Juan had tried to point out to me—in the spirit of a *warrior-traveler* whose only virtue, he had said, is to keep alive the memory of whatever has affected him, whose only way to say thank you and good-bye was by this act of magic: of storing in his silence whatever he has loved.

# Beyond Syntax

# The Usher

I WAS IN don Juan's house in Sonora, sound asleep in my bed, when he woke me up. I had stayed up practically all night, mulling over concepts that he had explained to me.

"You have rested enough," he said firmly, almost gruffly, as he shook me by the shoulders. "Don't indulge in being fatigued. Your fatigue is, more than fatigue, a desire not to be bothered. Something in you resents being bothered. But it's most important that you exacerbate that part of you until it breaks down. Let's go for a hike."

Don Juan was right. There was some part of me that resented immensely being bothered. I wanted to sleep for days and not think about don Juan's sorcery concepts anymore. Thoroughly against my will, I got up and followed him. Don Juan had prepared a meal, which I devoured as if I hadn't eaten for days, and then we walked out of the house and headed east, toward the mountains. I had been so dazed that I hadn't noticed that it was early morning until I saw the sun, which was right above the eastern range of mountains. I wanted to comment to don Juan that I had slept all night without moving, but he hushed me. He said that we were going to go on an expedition to the mountains to search for specific plants.

"What are you going to do with the plants you are going to collect, don Juan?" I asked him as soon as we had started off.

"They are not for me," he said with a grin. "They are for a friend of mine, a botanist and pharmacist. He makes potions with them."

"Is he a Yaqui, don Juan? Does he live here in Sonora?" I asked.

"No, he isn't a Yaqui, and he doesn't live here in Sonora. You'll meet him someday."

"Is he a sorcerer, don Juan?"

"Yes, he is," he replied dryly.

I asked him then if I could take some of the plants to be identified at the Botanical Garden at UCLA.

"Surely, surely!" he said.

I had found out in the past that whenever he said "surely," he didn't mean it. It was obvious that he had no intention whatsoever of giving me any specimens for identification. I became very curious about his sorcerer friend, and asked him to tell me more about him, perhaps describe him, telling me where he lived and how he got to meet him.

"Whoa, whoa, whoa, whoa!" don Juan said, as if I were a horse. "Hold it, hold it! Who are you? Professor Lorca? Do you want to study his cognitive system?"

We went deep into the arid foothills. Don Juan walked steadily for hours. I thought that the task of the day was going to be just to walk. He finally stopped and sat down on the shaded side of the foothills.

"It is time that you start on one of the biggest projects of sorcery," don Juan said.

"What is this project of sorcery that you're talking about, don Juan?" I inquired.

"It's called the *recapitulation*," he said. "The old sorcerers used to call it *recounting the events of your life*, and for them, it started as a simple technique, a device to aid them in remembering what they were doing and saying to their disciples. For their disciples, the technique had the same value: It allowed them to remember what their teachers had said and done to them. It took terrible social upheavals, like being conquered and vanquished several times, before the old sorcerers realized that their technique had far-reaching effects."

"Are you referring, don Juan, to the Spanish conquest?" I asked.

"No," he said. "That was just the icing on the cake. There were other upheavals before that, more devastating. When the Spaniards got here, the old sorcerers didn't exist any longer. The disciples of those who had survived other upheavals were very cagey by then. They knew how to take care of themselves. It is that new crop of sorcerers who renamed the old sorcerers' technique *recapitulation*.

"There's an enormous premium on time," he continued. "For sorcerers in general, time is of the essence. The challenge I am faced with is that in a very compact unit of time I must cram into you everything there is to know about sorcery as an abstract proposition, but in order to do that I have to build the necessary space in you."

"What space? What are you talking about, don Juan?"

"The premise of sorcerers is that in order to bring something in, there must be a space to put it in," he said. "If you are filled to the brim with the items of everyday life, there's no space for anything new. That space must be built. Do you see what I mean? The sorcerers of olden times believed that the *recapitulation* of your life made that space. It does, and much more, of course.

"The way sorcerers perform the *recapitulation* is very formal," he went on. "It consists of writing a list of all the people they have met, from the present to the very beginning of their lives. Once they have that list, they take the first person on it and recollect everything they can about that person. And I mean everything, every detail. It's better to recapitulate from the present to the past, because the memories of the present are fresh, and in this manner, the recollection ability is honed. What practitioners do is to recollect and breathe. They inhale slowly and deliberately, fanning the head from right to left, in a barely noticeable swing, and exhale in the same fashion."

He said that the inhalations and exhalations should be natural; if they were too rapid, one would enter into something that he called *tiring breaths:* breaths that required slower breathing afterward in order to calm down the muscles.

"And what do you want me to do, don Juan, with all this?" I asked.

"You begin making your list today," he said. "Divide it by years, by occupations, arrange it in any order you want to, but make it sequential, with the most recent person first, and end with Mommy and Daddy. And then, remember everything about them. No more ado than that. As you practice, you will realize what you're doing."

On my next visit to his house, I told don Juan that I had been meticulously going through the events of my life, and that it was very difficult for me to adhere to his strict format and follow my list of persons one by one. Ordinarily, my *recapitulation* took me every which way. I let the events decide the direction of my recollection. What I did, which was volitional, was to adhere to a general unit of time. For instance, I had begun with the people in the anthropology department, but I let my recollection pull me to anywhere in time, from the present to the day I started attending school at UCLA.

I told don Juan that an odd thing I'd found out, which I had completely forgotten, was that I had no idea that UCLA existed until one night when my girlfriend's roommate from college came to Los Angeles and we picked her up at the airport. She was going to study musicology at UCLA. Her plane arrived in the early evening, and she asked me if I could take her to the campus so she could take a look at the place where she was going to spend the next four years of her life. I knew where the campus was, for I had driven past its entrance on Sunset Boulevard endless times on my way to the beach. I had never been on the campus, though.

It was during the semester break. The few people that we found directed us to the music department. The campus was deserted, but what I witnessed subjectively was the most exquisite thing I have ever seen. It was a delight to my eyes. The buildings seemed to be alive with some energy of their own. What was going to be a very cursory visit to the music department turned out to be a gigantic tour of the entire campus. I fell in love with UCLA. I mentioned to don Juan that the only thing that marred my ecstasy was my girlfriend's annoyance at my insistence on walking through the huge campus.

"What the hell could there be in here?" she yelled at me in protest. "It's as if you have never seen a university campus in your life! You've seen one, you've seen them all. I think you're just trying to impress my friend with your sensitivity!"

I wasn't, and I vehemently told them that I was genuinely impressed by the beauty of my surroundings. I sensed so much hope in those buildings, so much promise, and yet I couldn't express my subjective state.

"I have been in school nearly all my life," my girlfriend said through clenched teeth, "and I'm sick and tired of it! Nobody's going to find shit in here! All you find is guff, and they don't even prepare you to meet your responsibilities in life."

When I mentioned that I would like to attend school here, she became even more furious.

"Get a job!" she screamed. "Go and meet life from eight to five, and cut the crap! That's what life is: a job from eight to five, forty hours a week! See what it does to you! Look at me—I'm super-educated now, and I'm not fit for a job."

All I knew was that I had never seen a place so beautiful. I made a promise then that I would go to school at UCLA, no matter what, come hell or high water. My desire had everything to do with me, and yet it was not driven by the need for immediate gratification. It was more in the realm of awe.

I told don Juan that my girlfriend's annoyance had been so jarring to me that it forced me to look at her in a different light, and that to my recollection, that was the first time ever that a commentary had aroused such a deep reaction in me. I saw facets of character in my girlfriend that I hadn't seen before, facets that scared me stiff.

"I think I judged her terribly," I said to don Juan. "After our visit to the campus, we drifted apart. It was as if UCLA had come between us like a wedge. I know that it's stupid to think this way."

"It isn't stupid," don Juan said. "It was a perfectly valid reaction. While you were walking on the campus, I am sure that you had a bout with *intent*. You *intended* being there, and anything that was opposed to it you had to let go.

"But don't overdo it," he went on. "The touch of *warrior-travelers* is very light, although it is cultivated. The hand of a *warrior-traveler* begins as a heavy, gripping, iron hand but becomes like the hand of a ghost, a hand made of gossamer. *Warrior-travelers* leave no marks, no tracks. That's the challenge for *warrior-travelers*."

Don Juan's comments made me sink into a deep, morose state of recriminations against myself, for I knew, from the little bit of my recounting, that I was extremely heavy-handed, obsessive, and domineering. I told don Juan about my ruminations.

"The power of the *recapitulation*," don Juan said, "is that it stirs up all the garbage of our lives and brings it to the surface."

Then don Juan delineated the intricacies of awareness and perception, which were the basis of the *recapitulation*. He began by saying that he was going to present an arrangement of concepts that I should not take as sorcerers' theories under any conditions, because it was an arrangement formulated by the shamans of ancient Mexico as a result of *seeing* energy directly as it flows in the universe. He warned me that he would present the units of this arrangement to me without any attempt at classifying them or ranking them by any predetermined standard.

"I'm not interested in classifications," he went on. "You have been classifying everything all your life. Now you are going to be forced to stay away from classifications. The other day, when I asked you if you knew anything about clouds, you gave me the names of all the clouds and the percentage of moisture that one should expect from each one of them. You were a veritable weatherman. But when I asked you if you knew what you could do with the clouds personally, you had no idea what I was talking about.

"Classifications have a world of their own," he continued. "After you begin to classify anything, the classification becomes alive, and it rules you. But since classifications never started as energy-giving affairs, they always remain like dead logs. They are not trees; they are merely logs."

He explained that the sorcerers of ancient Mexico *saw* that the universe at large is composed of energy fields in the form of luminous filaments. They *saw* zillions of them, wherever they turned to *see*. They also *saw* that those energy fields arrange themselves into currents of luminous fibers, streams that are constant, perennial forces in the universe, and that the current or stream of filaments that is related to the *recapitulation* was named by those sorcerers the *dark sea of awareness*, and also the *Eagle*.

He stated that those sorcerers also found out that every creature in the universe is attached to the *dark sea of awareness* at a round point of luminosity that was apparent when those creatures were perceived as energy. On that point of luminosity, which the sorcerers of ancient Mexico called the *assemblage point*, don Juan said that perception was assembled by a mysterious aspect of the *dark sea of awareness*.

Don Juan asserted that on the *assemblage point* of human beings, zillions of energy fields from the universe at large, in the form of luminous filaments, converge and go through it. These energy fields are converted into sensory data, and the sensory data is then interpreted and perceived as the world we know. Don Juan further explained that what turns the luminous fibers into sensory data is the *dark sea of awareness*. Sorcerers *see* this transformation and call it the *glow of awareness*, a sheen that extends like a halo around the *assemblage point*. He warned me then that he was going to make a statement which, in the understanding of sorcerers, was central to comprehending the scope of the *recapitulation*.

Putting an enormous emphasis on his words, he said that what we call the *senses* in organisms is nothing but degrees of awareness. He maintained that if we accept that the senses are the *dark sea of awareness*, we have to admit that the interpretation that the senses make of sensory data is also the *dark sea of awareness*. He explained at length that to face the world around us in the terms that we do is the result of the interpretation system of mankind with which every human being is equipped. He also said that every organism in existence has to have an interpretation system that permits it to function in its surroundings.

"The sorcerers who came after the apocalyptic upheavals I told you about," he continued, "*saw* that at the moment of death, the *dark sea of awareness* sucked in, so to speak, through the *assemblage point*, the awareness of living creatures. They also *saw* that the *dark sea of awareness* had a moment's, let's say, hesitation when it was faced with sorcerers who had done a recounting of their lives. Unbeknownst to them, some had done it so thoroughly that the *dark sea of awareness* took their awareness in the form of their life experiences, but didn't touch their life force. Sorcerers had found out a gigantic truth about the forces of the universe: The *dark sea of awareness* wants only our life experiences, not our life force."

The premises of don Juan's elucidation were incomprehensible to me. Or perhaps it would be more accurate to say that I was vaguely and yet deeply cognizant of how functional the premises of his explanation were.

"Sorcerers believe," don Juan went on, "that as we *recapitulate* our lives, all the debris, as I told you, comes to the surface. We realize our inconsistencies, our repetitions, but something in us puts up a tremendous resistance to *recapitulating*. Sorcerers say that the road is free only after a gigantic upheaval, after the appearance on our screen of the memory of an event that shakes our foundations with its terrifying clarity of detail. It's the event that drags us to the actual moment that we lived it. Sorcerers call that event the *usher,* because from then on every event we touch on is relived, not merely remembered.

"Walking is always something that precipitates memories," don Juan went on. "The sorcerers of ancient Mexico believed that everything we live we store as a sensation on the backs of the legs. They considered the backs of the legs to be the warehouse of man's personal history. So, let's go for a walk in the hills now."

We walked until it was almost dark.

"I think I have made you walk long enough," don Juan said when we were back at his house, "to have you ready to begin this sorcerers' maneuver of finding an *usher:* an event in your life that you will remember with such clarity that it will serve as a spotlight to illuminate everything else in your *recapitulation* with the same, or comparable, clarity. Do what sorcerers call *recapitulating pieces of a puzzle.* Something will lead you to remember the event that will serve as your *usher.*"

He left me alone, giving me one last warning.

"Give it your best shot," he said. "Do your best."

I was extremely silent for a moment, perhaps due to the silence around me. I experienced, then, a vibration, a sort of jolt in my chest. I had difficulty breathing, but suddenly something opened up in my chest that allowed me to take a deep breath, and a total view of a forgotten event of my childhood burst into my memory, as if it had been held captive and was suddenly released.

I was at my grandfather's studio, where he had a billiard table, and I was playing billiards with him. I was almost nine years old then. My grandfather was quite a skillful player, and compulsively he had taught me every play he knew until I was good enough to have a serious match with him. We spent endless hours playing billiards. I became so proficient at it that one day I defeated him. From that day on, he was incapable of winning. Many a time I deliberately threw the game, just to be nice to him, but he knew it and would become furious with me. Once, he got so upset that he hit me on the top of the head with the cue.

To my grandfather's chagrin and delight, by the time I was nine years old, I could make carom after carom without stopping. He became so frustrated and impatient in a game with me once that he threw down his cue and told me to play by myself. My compulsive nature made it possible for me to compete with myself and work the same play on and on until I got it perfectly.

One day, a man notorious in town for his gambling connections, the owner of a billiards house, came to visit my grandfather. They were talking and playing billiards as I happened to enter the room. I instantly tried to retreat, but my grandfather grabbed me and pulled me in.

"This is my grandson," he said to the man.

"Very pleased to meet you," the man said. He looked at me sternly, and then extended his hand, which was the size of the head of a normal person.

I was horrified. His enormous burst of laughter told me that he was cognizant of my discomfort. He told me that his name was Falelo Quiroga, and I mumbled my name.

He was very tall, and extremely well dressed. He was wearing a double-breasted blue pinstriped suit with beautifully tapered trousers. He must have been in his early fifties then, but he was trim and fit except for a slight bulge in his midsection. He wasn't fat; he seemed to cultivate the look of a man who is well fed and is not in need of anything. Most of the people in my hometown were gaunt. They were people who labored hard to earn a living and had no time for niceties. Falelo Quiroga appeared to be the opposite. His whole demeanor was that of a man who had time only for niceties.

He was pleasant-looking. He had a bland, well-shaven face with kind blue eyes. He had the air and the confidence of a doctor. People in my town used to say that he was capable of putting anyone at ease, and that he should have been a priest, a lawyer, or a doctor instead of a gambler. They also used to say that he made more money gambling than all the doctors and lawyers in town put together made by working.

His hair was black, and carefully combed. It was obviously thinning considerably. He tried to hide his receding hairline by combing his hair over his forehead. He had a square jaw and an absolutely winning smile. He had big, white teeth, which were well cared for, the ultimate novelty in an area where tooth decay was monumental. Two other remarkable features of Falelo Quiroga, for me, were his enormous feet and his handmade, black patent-leather shoes. I was fascinated by the fact that his shoes didn't squeak at all as he walked back and forth in the room. I was accustomed to hearing my grandfather's approach by the squeak of the soles of his shoes.

"My grandson plays billiards very well," my grandfather said nonchalantly to Falelo Quiroga. "Why don't I give him my cue and let him play with you while I watch?"

"This child plays billiards?" the big man asked my grandfather with a laugh.

"Oh, he does," my grandfather assured him. "Of course, not as well as you do, Falelo. Why don't you try him? And to make it interesting for you, so you won't be patronizing my grandson, let's bet a little money. What do you say if we bet this much?"

He put a thick wad of crumpled-up bills on the table and smiled at Falelo Quiroga, shaking his head from side to side as if daring the big man to take his bet.

"My oh my, that much, eh?" Falelo Quiroga said, looking at me questioningly. He opened his wallet then and pulled out some neatly folded bills. This, for me, was another surprising detail. My grandfather's habit was to carry his money in every one of his pockets, all crumpled up. When he needed to pay for something, he had to straighten out the bills in order to count them.

Falelo Quiroga didn't say it, but I knew that he felt like a highway robber. He smiled at my grandfather and, obviously out of respect for him, he put his money on the table. My grandfather, acting as the arbiter, set the game at a certain number of caroms and flipped a coin to see who would start first. Falelo Quiroga won.

"You better give it all you have, without holding back," my grandfather urged him. "Don't have any qualms about demolishing this twerp and winning my money!"

Falelo Quiroga, following my grandfather's advice, played as hard as he was able, but at one point he missed one carom by a hair. I took the cue. I thought I was going to faint, but seeing my grandfather's glee—he was jumping up and down—calmed me, and besides, it irked me to see Falelo Quiroga about to split his sides laughing when he saw the way I held the cue. I couldn't lean over the table, as billiards is normally played, because of my height. But my grandfather, with painstaking patience and determination, had taught me an alternative way of playing. By extending my arm all the way back, I held the cue nearly above my shoulders, to the side.

"What does he do when he has to reach the middle of the table?" Falelo Quiroga asked, laughing.

"He hangs on the edge of the table," my grandfather said matter-of-factly. "It's permissible, you know."

My grandfather came to me and whispered through clenched teeth that if I tried to be polite and lose he was going to break all the cues on my head. I knew he didn't mean it; this was just his way of expressing his confidence in me.

I won easily. My grandfather was delighted beyond description, but strangely enough, so was Falelo Quiroga. He laughed as he went around the pool table, slapping its edges. My grandfather praised me to the skies. He revealed to Quiroga my best score, and joked that I had excelled because he had found the way to lure me to practice: coffee with Danish pastries.

"You don't say, you don't say!" Quiroga kept repeating. He said good-bye; my grandfather picked up the bet money, and the incident was forgotten.

My grandfather promised to take me to a restaurant and buy me the best meal in town, but he never did. He was very stingy; he was known to be a lavish spender only with women.

Two days later, two enormous men affiliated with Falelo Quiroga came to me at the time that I got out from school and was leaving.

"Falelo Quiroga wants to see you," one of them said in a guttural tone. "He wants you to go to his place and have some coffee and Danish pastries with him."

If he hadn't said coffee and Danish pastries, I probably would have run away from them. I remembered then that my grandfather had told Falelo Quiroga that I would sell my soul for coffee and Danish pastries. I gladly went with them. However, I couldn't walk as fast as they did, so one of them, the one whose name was Guillermo Falcón, picked me up and cradled me in his huge arms. He laughed through crooked teeth.

"You better enjoy the ride, kid," he said. His breath was terrible. "Have you ever been carried by anyone? Judging by the way you wriggle, never!" He giggled grotesquely.

Fortunately, Falelo Quiroga's place was not too far from the school. Mr. Falcón deposited me on a couch in an office. Falelo Quiroga was there, sitting behind a huge desk. He stood up and shook hands with me. He immediately had some coffee and delicious pastries brought to me, and the two of us sat there chatting amiably about my grandfather's chicken farm. He asked me if I would like to have more pastries, and I said that I wouldn't mind if I did. He laughed, and he himself brought me a whole tray of unbelievably delicious pastries from the next room.

After I had veritably gorged myself, he politely asked me if I would consider coming to his billiards place in the wee hours of the night to play a couple of friendly games with some people of his choice. He casually mentioned that a considerable amount of money was going to be involved. He openly expressed his trust in my skill, and added that he was going to pay me, for my time and my effort, a percentage of the winning money. He further stated that he knew the mentality of my family; they would have found it improper that he give me money, even though it was pay. So he promised to put the money in the bank in a special account for me, or more practical yet, he would cover any purchase that I made in any of the stores in town, or the food I consumed in any restaurant in town.

I didn't believe a word of what he was saying. I knew that Falelo Quiroga was a crook, a racketeer. I liked, however, the idea of playing billiards with people I didn't know, and I struck a bargain with him.

"Will you give me some coffee and Danish pastries like the ones you gave me today?" I said.

"Of course, my boy," he replied. "If you come to play for me, I will buy you the bakery! I will have the baker bake them just for you. Take my word."

I warned Falelo Quiroga that the only drawback was my incapacity to get out of my house; I had too many aunts who watched me like hawks, and besides, my bedroom was on the second floor.

"That's no problem," Falelo Quiroga assured me. "You're quite small. Mr. Falcón will catch you if you jump from your window into his arms. He's as big as a house! I recommend that you go to bed early tonight. Mr. Falcón will wake you up by whistling and throwing rocks at your window. You have to watch out, though! He's an impatient man."

I went home in the midst of the most astounding excitement. I couldn't go to sleep. I was quite awake when I heard Mr. Falcón whistling and throwing small pebbles against the glass panes of the window. I opened the window. Mr. Falcón was right below me, on the street.

"Jump into my arms, kid," he said to me in a constricted voice, which he tried to modulate into a loud whisper. "If you don't aim at my arms, I'll drop you and you'll die. Remember that. Don't make me run around. Just aim at my arms. Jump! Jump!"

I did, and he caught me with the ease of someone catching a bag of cotton. He put me down and told me to run. He said that I was a child awakened from a deep sleep, and that he had to make me run so I would be fully awake by the time I got to the billiards house.

I played that night with two men, and I won both games. I had the most delicious coffee and pastries that one could imagine. Personally, I was in heaven. It was around seven in the morning when I returned home. Nobody had noticed my absence. It was time to go to school. For all practical purposes, everything was normal except for the fact that I was so tired that I couldn't keep my eyes open all day.

From that day on, Falelo Quiroga sent Mr. Falcón to pick me up two or three times a week, and I won every game that he made me play. And faithful to his promise, he paid for anything that I bought, including meals at my favorite Chinese restaurant, where I used to go daily. Sometimes, I even invited my friends, whom I mortified no end by running out of the restaurant screaming when the waiter brought the bill. They were amazed at the fact that they were never taken to the police for consuming food and not paying for it.

What was an ordeal for me was that I had never conceived of the fact that I would have to contend with the hopes and expectations of all the people who bet on me. The ordeal of ordeals, however, took place when a crack player from a nearby city challenged Falelo Quiroga and backed his challenge with a giant bet. The night of the game was an inauspicious night. My grandfather became ill and couldn't fall asleep. The entire family was in an uproar. It appeared that nobody went to bed. I doubted that I had any possibility of sneaking out of my bedroom, but Mr. Falcón's whistling and the pebbles hitting the glass of my window were so insistent that I took a chance and jumped from my window into Mr. Falcón's arms.

It seemed that every male in town had congregated at the billiards place. Anguished faces silently begged me not to lose. Some of the men boldly assured me that they had bet their houses and all their belongings. One man, in a half-joking tone, said that he had bet his wife; if I didn't win, he would be a cuckold that night, or a murderer. He didn't specify whether he meant he would kill his wife in order not to be a cuckold, or me, for losing the game.

Falelo Quiroga paced back and forth. He had hired a masseur to massage me. He wanted me relaxed. The masseur put hot towels on my arms and wrists and cold towels on my forehead. He put on my feet the most comfortable, soft shoes that I had ever worn. They had hard, military heels and arch supports. Falelo Quiroga even outfitted me with a beret to keep my hair from falling in my face, as well as a pair of loose overalls with a belt.

Half of the people around the billiard table were strangers from another town. They glared at me. They gave me the feeling that they wanted me dead.

Falelo Quiroga flipped a coin to decide who would go first. My opponent was a Brazilian of Chinese descent, young, round-faced, very spiffy and confident. He started first, and he made a staggering amount of caroms. I knew by the color of his face that Falelo Quiroga was about to have a heart attack, and so were the other people who had bet everything they had on me.

I played very well that night, and as I approached the number of caroms that the other man had made, the nervousness of the ones who had bet on me reached its peak. Falelo Quiroga was the most hysterical of them all. He yelled at everybody and demanded that someone open the windows because the cigarette smoke made the air unbreathable for me. He wanted the masseur to relax my arms and shoulders. Finally, I had to stop everyone, and in a real hurry, I made the eight caroms that I needed to win. The euphoria of those who had bet on me was indescribable. I was oblivious to all that, for it was already morning and they had to take me home in a hurry.

My exhaustion that day knew no limits. Very obligingly, Falelo Quiroga didn't send for me for a whole week. However, one afternoon, Mr. Falcón picked me up from school and took me to the billiards house. Falelo Quiroga was extremely serious. He didn't even offer me coffee or Danish pastries. He sent everybody out of his office and got directly to the point. He pulled his chair close to me.

"I have put a lot of money in the bank for you," he said very solemnly. "I am true to what I promised you. I give you my word that I will always look after you. You know that! Now, if you do what I am going to tell you to do, you will make so much money that you won't have to work a day in your life. I want you to lose your next game by one carom. I know that you can do it. But I want you to miss by only a hair. The more dramatic, the better."

I was dumbfounded. All of this was incomprehensible to me. Falelo Quiroga repeated his request and further explained that he was going to bet anonymously all he had against me, and that that was the nature of our new deal.

"Mr. Falcón has been guarding you for months," he said. "All I need to tell you is that Mr. Falcón uses all his force to protect you, but he could do the opposite with the same strength."

Falelo Quiroga's threat couldn't have been more obvious. He must have seen in my face the horror that I felt, for he relaxed and laughed.

"Oh, but don't you worry about things like that," he said reassuringly, "because we are brothers."

This was the first time in my life that I had been placed in an untenable position. I wanted with all my might to run away from Falelo Quiroga, from the fear that he had evoked in me. But at the same time, and with equal force, I wanted to stay; I wanted the ease of being able to buy anything I wanted from any store, and above all, the ease of being able to eat at any restaurant of my choice, without paying. I was never confronted, however, with having to choose one or the other.

Unexpectedly, at least for me, my grandfather moved to another area, quite distant. It was as if he knew what was going on, and he sent me ahead of everyone else. I doubted that he actually knew what was taking place. It seemed that sending me away was one of his usual intuitive actions.

◎◎

Don Juan's return brought me out of my recollection. I had lost track of time. I should have been famished but I wasn't hungry at all. I was filled with nervous energy. Don Juan lit a kerosene lantern and hung it from a nail on the wall. Its dim light cast strange, dancing shadows in the room. It took a moment for my eyes to adjust to the semidarkness. I entered then into a state of profound sadness. It was a strangely detached feeling, a far-reaching longing that came from that semidarkness, or perhaps from the sensation of being trapped. I was so tired that I wanted to leave, but at the same time, and with the same force, I wanted to stay.

Don Juan's voice brought me a measure of control. He appeared to know the reason for and the depth of my turmoil, and modulated his voice to fit the occasion. The severity of his tone helped me to gain control over something that could easily have turned into a hysterical reaction to fatigue and mental stimulation.

"To recount events is magical for sorcerers," he said. "It isn't just telling stories. It is *seeing* the underlying fabric of events. This is the reason recounting is so important and vast."

At his request, I told don Juan the event I had recollected.

"How appropriate," he said, and chuckled with delight. "The only commentary I can make is that *warrior-travelers* roll with the punches. They go wherever the impulse may take them. The power of *warrior-travelers* is to be alert, to get maximum effect from minimal impulse. And above all, their power lies in not interfering. Events have a force, a gravity of their own, and travelers are just travelers. Everything around them is for their eyes alone. In this fashion, travelers construct the meaning of every situation, without ever asking how it happened this way or that way.

"Today, you remembered an event that sums up your total life," he continued. "You are always faced with a situation that is the same as the one that you never resolved. You never really had to choose whether to accept or reject Falelo Quiroga's crooked deal.

"*Infinity* always puts us in this terrible position of having to choose," he went on. "We want *infinity*, but at the same time, we want to run away from it. You want to tell me to go and jump in a lake, but at the same time you are compelled to stay. It would be infinitely easier for you to just be compelled to stay."

# The Interplay of Energy on the Horizon

THE CLARITY OF the *usher* brought a new impetus to my *recapitulation*. A new mood replaced the old one. From then on, I began to recollect events in my life with maddening clarity. It was exactly as if a barrier had been built inside me that had kept me holding rigidly on to meager and unclear memories, and the *usher* had smashed it. My memory faculty had been for me, prior to that event, a vague way of referring to things that had happened, but which I wanted most of the time to forget. Basically, I had no interest whatsoever in remembering anything of my life. Therefore, I honestly saw absolutely no point in this futile exercise of *recapitulating*, which don Juan had practically imposed on me. For me, it was a chore that tired me instantly and did nothing but point out my incapacity for concentrating.

I had dutifully made, nevertheless, lists of people, and I had engaged in a haphazard effort of quasi-remembering my interactions with them. My lack of clarity in bringing those people into focus didn't dissuade me. I fulfilled what I considered to be my duty, regardless of the way I really felt. With practice, the clarity of my recollection improved, I thought remarkably. I was able to descend, so to speak, on certain choice events with a fair amount of keenness that was at once scary and rewarding. After don Juan presented me with the idea of the *usher*, however, the power of my recollection became something for which I had no name.

Following my list of people made the *recapitulation* extremely formal and exigent, the way don Juan wanted it. But from time to time, something in me got loose, something that forced me to focus on events unrelated to my list, events whose clarity was so maddening that I was caught and submerged in them, perhaps even more intensely than I had been when I had lived the experiences themselves. Every time I *recapitulated* in such a fashion, I had a degree of detachment which allowed me to see things I had disregarded when I had really been in the throes of them.

The first time in which the recollection of an event shook me to my foundations happened after I had given a lecture at a college in Oregon. The students in charge of organizing the lecture took me and another anthropology friend of mine to a house to spend the night. I was going to go to a motel, but they insisted, for our comfort, on taking us to this house. They said that it was in the country, and there were no noises, the quietest place in the world, with no telephones, no interference from the outside world. I, like the fool that I was, agreed to go with them. Don Juan had not only warned me to always be a solitary bird, he had demanded that I observe his recommendation, something that I did most of the time, but there were occasions when the gregarious creature in me took the upper hand.

The committee took us to the house, quite a distance from Portland, of a professor who was on sabbatical. Very swiftly, they turned on the lights inside and outside of the house, which was located on a hill with spotlights all around it. With the spotlights on, the house must have been visible from five miles away.

After that, the committee took off as fast as they could, something that surprised me because I thought they were going to stay and talk. The house was a wooden A-frame, small, but very well constructed. It had an enormous living room and a mezzanine above it where the bedroom was. Right above, at the apex of the A-frame, there was a life-size crucifix hanging from a strange rotating hinge, which was drilled into the head of the figure. The spotlights on the wall were focused on the crucifix. It was quite an impressive sight, especially when it rotated, squeaking as if the hinge needed oil.

The bathroom of the house was another sight. It had mirrored tiles on the ceiling, the walls, and the floor, and it was illuminated with a reddish light. There was no way to go to the bathroom without seeing yourself from every conceivable angle. I enjoyed all those features of the house, which seemed to me stupendous.

When the time came for me to go to sleep, however, I encountered a serious problem because there was only one narrow, hard, quite monastic bed and my anthropologist friend was close to having pneumonia, wheezing and retching phlegm every time he coughed. He went straight for the bed and passed out. I looked for a place to sleep. I couldn't find one. That house was barren of comforts. Besides, it was cold. The committee had turned on the lights, but not the heater. I looked for the heater. My search was fruitless, as was my search for the switch to the spotlights or to any of the lights in the house, for that matter. The switches were there on the walls, but they seemed to be overruled by the effect of some main switch. The lights were on, and I had no way to turn them off.

The only place I could find to sleep was on a thin throw rug, and the only thing I found with which I could cover myself was the tanned hide of a giant French poodle. Obviously, it had been the pet of the house and had been preserved; it had shiny black-marble eyes and an open mouth with the tongue hanging out. I put the head of the poodle skin toward my knees. I still had to cover myself with the tanned rear end, which was on my neck. Its preserved head was like a hard object between my knees, quite unsettling! If it had been dark, it wouldn't have been as bad. I gathered a bundle of washcloths and used them as a pillow. I used as many as possible to cover the hide of the French poodle the best way I could. I couldn't sleep all night.

It was then, as I lay there cursing myself silently for being so stupid and not following don Juan's recommendation, that I had the first maddeningly clear recollection of my entire life. I had recollected the event that don Juan had called the *usher* with equal clarity, but my tendency had always been to half-disregard what happened to me when I was with don Juan, on the basis that in his presence anything was possible. This time, however, I was alone.

Years before I met don Juan, I had worked painting signs on buildings. My boss's name was Luigi Palma. One day Luigi got a contract to paint a sign, advertising the sale and rental of bridal gowns and tuxedos, on the back wall of an old building. The owner of the store in the building wanted to catch the eye of possible customers with a large display. Luigi was going to paint a bride and groom, and I was going to do the lettering. We went to the flat roof of the building and set up a scaffold.

I was quite apprehensive although I had no overt reason to be so. I had painted dozens of signs on high buildings. Luigi thought that I was beginning to be afraid of heights, but that my fear was going to pass. When the time came to start working, he lowered the scaffold a few feet from the roof and jumped onto its flat boards. He went to one side, while I stood on the other in order to be totally out of his way. He was the artist.

Luigi began to show off. His painting movements were so erratic and agitated that the scaffold moved back and forth. I became dizzy. I wanted to go back to the flat roof, using the pretext that I needed more paint and other painters' paraphernalia. I grabbed the edge of the wall that fringed the flat roof and tried to hoist myself up, but the tips of my feet got stuck in the boards of the scaffold. I tried to pull my feet and the scaffold toward the wall; the harder I pulled, the farther away I pushed the scaffold from the wall. Instead of helping me untangle my feet, Luigi sat down and braced himself with the cords that attached the scaffold to the flat roof. He crossed himself and looked at me in horror. From his sitting position, he knelt, weeping quietly as he recited the Lord's Prayer.

I held on to the edge of the wall for dear life; what gave me the desperate strength to endure was the certainty that if I was in control, I could keep the scaffold from moving farther and farther away. I wasn't going to lose my grip and fall thirteen floors to my death. Luigi, being a compulsive taskmaster to the bitter end, yelled to me, in the midst of tears, that I should pray. He swore that both of us were going to fall to our deaths, and that the least we could do was to pray for the salvation of our souls. For a moment, I deliberated about whether it was functional to pray. I opted to yell for help. People in the building must have heard my yelling and sent for the firemen. I sincerely thought that it had taken only two or three seconds after I began to yell for the firemen to come onto the roof and grab Luigi and me and secure the scaffold.

In reality, I had hung on to the side of the building for at least twenty minutes. When the firemen finally pulled me onto the roof, I had lost any vestige of control. I vomited on the hard floor of the roof, sick to my stomach from fear and the odious smell of melted tar. It was a very hot day; the tar on the cracks of the scratchy roofing sheets was melting in the heat. The ordeal had been so frightening and embarrassing that I didn't want to remember it, and I ended up hallucinating that the firemen had pulled me into a warm, yellow room; they had then put me in a supremely comfortable bed, and I had fallen peacefully asleep, safe, wearing my pajamas, delivered from danger.

My second recollection was another blast of incommensurable force. I was talking amiably to a group of friends when, for no apparent reason I could account for, I suddenly lost my breath under the impact of a thought, a memory, which was vague for an instant and then became an engrossing experience. Its force was so intense that I had to excuse myself and retreat for a moment to a corner. My friends seemed to understand my reaction; they disbanded without any comments. What I was remembering was an incident that had taken place in my last year of high school.

My best friend and I used to walk to school, passing a big mansion with a black wrought-iron fence at least seven feet high and ending in pointed spikes. Behind the fence was an extensive, well-kept green lawn, and a huge, ferocious German shepherd dog. Every day, we used to tease the dog and let him charge at us. He stopped physically at the wrought-iron fence, but his rage seemed to cross over to us. My friend delighted in engaging the dog every day in a contest of mind over matter. He used to stand a few inches from the dog's snout, which protruded between the iron bars at least six inches into the street, and bare his teeth, just like the dog did.

"Yield, yield!" my friend shouted every time. "Obey! Obey! I am more powerful than you!"

His daily displays of mental power, which lasted at least five minutes, never affected the dog, outside of leaving him more furious than ever. My friend assured me daily, as part of his ritual, that the dog was either going to obey him or die in front of us of heart failure brought about by rage. His conviction was so intense that I believed that the dog was going to drop dead any day.

One morning, when we came around, the dog wasn't there. We waited for a moment, but he didn't show up; then we saw him, at the end of the extensive lawn. He seemed to be busy there, so we slowly began to walk away. From the corner of my eye, I noticed that the dog was running at full speed, toward us. When he was perhaps six or seven feet from the fence, he took a gigantic leap over it. I was sure that he was going to rip his belly on the spikes. He barely cleared them and fell onto the street like a sack of potatoes.

I thought for a moment that he was dead, but he was only stunned. Suddenly, he got up, and instead of chasing after the one who had brought about his rage, he ran after me. I jumped onto the roof of a car, but the car was nothing for the dog. He took a leap and was nearly on top of me. I scrambled down and climbed the first tree that was within reach, a flimsy little tree that could barely support my weight. I was sure that it would snap in the middle, sending me right into the dog's jaws to be mauled to death.

In the tree, I was nearly out of his reach. But the dog jumped again, and snapped his teeth, catching me by the seat of my pants and ripping them. His teeth actually nicked my buttocks. The moment I was safe at the top of the tree, the dog left. He just ran up the street, perhaps looking for my friend.

At the infirmary in school, the nurse told me that I had to ask the owner of the dog for a certificate of rabies vaccination.

"You must look into this," she said severely. "You may have rabies already. If the owner refuses to show you the vaccination certificate, you are within your rights to call the police."

I talked to the caretaker of the mansion where the dog lived. He accused me of luring the owner's most valuable dog, a pedigreed animal, out into the street.

"You better watch out, boy!" he said in an angry tone. "The dog got lost. The owner will send you to jail if you keep on bothering us."

"But I may have rabies," I said in a sincerely terrified tone.

"I don't give a shit if you have the bubonic plague," the man snapped. "Scram!"

"I'll call the police," I said.

"Call whoever you like," he retorted. "You call the police, we'll turn them against you. In this house, we have enough clout to do that!"

I believed him, so I lied to the nurse and said that the dog could not be found, and that it had no owner.

"Oh my god!" the woman exclaimed. "Then brace yourself for the worst. I may have to send you to the doctor." She gave me a long list of symptoms that I should look for or wait for until they manifested themselves. She said that the injections for rabies were extremely painful, and that they had to be administered subcutaneously on the area of the abdomen.

"I wouldn't wish that treatment on my worst enemy," she said, plunging me into a horrid nightmare.

What followed was my first real depression. I just lay in my bed feeling every one of the symptoms enumerated by the nurse. I ended up going to the school infirmary and begging the woman to give me the treatment for rabies, no matter how painful. I made a huge scene. I became hysterical. I didn't have rabies, but I had totally lost my control.

I related to don Juan my two recollections in all their detail, sparing nothing. He didn't make any comments. He nodded a few times.

"In both recollections, don Juan," I said, feeling myself the urgency of my voice, "I was as hysterical as anyone could be. My body was trembling. I was sick to my stomach. I don't want to say it was *as if* I were in the experiences, because that's not the truth. I *was* in the experiences themselves both times. And when I couldn't take them anymore, I jumped into my life now. For me, that was a jump into the future. I had the power of going over time. My jump into the past was not abrupt; the event developed slowly, as memories do. It was at the end that I did jump abruptly into the future: my life now."

"Something in you has begun to collapse for sure," he finally said. "It has been collapsing all along, but it repaired itself very quickly every time its supports failed. My feeling is that it is now collapsing totally."

After another long silence, don Juan explained that the sorcerers of ancient Mexico believed that, as he had told me already, we had two minds, and only one of them was truly ours. I had always understood don Juan as saying that there were two parts to our minds, and one of them was always silent because expression was denied to it by the force of the other part. Whatever don Juan had said, I had taken as a metaphorical way to explain, perhaps, the apparent dominance of the left hemisphere of the brain over the right, or something of the like.

"There is a secret option to the *recapitulation*," don Juan said.

167

"Just like I told you that there is a secret option to dying, an option that only sorcerers take. In the case of dying, the secret option is that human beings could retain their life force and relinquish only their awareness, the product of their lives. In the case of the *recapitulation*, the secret option that only sorcerers take is to choose to enhance their true minds.

"The haunting memory of your recollections," he went on, "could come only from your true mind. The other mind that we all have and share is, I would say, a cheap model: economy strength, one size fits all. But this is a subject that we will discuss later. What is at stake now is the advent of a disintegrating force. But not a force that is disintegrating you—I don't mean it that way. It is disintegrating what the sorcerers call the *foreign installation*, which exists in you and in every other human being. The effect of the force that is descending on you, which is disintegrating the *foreign installation*, is that it pulls sorcerers out of their syntax."

I had listened carefully to don Juan, but I couldn't say that I had understood what he had said. For some strange reason, which was to me as unknown as the cause of my vivid recollections, I couldn't ask him any questions.

"I know how difficult it is for you," don Juan said all of a sudden, "to deal with this facet of your life. Every sorcerer that I know has gone through it. The males going through it suffer infinitely more damage than the females. I suppose it's the condition of women to be more durable. The sorcerers of ancient Mexico, acting as a group, tried their best to buttress the impact of this disintegrating force. In our day, we have no means of acting as a group, so we must brace ourselves to face in solitude a force that will sweep us away from language, for there is no way to describe adequately what is going on."

Don Juan was right in that I was at a loss for explanations or ways of describing the effect that those recollections had had on me. Don Juan had told me that sorcerers face the unknown in the most common incidents one can imagine. When they are confronted with it, and cannot interpret what they are perceiving, they have to rely on an outside source for direction. Don Juan had called that source *infinity*, or the *voice of the spirit*, and had said that if sorcerers don't try to be rational about what can't be rationalized, the *spirit* unerringly tells them what's what.

Don Juan had guided me to accept the idea that *infinity* was a force that had a voice and was conscious of itself. Consequently, he had prepared me to be ready to listen to that voice and act efficiently always, but without antecedents, using as little as possible the railings of the a priori. I waited impatiently for the *voice of the spirit* to tell me the meaning of my recollections, but nothing happened.

I was in a bookstore one day when a girl recognized me and came over to talk to me. She was tall and slim, and had an insecure, little girl's voice. I was trying to make her feel at ease when I was suddenly accosted by an instantaneous energetic change. It was as if an alarm had been triggered in me, and as it had happened in the past, without any volition on my part whatsoever, I recollected another completely forgotten event in my life. The memory of my grandparents' house flooded me. It was a veritable avalanche so intense that it was devastating, and once more, I had to retreat to a corner. My body shook, as if I had taken a chill.

I must have been eight years old. My grandfather was talking to me. He had begun by telling me that it was his utmost duty to set me straight. I had two cousins who were my age: Alfredo and Luis. My grandfather demanded mercilessly that I admit that my cousin Alfredo was really beautiful. In my vision, I heard my grandfather's raspy, constricted voice.

"Alfredo doesn't need any introductions," he had said to me on that occasion. "He needs only to be present and the doors will fly open for him because everybody practices the cult of beauty. Everybody likes beautiful people. They envy them, but they certainly seek their company. Take it from me. I am handsome, wouldn't you say?"

I sincerely agreed with my grandfather. He was certainly a very handsome man, small-boned, with laughing blue eyes and an exquisitely chiseled face with beautiful cheekbones. Everything seemed to be perfectly balanced in his face—his nose, his mouth, his eyes, his pointed jaw. He had blond hair growing on his ears, a feature that gave him an elflike appearance. He knew everything about himself, and he exploited his attributes to the maximum. Women adored him; first, according to him, for his beauty, and second, because he posed no threat to them. He, of course, took full advantage of all this.

"Your cousin Alfredo is a winner," my grandfather went on. "He will never have to crash a party because he'll be the first one on the list of guests. Have you ever noticed how people stop in the street to look at him, and how they want to touch him? He's so beautiful that I'm afraid he's going to turn out to be an asshole, but that's a different story. Let us say that he'll be the most welcome asshole you have ever met."

My grandfather compared my cousin Luis with Alfredo. He said that Luis was homely, and a little bit stupid, but that he had a heart of gold. And then he brought me into the picture.

"If we are going to proceed with our explanation," he continued, "you have to admit in sincerity that Alfredo is beautiful and Luis is good. Now, let's take you; you are neither handsome nor good. You are a veritable son of a bitch. Nobody's going to invite you to a party. You'll have to get used to the idea that if you want to be at a party, you will have to crash it. Doors will never be open for you the way they will be open for Alfredo for being beautiful, and for Luis for being good, so you will have to get in through the window."

His analysis of his three grandsons was so accurate that he made me weep with the finality of what he had said. The more I wept, the happier he became. He finished his case with a most deleterious admonition.

"There's no need to feel bad," he said, "because there's nothing more exciting than getting in through the window. To do that, you have to be clever and on your toes. You have to watch every-thing, and be prepared for endless humiliations.

"If you have to go in through the window," he went on, "it's because you're definitely not on the list of guests; therefore, your presence is not welcome at all, so you have to work your butt off to stay. The only way I know is by possessing everybody. Scream! Demand! Advise! Make them feel that you are in charge! How could they throw you out if you're in charge?"

Remembering this scene caused a profound upheaval in me. I had buried this incident so deeply that I had forgotten all about it. What I had remembered all along, however, was his admoni-tion to be in charge, which he must have repeated to me over and over throughout the years.

I didn't have a chance to examine this event, or ponder it, because another forgotten memory surfaced with the same force. In it, I was with the girl I had been engaged to. At that time, both of us were saving money to be married and have a house of our own. I heard myself demanding that we have a joint checking account; I wouldn't have it any other way. I felt an imperative need to lecture her on frugality. I heard myself telling her where to buy her clothes, and what the top affordable price should be.

Then I saw myself giving driving lessons to her younger sister and going veritably berserk when she said that she was planning to move out of her parents' house. Forcefully, I threatened her with canceling my lessons. She wept, confessing that she was having an affair with her boss. I jumped out of the car and began kicking the door.

However, that was not all. I heard myself telling my fiancée's father not to move to Oregon, where he planned to go. I shouted at the top of my voice that it was a stupid move. I really believed that my reasonings against it were unbeatable. I presented him with budget figures in which I had meticulously calculated his losses. When he didn't pay any attention to me, I slammed the door and left, shaking with rage. I found my fiancée in the living room, playing her guitar. I pulled it out of her hands and yelled at her that she embraced the guitar instead of playing it, as if it were more than an object.

My desire to impose my will extended all across the board. I made no distinctions; whoever was close to me was there for me to possess and mold, following my whims.

I didn't have to ponder anymore the significance of my vivid visions. For an unquestionable certainty invaded me, as if coming from outside me. It told me that my weak point was the idea that I had to be the man in the director's chair at all times. It had been a deeply ingrained concept with me that I not only had to be in charge, but I had to be in control of any situation. The way in which I had been brought up had reinforced this drive, which must have been arbitrary at its onset, but had turned, in my adulthood, into a deep necessity.

I was aware, beyond any doubt, that what was at stake was *infinity*. Don Juan had portrayed it as a conscious force that deliberately intervenes in the lives of sorcerers. And now it was intervening in mine. I knew that *infinity* was pointing out to me, through the vivid recollection of those forgotten experiences, the intensity and the depth of my drive for control, and thus preparing me for something transcendental to myself. I knew with frightening certainty that something was going to bar any possibility of my being in control, and that I needed, more than anything else, sobriety, fluidity, and abandon in order to face the things that I felt were coming to me.

Naturally, I told all this to don Juan, elaborating to my heart's content on my speculations and inspirational insights about the possible significance of my recollections.

Don Juan laughed good-humoredly. "All this is psychological exaggeration on your part, wishful thinking," he said. "You are, as usual, seeking explanations with linear cause and effect. Each of your recollections becomes more and more vivid, more and more maddening to you, because as I told you already, you have entered an irreversible process. Your true mind is emerging, waking up from a state of lifelong lethargy.

"*Infinity* is claiming you," he continued. "Whatever means it uses to point that out to you cannot have any other reason, any other cause, any other value than that. What you should do, however, is to be prepared for the onslaughts of *infinity*. You must be in a state of continuously bracing yourself for a blow of tremendous magnitude. That is the sane, sober way in which sorcerers face *infinity*."

Don Juan's words left me with a bad taste in my mouth. I actually sensed the assault coming on me, and feared it. Since I had spent my entire life hiding behind some superfluous activity, I immersed myself in work. I gave lectures in classes taught by my friends in different schools in southern California. I wrote copiously. I could say without exaggeration that I threw dozens of manuscripts into the garbage can because they didn't fulfill an indispensable requirement that don Juan had described to me as the mark of something that is acceptable by *infinity*.

He had said that everything I did had to be an act of sorcery. An act free from encroaching expectations, fears of failure, hopes of success. Free from the cult of *me*; everything I did had to be impromptu, a work of magic where I freely opened myself to the impulses of the infinite.

One night, I was sitting at my desk preparing myself for my daily activity of writing. I felt a moment of grogginess. I thought that I was feeling dizzy because I had gotten up too quickly from my mat where I had been doing my exercises. My vision blurred. I saw yellow spots in front of my eyes. I thought I was going to faint. The fainting spell got worse. There was an enormous red spot in front of me. I began to breathe deeply, trying to quiet whatever agitation was causing this visual distortion. I became extraordinarily silent, to the point where I noticed that I was surrounded by impenetrable darkness. The thought crossed my mind that I had fainted. However, I could feel the chair, my desk; I could feel everything around me from inside the darkness that surrounded me.

Don Juan had said that the sorcerers of his lineage considered that one of the most coveted results of *inner silence* was a specific interplay of energy, which is always heralded by a strong emotion. He felt that my recollections were the means to agitate me to the extreme, where I would experience this interplay. Such an interplay manifested itself in terms of hues that were projected on any horizon in the world of everyday life, be it a mountain, the sky, a wall, or simply the palms of the hands. He had explained that this interplay of hues begins with the appearance of a tenuous brushstroke of lavender on the horizon. In time, this lavender brushstroke starts to expand until it covers the visible horizon, like advancing storm clouds.

He assured me that a dot of a peculiar, rich, pomegranate red shows up, as if bursting from the lavender clouds. He stated that as sorcerers become more disciplined and experienced, the dot of pomegranate expands and finally explodes into thoughts or visions, or in the case of a literate man, into written words; sorcerers either see visions engendered by energy, hear thoughts being voiced as words, or read written words.

That night at my desk, I didn't see any lavender brushstrokes, nor did I see any advancing clouds. I was sure that I didn't have the discipline that sorcerers require for such an interplay of energy, but I had an enormous dot of pomegranate red in front of me. This enormous dot, without any preliminaries, exploded into disassociated words that I read as if they were on a sheet of paper coming out of a typewriter. The words moved at such tremendous speed in front of me that it was impossible to read anything. Then I heard a voice describing something to me. Again, the speed of the voice was wrong for my ears. The words were garbled, making it impossible to hear anything that would make sense.

As if that weren't enough, I began to see liverish scenes like one sees in dreams after a heavy meal. They were baroque, dark, ominous. I began to twirl, and I did so until I got sick to my stomach. The whole event ended there. I felt the effect of whatever had happened to me in every muscle of my body. I was exhausted. This violent intervention had made me angry and frustrated.

I rushed to don Juan's house to tell him about this happening. I sensed that I needed his help more than ever.

"There's nothing gentle about sorcerers or sorcery," don Juan commented after he heard my story. "This was the first time that *infinity* descended on you in such a fashion. It was like a blitz. It was a total takeover of your faculties. Insofar as the speed of your visions is concerned, you yourself will have to learn to adjust it. For some sorcerers, that's the job of a lifetime. But from now on, energy will appear to you as if it were being projected onto a movie screen.

"Whether or not you understand the projection," he went on, "is another matter. In order to make an accurate interpretation, you need experience. My recommendation is that you shouldn't be bashful, and you should begin now. Read energy on the wall! Your true mind is emerging, and it has nothing to do with the mind that is a *foreign installation*. Let your true mind adjust the speed. Be silent, and don't fret, no matter what happens."

"But, don Juan, is all this possible? Can one actually read energy as if it were a text?" I asked, overwhelmed by the idea.

"Of course it's possible!" he retorted. "In your case, it's not only possible, it's happening to you."

"But why reading it, as if it were a text?" I insisted, but it was a rhetorical insistence.

"It's an affectation on your part," he said. "If you read the text, you could repeat it verbatim. However, if you tried to be a *viewer of infinity* instead of a *reader of infinity*, you would find that you could not describe whatever you were viewing, and you would end up babbling inanities, incapable of verbalizing what you witness. The same thing if you tried to hear it. This is, of course, specific to you. Anyway, *infinity* chooses. The *warrior-traveler* simply acquiesces to the choice.

"But above all," he added after a calculated pause, "don't be overwhelmed by the event because you cannot describe it. It is an event beyond the syntax of our language."

# Journeys Through the Dark Sea of Awareness

"WE CAN SPEAK a little more clearly now about *inner silence*," don Juan said.

His statement was such a non sequitur that it startled me. He had been talking to me all afternoon about the vicissitudes that the Yaqui Indians had suffered after the big Yaqui wars of the twenties, when they were deported by the Mexican government from their native homeland in the state of Sonora, in northern Mexico, to work in sugarcane plantations in central and southern Mexico. The Mexican government had had problems with endemic wars with the Yaqui Indians for years. Don Juan told me some astounding, poignant Yaqui stories of political intrigue and betrayal, deprivation and human misery.

I had the feeling that don Juan was setting me up for something, because he knew that those stories were my cup of tea, so to speak. I had at that time an exaggerated sense of social justice and fair play.

"Circumstances around you have made it possible for you to have more energy," he went on. "You have started the *recapitulation* of your life; you have looked at your friends for the first time as if they were in a display window; you arrived at your breaking point, all by yourself, driven by your own needs; you canceled your business; and above all, you have accrued enough *inner silence*. All of these made it possible for you to make a journey through the *dark sea of awareness*.

"Meeting me in that town of our choice was that journey," he continued. "I know that a crucial question almost reached the surface in you, and that for an instant, you wondered if I really came to your house. My coming to see you wasn't a dream for you. I was real, wasn't I?"

"You were as real as anything could be," I said.

I had nearly forgotten about those events, but I remembered that it did seem strange to me that he had found my apartment. I had discarded my astonishment by the simple process of assuming that he had asked someone for my new address, although, if I had been pressed, I wouldn't have been able to come up with the identity of anyone who would have known where I lived.

"Let us clarify this point," he continued. "In my terms, which are the terms of the sorcerers of ancient Mexico, I was as real as I could have been, and as such, I actually went to your place from my *inner silence* to tell you about the requisite of *infinity*, and to warn you that you were about to run out of time. And you, in turn, from your *inner silence*, veritably went to that town of our choice to tell me that you had succeeded in fulfilling the requisite of *infinity*.

"In your terms, which are the terms of the average man, it was a dream-fantasy in both instances. You had a dream-fantasy that I came to your place without knowing the address, and then you had a dream-fantasy that you went to see me. As far as I'm concerned, as a sorcerer, what you consider your dream-fantasy of meeting me in that town was as real as the two of us talking here today."

I confessed to don Juan that there was no possibility of my framing those events in a pattern of thought proper to Western man. I said that to think of them in terms of dream-fantasy was to create a false category that couldn't stand up under scrutiny, and that the only quasi-explanation that was vaguely possible was another aspect of his knowledge: *dreaming*.

"No, it is not *dreaming*," he said emphatically. "This is something more direct, and more mysterious. By the way, I have a new definition of *dreaming* for you today, more in accordance with your state of being. *Dreaming* is the act of changing the point of attachment with the *dark sea of awareness*. If you view it in this fashion, it's a very simple concept, and a very simple maneuver. It takes all you have to realize it, but it's not an impossibility, nor is it something surrounded with mystical clouds.

"*Dreaming* is a term that has always bugged the hell out of me," he continued, "because it weakens a very powerful act. It makes it sound arbitrary; it gives it a sense of being a fantasy, and this is the only thing it is not. I tried to change the term myself, but it's too ingrained. Maybe someday you could change it yourself, although, as with everything else in sorcery, I am afraid that by the time you could actually do it, you won't give a damn about it because it won't make any difference what it is called anymore."

Don Juan had explained at great length, during the entire time that I had known him, that *dreaming* was an art, discovered by the sorcerers of ancient Mexico, by means of which ordinary dreams were transformed into bona-fide entrances to other worlds of *perception*. He advocated, in any way he could, the advent of something he called *dreaming attention*, which was the capacity to pay a special kind of attention, or to place a special kind of awareness on the elements of an ordinary dream.

I had followed meticulously all his recommendations and had succeeded in commanding my awareness to remain fixed on the elements of a dream. The idea that don Juan proposed was not to set out deliberately to have a desired dream, but to fix one's attention on the component elements of whatever dream presented itself.

Then don Juan had showed me energetically what the sorcerers of ancient Mexico considered to be the origin of *dreaming:* the displacement of the *assemblage point.* He said that the *assemblage point* was displaced very naturally during sleep, but that to *see* the displacement was a bit difficult because it required an aggressive mood, and that such an aggressive mood had been the predilection of the sorcerers of ancient Mexico. Those sorcerers, according to don Juan, had found all the premises of their sorcery by means of this mood.

"It is a very predatory mood," don Juan went on. "It's not difficult at all to enter into it, because man is a predator by nature. You could *see,* aggressively, anybody in this little village, or perhaps someone far away, while they are asleep; anyone would do for the purpose at hand. What's important is that you arrive at a complete sense of indifference. You are in search of something, and you are out to get it. You're going to go out looking for a person, searching like a feline, like an animal of prey, for someone to descend on."

Don Juan had told me, laughing at my apparent chagrin, that the difficulty with this technique was the mood, and that I couldn't be passive in the act of *seeing,* for the sight was not something to watch but to act upon. It might have been the power of his suggestion, but that day, when he had told me all this, I felt astoundingly aggressive. Every muscle of my body was filled to the brim with energy, and in my *dreaming* practice I did go after someone. I was not interested in who that someone might have been. I needed someone who was asleep, and some force I was aware of, without being fully conscious of it, had guided me to find that someone.

I never knew who the person was, but while I was *seeing* that person, I felt don Juan's presence. It was a strange sensation of knowing that someone was with me by an undetermined sensation of proximity that was happening at a level of awareness that wasn't part of anything that I had ever experienced. I could only focus my attention on the individual at rest. I knew that he was a male, but I don't know how I knew that. I knew that he was asleep because the ball of energy that human beings ordinarily are was a little bit flat; it was expanded laterally.

And then I *saw* the *assemblage point* at a position different from the habitual one, which is right behind the shoulder blades. In this instance, it had been displaced to the right of where it should have been, and a bit lower. I calculated that in this case it had moved to the side of the ribs. Another thing that I noticed was that there was no stability to it. It fluctuated erratically and then abruptly went back to its normal position. I had the clear sensation that, obviously, my presence, and don Juan's, had awakened the individual. I had experienced a profusion of blurred images right after that, and then I woke up back in the place where I had started.

Don Juan had also told me all along that sorcerers were divided into two groups: one group was *dreamers;* the other was *stalkers.* The *dreamers* were those who had a great facility for displacing the *assemblage point.* The *stalkers* were those who had a great facility for maintaining the *assemblage point* fixed on that new position. *Dreamers* and *stalkers* complemented each other, and worked in pairs, affecting one another with their given proclivities.

Don Juan had assured me that the displacement and the fixation of the *assemblage point* could be realized at will by means of the sorcerers' iron-handed discipline. He said that the sorcerers of his lineage believed that there were at least six hundred points within the luminous sphere that we are, that when reached at will by the *assemblage point,* can each give us a totally inclusive world; meaning that, if our *assemblage point* is displaced to any of those points and remains fixed on it, we will perceive a world as inclusive and total as the world of everyday life, but a different world nevertheless.

Don Juan had further explained that the art of sorcery is to manipulate the *assemblage point* and make it change positions at will on the luminous spheres that human beings are. The result of this manipulation is a shift in the point of contact with the *dark sea of awareness*, which brings as its concomitant a different bundle of zillions of energy fields in the form of luminous filaments that converge on the *assemblage point*. The consequence of new energy fields converging on the *assemblage point* is that awareness of a different sort than that which is necessary for perceiving the world of everyday life enters into action, turning the new energy fields into sensory data, sensory data that is interpreted and perceived as a different world because the energy fields that engender it are different from the habitual ones.

He had asserted that an accurate definition of sorcery as a practice would be to say that sorcery is the manipulation of the *assemblage point* for purposes of changing its focal point of contact with the *dark sea of awareness*, thus making it possible to perceive other worlds.

Don Juan had said that the art of the *stalkers* enters into play after the *assemblage point* has been displaced. Maintaining the *assemblage point* fixed in its new position assures sorcerers that they will perceive whatever new world they enter in its absolute completeness, exactly as we do in the world of ordinary affairs. For the sorcerers of don Juan's lineage, the world of everyday life was but one fold of a total world consisting of at least six hundred folds.

Don Juan went back again to the topic under discussion: my journeys through the *dark sea of awareness*, and said that what I had done from my *inner silence* was very similar to what is done in *dreaming* when one is asleep. However, when journeying through the *dark sea of awareness*, there was no interruption of any sort caused by going to sleep, nor was there any attempt whatsoever at controlling one's attention while having a dream. The journey through the *dark sea of awareness* entailed an immediate response. There was an overpowering sensation of the here and now. Don Juan lamented the fact that some idiotic sorcerers had given the name *dreaming-awake* to this act of reaching the dark *sea of aware-*

*ness* directly, making the term *dreaming* even more ridiculous.

"When you thought that you had the dream-fantasy of going to that town of our choice," he continued, "you had actually placed your *assemblage point* directly on a specific position on the *dark sea of awareness* that allows the journey. Then the *dark sea of awareness* supplied you with whatever was necessary to carry on that journey. There's no way whatsoever to choose that place at will. Sorcerers say that *inner silence* selects it unerringly. Simple, isn't it?"

He explained to me then the intricacies of choice. He said that choice, for *warrior-travelers*, was not really the act of choosing, but rather the act of acquiescing elegantly to the solicitations of *infinity*.

"*Infinity* chooses," he said. "The art of the *warrior-traveler* is to have the ability to move with the slightest insinuation, the art of acquiescing to every command of *infinity*. For this, a *warrior-traveler* needs prowess, strength, and above everything else, sobriety. All those three put together give, as a result, elegance!"

After a moment's pause, I went back to the subject that intrigued me the most.

"But it's unbelievable that I actually went to that town, don Juan, in body and soul," I said.

"It is unbelievable, but it's not unlivable," he said. "The universe has no limits, and the possibilities at play in the universe at large are indeed incommensurable. So don't fall prey to the axiom, 'I believe only what I see,' because it is the dumbest stand one can possibly take."

Don Juan's elucidation had been crystal clear. It made sense, but I didn't know where it made sense; certainly not in my daily world of usual affairs. Don Juan assured me then, unleashing a great trepidation in me, that there was only one way in which sorcerers could handle all this information: to taste it through experience, because the mind was incapable of taking in all that stimulation.

"What do you want me to do, don Juan?" I asked.

"You must deliberately journey through the *dark sea of awareness*," he replied, "but you'll never know how this is done. Let's say that *inner silence* does it, following inexplicable ways, ways that cannot be understood, but only practiced."

Don Juan had me sit down on my bed and adopt the position that fostered *inner silence*. I usually fell asleep instantly whenever I adopted this position. However, when I was with don Juan, his presence always made it impossible for me to fall asleep; instead, I entered into a veritable state of complete quietude. This time, after an instant of silence, I found myself walking. Don Juan was guiding me by holding my arm as we walked.

We were no longer in his house; we were walking in a Yaqui town I had never been in before. I knew of the town's existence; I had been close to it many times, but I had been made to turn around by the sheer hostility of the people who lived around it. It was a town where it was nearly impossible for a stranger to enter. The only non-Yaquis who had free access to that town were the supervisors from the federal bank because of the fact that the bank bought the crops from the Yaqui farmers. The endless negotiations of the Yaqui farmers revolved around getting cash advances from the bank on the basis of a near-speculation process about future crops.

I instantly recognized the town from the descriptions of people who had been there. As if to increase my astonishment, don Juan whispered in my ear that we were in the Yaqui town in question. I wanted to ask him how we had gotten there, but I couldn't articulate my words. There were a large number of Indians talking in argumentative tones; tempers seemed to flare. I didn't understand a word of what they were saying, but the moment I conceived of the thought that I couldn't understand, something cleared up. It was very much as if more light went into the scene. Things became very defined and neat, and I understood what the people were saying although I didn't know how; I didn't speak their language. The words were definitely understandable to me, not singularly, but in clusters, as if my mind could pick up whole patterns of thought.

I could say in earnest that I got the shock of a lifetime, not so much because I understood what they were saying but because of the content of what they were saying. Those people were indeed warlike. They were not Western men at all. Their propositions were propositions of strife, warfare, strategy. They were measuring their strength, their striking resources, and lamenting the fact that they had no power to deliver their blows. I registered in my body the anguish of their impotence. All they had were sticks and stones to fight high-technology weapons. They mourned the fact that they had no leaders. They coveted, more than anything else one could imagine, the rise of some charismatic fighter who could galvanize them.

I heard then the voice of cynicism; one of them expressed a thought that seemed to devastate everyone equally, including me, for I seemed to be an indivisible part of them. He said that they were defeated beyond salvation, because if at a given moment one of them had the charisma to rise up and rally them, he would be betrayed because of envy and jealousy and hurt feelings.

I wanted to comment to don Juan on what was happening to me, but I couldn't voice a single word. Only don Juan could talk.

"The Yaquis are not unique in their pettiness," he said in my ear. "It is a condition in which human beings are trapped, a condition that is not even human, but imposed from the outside."

I felt my mouth opening and closing involuntarily as I tried desperately to ask a question that I could not even conceive of. My mind was blank, void of thoughts. Don Juan and I were in the middle of a circle of people, but none of them seemed to have noticed us. I did not record any movement, reaction, or furtive glance that may have indicated that they were aware of us.

The next instant, I found myself in a Mexican town built around a railroad station, a town located about a mile and a half east of where don Juan lived. Don Juan and I were in the middle of the street by the government bank. Immediately afterward, I saw one of the strangest sights I had ever been witness to in don Juan's world. I was *seeing* energy as it flows in the universe, but I wasn't *seeing* human beings as spherical or oblong blobs of energy. The people around me were, in one instant, the normal beings of everyday life, and in the next instant, they were strange creatures. It was as if the ball of energy that we are were transparent; it was like a halo around an insectlike core. That core did not have a primate's shape. There were no skeletal pieces, so I wasn't *seeing* people as if I had X-ray vision that went to the bone core. At the core of people there were, rather, geometric shapes made of what seemed to be hard vibrations of matter. That core was like letters of the alphabet—a capital *T* seemed to be the main structural support. An inverted thick *L* was suspended in front of the *T*; the Greek letter for delta, which went almost to the floor, was at the bottom of the vertical bar of the *T*, and seemed to be a support for the whole structure. On top of the letter *T*, I saw a ropelike strand, perhaps an inch in diameter; it went through the top of the luminous sphere, as if what I was *seeing* were indeed a gigantic bead hanging from the top like a drooping gem.

Once, don Juan had presented to me a metaphor to describe the energetic union of strands of human beings. He had said that the sorcerers of ancient Mexico described those strands as a curtain made from beads strung on a string. I had taken this description literally, and thought that the string went through the conglomer-ate of energy fields that we are from head to toe. The attaching string I was *seeing* made the round shape of the energy fields of human beings look more like a pendant. I didn't *see*, however, any other creature being strung by the same string. Every single crea-ture that I *saw* was a geometrically patterned being that had a sort of string on the upper part of its spherical halo. The string reminded me immensely of the segmented wormlike shapes that some of us see with the eyelids half closed when we are in sunlight.

Don Juan and I walked in the town from one end to the other, and I *saw* literally scores of geometrically patterned creatures. My ability to *see* them was unstable in the extreme. I would *see* them for an instant, and then I would lose sight of them and I would be faced with average people.

Soon, I became exhausted, and I could see only normal people. Don Juan said that it was time to go back home, and again, something in me lost my usual sense of continuity. I found myself in don Juan's house without having the slightest notion as to how I had covered the distance from the town to the house. I lay down in my bed and tried desperately to recollect, to call back my memory, to probe the depths of my very being for a clue as to how I had gone to the Yaqui town, and to the railroad-station town. I didn't believe that they had been dream-fantasies, because the scenes were too detailed to be anything but real, and yet they couldn't possibly have been real.

"You're wasting your time," don Juan said, laughing. "I guarantee you that you will never know how we got from the house to the Yaqui town, and from the Yaqui town to the railroad station, and from the railroad station to the house. There was a break in the continuity of time. That is what *inner silence* does."

He patiently explained to me that the interruption of that flow of continuity that makes the world understandable to us is sorcery. He remarked that I had journeyed that day through the *dark sea of awareness*, and that I had *seen* people as they are, engaged in people's business. And then I had *seen* the strand of energy that joins specific lines of human beings.

Don Juan reiterated to me over and over that I had witnessed something specific and inexplicable. I had understood what people were saying, without knowing their language, and I had *seen* the strand of energy that connected human beings to certain other beings, and I had selected those aspects through an act of *intending* it. He stressed the fact that this *intending* I had done was not something conscious or volitional; the *intending* had been done at a deep level, and had been ruled by necessity. I needed to become cognizant of some of the possibilities of journeying through the *dark sea of awareness*, and my *inner silence* had guided *intent*—a perennial force in the universe—to fulfill that need.

# Inorganic Awareness

AT A GIVEN moment in my apprenticeship, don Juan revealed to me the complexity of his life situation. He had maintained, to my chagrin and despondency, that he lived in the shack in the state of Sonora, Mexico, because that shack depicted my state of awareness. I didn't quite believe that he really meant that I was so meager, nor did I believe that he had other places to live, as he was claiming.

It turned out that he was right on both counts. My state of awareness was very meager, and he did have other places where he could live, infinitely more comfortable than the shack where I had first found him. Nor was he the solitary sorcerer that I had thought him to be, but the leader of a group of fifteen other *warrior-travelers*: ten women and five men. My surprise was gigantic when he took me to his house in central Mexico, where he and his companion sorcerers lived.

"Did you live in Sonora just because of me, don Juan?" I asked him, unable to stand the responsibility, which filled me with guilt and remorse and a sensation of worthlessness.

"Well, I didn't actually live there," he said, laughing. "I just met you there."

"But-but-but you never knew when I was coming to see you, don Juan," I said. "I had no means to let you know!"

"Well, if you remember correctly," he said, "there were many, many times when you didn't find me. You had to sit patiently and wait for me, for days sometimes."

"Did you fly from here to Guaymas, don Juan?" I asked him in earnest. I thought that the shortest way would have been to take a plane.

"No, I didn't fly to Guaymas," he said with a big smile. "I flew directly, to the shack where you were waiting."

I knew that he was purposefully telling me something that my linear mind could not understand or accept, something that was confusing me no end. I was at the level of awareness, in those days, when I asked myself incessantly a fatal question: What if all that don Juan says is true?

I didn't want to ask him any more questions, because I was hopelessly lost, trying to bridge our two tracks of thought and action.

In his new surroundings, don Juan began painstakingly to instruct me in a more complex facet of his knowledge, a facet that required all my attention, a facet in which merely suspending judgment was not enough. This was the time when I had to plummet down into the depths of his knowledge. I had to cease to be objective, and at the same time I had to desist from being subjective.

One day, I was helping don Juan clean some bamboo poles in the back of his house. He asked me to put on some working gloves, because, he said, the splinters of bamboo were very sharp and easily caused infections. He directed me on how to use a knife to clean the bamboo. I became immersed in the work. When don Juan began to talk to me, I had to stop working in order to pay attention. He told me that I had worked long enough, and that we should go into the house.

He asked me to sit down in a very comfortable armchair in his spacious, almost empty living room. He gave me some nuts, dried apricots, and slices of cheese, neatly arranged on a plate. I protested that I wanted to finish cleaning the bamboo. I didn't want to eat. But he didn't pay attention to me. He recommended that I nibble slowly and carefully, for I would need a steady supply of food in order to be alert and attentive to what he was going to tell me.

"You already know," he began, "that there exists in the universe a perennial force, which the sorcerers of ancient Mexico called the *dark sea of awareness*. While they were at the maximum of their perceiving power, they *saw* something that made them shake in their pantaloonies, if they were wearing any. They *saw* that the *dark sea of awareness* is responsible not only for the awareness of organisms, but also for the awareness of entities that don't have an organism."

"What is this, don Juan, beings without an organism that have awareness?" I asked, astonished, for he had never mentioned such an idea before.

"The old shamans discovered that the entire universe is composed of twin forces," he began, "forces that are at the same time opposed and complementary to each other. It is inescapable that our world is a twin world. Its opposite and complementary world is one populated by beings that have awareness, but not an organism. For this reason, the old shamans called them *inorganic beings*."

"And where is this world, don Juan?" I asked, munching unconsciously on a piece of dried apricot.

"Here, where you and I are sitting," he replied matter-of-factly, but laughing outright at my nervousness. "I told you that it's our twin world, so it's intimately related to us. The sorcerers of ancient Mexico didn't think like you do in terms of space and time. They thought exclusively in terms of awareness. Two types of awareness coexist without ever impinging on each other, because each type is entirely different from the other. The old shamans faced this problem of coexistence without concerning themselves with time and space. They reasoned that the degree of awareness of *organic beings* and the degree of awareness of *inorganic beings* were so different that both could coexist with the most minimal interference."

"Can we perceive those *inorganic beings*, don Juan?" I asked.

"We certainly can," he replied. "Sorcerers do it at will. Average people do it, but they don't realize that they're doing it because they are not conscious of the existence of a twin world. When they think of a twin world, they enter into all kinds of mental masturbation, but it has never occurred to them that their fantasies have their origin in a subliminal knowledge that all of us have: that we are not alone."

I was riveted by don Juan's words. Suddenly, I had become voraciously hungry. There was an emptiness in the pit of my stomach. All I could do was to listen as carefully as I could, and eat.

"The difficulty with your facing things in terms of time and space," he continued, "is that you only notice if something has landed in the space and time at your disposal, which is very limited. Sorcerers, on the other hand, have a vast field on which they can notice if something extraneous has landed. Lots of entities from the universe at large, entities that possess awareness but not an organism, land in the field of awareness of our world, or the field of awareness of its twin world, without an average human being ever noticing them. The entities that land on our field of awareness, or the field of awareness of our twin world, belong to other worlds that exist besides our world and its twin. The universe at large is crammed to the brim with worlds of awareness, *organic* and *inorganic*."

Don Juan continued talking and said that those sorcerers knew when *inorganic awareness* from other worlds besides our twin world had landed in their field of awareness. He said that as every human being on this earth would do, those shamans made endless classifications of different types of this energy that has awareness. They knew them by the general term *inorganic beings*.

"Do those *inorganic beings* have life like we have life?" I asked.

"If you think that life is to be aware, then they do have life," he said. "I suppose it would be accurate to say that if life can be measured by the intensity, the sharpness, the duration of that awareness, I can sincerely say that they are more alive than you and I."

"Do those *inorganic beings* die, don Juan?" I asked.

Don Juan chuckled for a moment before he answered. "If you call death the termination of awareness, yes, they die. Their awareness ends. Their death is rather like the death of a human being, and at the same time, it isn't, because the death of human beings has a hidden option. It is something like a clause in a legal document, a clause that is written in tiny letters that you can barely see. You have to use a magnifying glass to read it, and yet it's the most important clause of the document."

"What's the hidden option, don Juan?"

"Death's hidden option is exclusively for sorcerers. They are the only ones who have, to my knowledge, read the fine print. For them, the option is pertinent and functional. For average human beings, death means the termination of their awareness, the end of their organisms. For the *inorganic beings*, death means the same: the end of their awareness. In both cases, the impact of death is the act of being sucked into the *dark sea of awareness*. Their individual awareness, loaded with their life experiences, breaks its boundaries, and awareness as energy spills out into the *dark sea of awareness*."

"But what is death's hidden option that is picked up only by sorcerers, don Juan?" I asked.

"For a sorcerer, death is a unifying factor. Instead of disintegrating the organism, as is ordinarily the case, death unifies it."

"How can death unify anything?" I protested.

"Death for a sorcerer," he said, "terminates the reign of individual moods in the body. The old sorcerers believed it was the dominion of the different parts of the body that ruled the moods and the actions of the total body; parts that become dysfunctional drag the rest of the body to chaos, such as, for instance, when you yourself get sick from eating junk. In that case, the mood of your stomach affects everything else. Death eradicates the dominion of those individual parts. It unifies their awareness into one single unit."

"Do you mean that after they die, sorcerers are still aware?" I asked.

"For sorcerers, death is an act of unification that employs every bit of their energy. You are thinking of death as a corpse in front of you, a body on which decay has settled. For sorcerers, when the act of unification takes place, there is no corpse. There is no decay. Their bodies in their entirety have been turned into energy, energy possessing awareness that is not fragmented. The boundaries that are set up by the organism, boundaries which are broken down by death, are still functioning in the case of sorcerers, although they are no longer visible to the naked eye.

"I know that you are dying to ask me," he continued with a broad smile, "if whatever I'm describing is the soul that goes to hell or heaven. No, it is not the soul. What happens to sorcerers, when they pick up that hidden option of death, is that they turn into *inorganic beings*, very specialized, high-speed *inorganic beings*, beings capable of stupendous maneuvers of perception. Sorcerers enter then into what the shamans of ancient Mexico called their *definitive journey*. *Infinity* becomes their realm of action."

"Do you mean by this, don Juan, that they become eternal?"

"My sobriety as a sorcerer tells me," he said, "that their awareness will terminate, the way *inorganic beings*' awareness terminates, but I haven't *seen* this happen. I have no firsthand knowledge of it. The old sorcerers believed that the awareness of this type of *inorganic being* would last as long as the earth is alive. The earth is their matrix. As long as it prevails, their awareness continues. To me, this is a most reasonable statement."

The continuity and order of don Juan's explanation had been, for me, superb. I had no way whatsoever in which to contribute. He left me with a sensation of mystery and unvoiced expectations to be fulfilled.

◈◈

On my next visit to don Juan, I began my conversation by asking him eagerly a question that was foremost in my mind.

"Is there a possibility, don Juan, that ghosts and apparitions really exist?"

"Whatever you may call a ghost or an apparition," he said, "when it is scrutinized by a sorcerer, boils down to one issue—it is possible that any of those ghostlike apparitions may be a conglomeratation of energy fields that have awareness, and which we turn into things we know. If that's the case, then the apparitions have energy. Sorcerers call them *energy-generating configurations.* Or, no energy emanates from them, in which case they are phantasmagorical creations, usually of a very strong person—strong in terms of awareness.

"One story that intrigued me immensely," don Juan continued, "was the story you told me once about your aunt. Do you remember it?"

I had told don Juan that when I was fourteen years old I had gone to live in my father's sister's house. She lived in a gigantic house that had three patios with living accommodations in between each of them—bedrooms, living rooms, etc. The first patio was very austere, cobblestoned. They told me that it was a colonial house and this first patio was where horse-drawn carriages had gone in. The second patio was a beautiful orchard zigzagged by brick lanes of Moorish design and filled with fruit trees. The third patio was covered with flowerpots hanging from the eaves of the roof, birds in cages, and a colonial-style fountain in the middle of it with running water, as well as a large area fenced with chicken wire, set aside for my aunt's prized fighting cocks, her predilection in life.

My aunt made available to me a whole apartment right in front of the fruit orchard. I thought I was going to have the time of my life there. I could eat all the fruit that I wanted. No one else in the household touched the fruit of any of those trees, for reasons that were never revealed to me. The household was composed of my aunt, a tall, round-faced chubby lady in her fifties, very jovial, a great raconteur, and full of eccentricities that she hid behind a formal facade and the appearance of devout Catholicism. There was a butler, a tall, imposing man in his early forties who had been a sergeant-major in the army and had been lured out of the service to occupy the better-paid position of butler, bodyguard, and all-around man in my aunt's house. His wife, a beautiful young woman, was my aunt's companion, cook, and confidante. The couple also had a daughter, a chubby little girl who looked exactly like my aunt. The likeness was so strong that my aunt had adopted her legally.

Those four were the quietest people I had ever met. They lived a very sedate life, punctuated only by the eccentricities of my aunt, who, on the spur of the moment, would decide to take trips, or buy promising new fighting cocks, train them, and actually have serious contests in which enormous sums of money were involved. She tended her fighting cocks with loving care, sometimes all day long. She wore thick leather gloves and stiff leather leggings to keep the fighting cocks from spurring her.

I spent two stupendous months living in my aunt's house. She taught me music in the afternoons, and told me endless stories about my family's ancestors. My living situation was ideal for me because I used to go out with my friends and didn't have to report the time I came back to anybody. Sometimes I used to spend hours without falling asleep, lying on my bed. I used to keep my window open to let the smell of orange blossoms fill my room. Whenever I was lying there awake, I would hear someone walking down a long corridor that ran the length of the whole property on the north side, joining all the patios of the house. This corridor had beautiful arches and a tiled floor. There were four light bulbs of minimal voltage that dimly illuminated the corridor, lights that were turned on at six o'clock every evening and turned off at six in the morning.

I asked my aunt if anyone walked at night and stopped at my

window, because whoever was walking always stopped by my window, turned around, and walked back again toward the main entrance of the house.

"Don't trouble yourself with nonsense, dear," my aunt said, smiling. "It's probably my butler, making his rounds. Big deal! Were you frightened?"

"No, I was not frightened," I said, "I just got curious, because your butler walks up to my room every night. Sometimes his steps wake me up."

She discarded my inquiry in a matter-of-fact fashion, saying that the butler had been a military man and was habituated to making his rounds, as a sentry would. I accepted her explanation.

One day, I mentioned to the butler that his steps were just too loud, and asked if he would make his rounds by my window with a little more care so as to let me sleep.

"I don't know what you're talking about!" he said in a gruff voice.

"My aunt told me that you make your rounds at night," I said.

"I never do such a thing!" he said, his eyes flaring with disgust.

"But who walks by my window then?"

"Nobody walks by your window. You're imagining things. Just go back to sleep. Don't go around stirring things up. I'm telling you this for your own good."

Nothing could have been worse for me in those years than someone telling me that they were doing something for my own good. That night, as soon as I began to hear the footsteps, I got out of my bed and stood behind the wall that led to the entrance of my apartment. When I calculated that whoever was walking was by the second bulb, I just stuck my head out to look down the corridor. The steps stopped abruptly, but there was no one in sight. The dimly illuminated corridor was deserted. If somebody had been walking there, they wouldn't have had time to hide because there was no place to hide. There were only bare walls.

My fright was so immense that I woke up the whole household screaming my head off. My aunt and her butler tried to calm me down by telling me that I was imagining all that, but my agitation was so intense that both of them sheepishly confessed, in the end, that something which was unknown to them walked in that house every night.

Don Juan had said that it was almost surely my aunt who walked at night; that is to say, some aspect of her awareness over which she had no volitional control. He believed that this phenomenon obeyed a sense of playfulness or mystery that she cultivated. Don Juan was sure that it was not a far-fetched idea that my aunt, at a subliminal level, was not only making all those noises happen, but that she was capable of much more complex manipulations of awareness. Don Juan had also said that to be completely fair, he had to admit the possibility that the steps were the product of *inorganic awareness*.

Don Juan said that the *inorganic beings* who populated our twin world were considered, by the sorcerers of his lineage, to be our relatives. Those shamans believed that it was futile to make friends with our family members because the demands levied on us for such friendships were always exorbitant. He said that that type of *inorganic being*, who are our *first cousins*, communicate with us incessantly, but that their communication with us is not at the level of conscious awareness. In other words, we know all about them in a subliminal way, while they know all about us in a deliberate, conscious manner.

"The energy from our *first cousins* is a drag!" don Juan went on. "They are as fucked up as we are. Let's say that the *organic* and *inorganic beings* of our twin worlds are the children of two sisters who live next door to each other. They are exactly alike although they look different. They cannot help us, and we cannot help them. Perhaps we could join together, and make a fabulous family business corporation, but that hasn't happened. Both branches of the family are extremely touchy and take offense over nothing, a typical relationship between touchy first cousins. The crux of the matter, the sorcerers of ancient Mexico believed, is that both human beings and *inorganic beings* from the twin worlds are profound egomaniacs."

According to don Juan, another classification that the sorcerers of ancient Mexico made of the *inorganic beings* was that of *scouts*, or *explorers*, and by this they meant *inorganic beings* that came from the depths of the universe, and which were possessors of awareness infinitely sharper and faster than that of human beings. Don Juan asserted that the old sorcerers had spent generations polishing their classification schemes, and their conclusions were that certain types of *inorganic beings* from the category of *scouts* or *explorers*, because of their vivaciousness, were akin to man. They could make liaisons and establish a symbiotic relation with men. The old sorcerers called these kinds of *inorganic beings* the *allies*.

Don Juan explained that the crucial mistake of those shamans with reference to this type of *inorganic being* was to attribute human characteristics to that impersonal energy and to believe that they could harness it. They thought of those blocks of energy as their helpers, and they relied on them without comprehending that, being pure energy, they didn't have the power to sustain any effort.

"I've told you all there is to know about *inorganic beings*," don Juan said abruptly. "The only way you can put this to the test is by means of direct experience."

I didn't ask him what he wanted me to do. A deep fear made my body rattle with nervous spasms that burst like a volcanic eruption from my solar plexus and extended down to the tips of my toes and up to my upper trunk.

"Today, we will go to look for some *inorganic beings*," he announced.

Don Juan ordered me to sit on my bed and adopt again the position that fostered *inner silence*. I followed his command with unusual ease. Normally, I would have been reluctant, perhaps not overtly, but I would have felt a twinge of reluctance nonetheless. I had a vague thought that by the time I sat down, I was already in a state of *inner silence*. My thoughts were no longer clear. I felt an impenetrable darkness surrounding me, making me feel as if I were falling asleep. My body was utterly motionless, either because I had no intention of setting up any commands to move or because I just couldn't formulate them.

A moment later, I found myself with don Juan, walking in the Sonoran desert. I recognized the surroundings; I had been there with him so many times that I had memorized every feature of it. It was the end of the day, and the light of the setting sun created in me a mood of desperation. I walked automatically, aware that I was feeling in my body sensations that were not accompanied by thoughts. I was not describing to myself my state of being. I wanted to tell this to don Juan, but the desire to communicate my bodily sensations to him vanished in an instant.

Don Juan said, very slowly, and in a low, grave voice, that the dry riverbed on which we were walking was a most appropriate place for our business at hand, and that I should sit on a small boulder, alone, while he went and sat on another boulder about fifty feet away. I didn't ask don Juan, as I ordinarily would have, what I was supposed to do. I knew what I had to do. I heard then the rustling steps of people walking through the bushes that were sparsely scattered around. There wasn't enough moisture in the area to allow the heavy growth of underbrush. Some sturdy bushes grew there, with a space of perhaps ten or fifteen feet between them.

I saw then two men approaching. They seemed to be local men, perhaps Yaqui Indians from one of the Yaqui towns in the vicinity. They came and stood by me. One of them nonchalantly asked me how I had been. I wanted to smile at him, laugh, but I couldn't. My face was extremely rigid. Yet I was ebullient. I wanted to jump up and down, but I couldn't. I told him that I had been fine. Then I asked them who they were. I said to them that I didn't know them, and yet I sensed an extraordinary familiarity with them. One of the men said, matter-of-factly, that they were my *allies*.

I stared at them, trying to memorize their features, but their features changed. They seemed to mold themselves to the mood of my stare. No thoughts were involved. Everything was a matter guided by visceral sensations. I stared at them long enough to erase their features completely, and finally, I was facing two shiny blobs of luminosity that vibrated. The blobs of luminosity did not have boundaries. They seemed to sustain themselves cohesively from within. At times, they became flat, wide. Then they would take on a verticality again, at the height of a man.

Suddenly, I felt don Juan's arm hooking my right arm and pulling me from the boulder. He said that it was time to go. The next moment, I was in his house again, in central Mexico, more bewildered than ever.

"Today, you found *inorganic awareness*, and then you *saw* it as it really is," he said. "Energy is the irreducible residue of everything. As far as we are concerned, to *see* energy directly is the bottom line for a human being. Perhaps there are other things beyond that, but they are not available to us."

Don Juan asserted all this over and over, and every time he said it, his words seemed to solidify me more and more, to help me return to my normal state.

I told don Juan everything I had witnessed, everything I had heard. Don Juan explained to me that I had succeeded that day in transforming the anthropomorphic shape of the *inorganic beings* into their essence: impersonal energy aware of itself.

"You must realize," he said, "that it is our cognition, which is in essence an interpretation system, that curtails our resources. Our interpretation system is what tells us what the parameters of our possibilities are, and since we have been using that system of interpretation all our lives, we cannot possibly dare to go against its dictums.

"The energy of those *inorganic beings* pushes us," don Juan went on, "and we interpret that push as we may, depending on our mood. The most sober thing to do, for a sorcerer, is to relegate those entities to an abstract level. The fewer interpretations sorcerers make, the better off they are.

"From now on," he continued, "whenever you are confronted with the strange sight of an apparition, hold your ground and gaze at it with an inflexible attitude. If it is an *inorganic being*, your interpretation of it will fall off like dead leaves. If nothing happens, it is just a chicken-shit aberration of your mind, which is not your mind anyway."

# The Clear View

FOR THE FIRST time in my life, I found myself in a total quandary as to how to behave in the world. The world around me had not changed. It definitely stemmed from a flaw in me. Don Juan's influence and all the activities stemming from his practices, into which he had engaged me so deeply, were taking their toll on me and were causing in me a serious incapacity to deal with my fellow men. I examined my problem and concluded that my flaw was my compulsion to measure everyone using don Juan as a yardstick.

Don Juan was, in my estimate, a being who lived his life professionally, in every aspect of the term, meaning that every one of his acts, no matter how insignificant, counted. I was surrounded by people who believed that they were immortal beings, who contradicted themselves every step of the way; they were beings whose acts could never be accounted for. It was an unfair game; the cards were stacked against the people I encountered. I was accustomed to don Juan's unalterable behavior, to his total lack of self-importance, and to the unfathomable scope of his intellect; very few of the people I knew were even aware that there existed another pattern of behavior that fostered those qualities. Most of them knew only the behavioral pattern of self-reflection, which renders men weak and contorted.

Consequently, I was having a very difficult time in my academic studies. I was losing sight of them. I tried desperately to find a rationale that would justify my academic endeavors. The only thing that came to my aid and gave me a connection, however flimsy, to academia was the recommendation that don Juan had made to me once that *warrior-travelers* should have a romance with knowledge, in whatever form knowledge was presented.

He had defined the concept of *warrior-travelers*, saying that it referred to sorcerers who, by being warriors, traveled in the *dark sea of awareness*. He had added that human beings were travelers of the *dark sea of awareness*, and that this Earth was but a station on their journey; for extraneous reasons, which he didn't care to divulge at the time, the travelers had interrupted their voyage. He said that human beings were caught in a sort of eddy, a current that went in circles, giving them the impression of moving while they were, in essence, stationary. He maintained that sorcerers were the only opponents of whatever force kept human beings prisoners, and that by means of their discipline sorcerers broke loose from its grip and continued their *journey of awareness*.

What precipitated the final chaotic upheaval in my academic life was my incapacity to focus my interest on topics of anthropological concern that didn't mean a hoot to me, not because of their lack of appeal but because they were mostly matters where words and concepts had to be manipulated, as in a legal document, to obtain a given result that would establish precedents. It was argued that human knowledge is built in such a fashion, and that the effort of every individual was a building block in constructing a system of knowledge. The example that was put to me was that of the legal system by which we live, and which is of invaluable importance to us. However, my romantic notions at the time impeded me from conceiving of myself as a barrister-at-anthropology. I had bought, lock, stock, and barrel, the concept that anthropology should be the matrix of all human endeavor, or the measure of man.

Don Juan, a consummate pragmatist, a true *warrior-traveler* of the unknown, said that I was full of prunes. He said that it didn't matter that the anthropological topics proposed to me were maneuvers of words and concepts, that what was important was the exercise of discipline.

"It doesn't make any difference," he said to me one time, "how good a reader you are, and how many wonderful books you can read. What's important is that you have the discipline to read what you don't want to read. The crux of the sorcerers' exercise of going to school is in what you refuse, not in what you accept."

I decided to take some time off from my studies and went to work in the art department of a company that made decals. My job engaged my efforts and thoughts to their fullest extent. My challenge was to carry out the tasks assigned to me as perfectly and as rapidly as I could. To set up the vinyl sheets with the images to be processed by silk-screening into decals was a standard procedure that wouldn't admit of any innovation, and the efficiency of the worker was measured by exactness and speed. I became a workaholic and enjoyed myself tremendously.

The director of the art department and I became fast friends. He practically took me under his wing. His name was Ernest Lipton. I admired and respected him immensely. He was a fine artist and a magnificent craftsman. His flaw was his softness, his incredible consideration for others, which bordered on passivity.

For example, one day we were driving out of the parking lot of a restaurant where we had eaten lunch. Very politely, he waited for another car to pull out of the parking space in front of him. The driver obviously didn't see us and began to back out at a considerable speed. Ernest Lipton could easily have blown his horn to attract the man's attention to watch where he was going. Instead, he sat, grinning like an idiot as the guy crashed into his car. Then he turned and apologized to me.

"Gee, I could have blown my horn," he said, "but it's so fucking loud, it embarrasses me."

The guy who had backed up into Ernest's car was furious and had to be placated.

"Don't worry," Ernest said. "There is no damage to your car. Besides, you only smashed my headlights; I was going to replace them anyway."

Another day, in the same restaurant, some Japanese people, clients of the decal company and his guests for lunch, were talking animatedly to us, asking questions. The waiter came with the food and cleared the table of some of the salad plates, making room, the best way he could on the narrow table, for the huge hot plates of the entree. One of the Japanese clients needed more space. He pushed his plate forward; the push set Ernest's plate in motion and it began to slide off the table. Again, Ernest could have warned the man, but he didn't. He sat there grinning until the plate fell in his lap.

On another occasion, I went to his house to help him put up some rafters over his patio, where he was going to let a grape vine grow for partial shade and fruit. We prearranged the rafters into a huge frame and then lifted one side and bolted it to some beams. Ernest was a tall, very strong man, and using a length of two-by-four as a hoisting device, he lifted the other end for me to fit the bolts into holes that were already drilled into the supporting beams. But before I had a chance to put in the bolts there was an insistent knock on the door and Ernest asked me to see who it was while he held the frame of rafters.

His wife was at the door with her grocery packages. She engaged me in a lengthy conversation and I forgot about Ernest. I even helped her to put her groceries away. In the middle of arranging her celery bundles, I remembered that my friend was still holding the frame of rafters, and knowing him, I knew that he would still be at the job, expecting everybody else to have the consideration that he himself had. I rushed desperately to the backyard, and there he was on the ground. He had collapsed from the exhaustion of holding the heavy wooden frame. He looked like a rag doll. We had to call his friends to lend a hand and hoist up the frame of rafters—he couldn't do it anymore. He had to go to bed. He thought for sure that he had a hernia.

The classic story about Ernest Lipton was that one day he went hiking for the weekend in the San Bernardino Mountains with some friends. They camped in the mountains for the night. While everybody was sleeping, Ernest Lipton went to the bushes, and being such a considerate man, he walked some distance from the camp so as not to bother anybody. He slipped in the darkness and rolled down the side of the mountain. He told his friends afterward that he knew for a fact that he was falling to his death at the bottom of the valley. He was lucky in that he grabbed on to a ledge with the tips of his fingers; he held on to it for hours, searching in the dark with his feet for any support, because his arms were about to give in—he was going to hold on until his death. By extending his legs as wide as he could, he found tiny protuberances in the rock that helped him to hold on. He stayed stuck to the rock, like the decals that he made, until there was enough light for him to realize that he was only a foot from the ground.

"Ernest, you could have yelled for help!" his friends complained.

"Gee, I didn't think there was any use," he replied. "Who could have heard me? I thought I had rolled down at least a mile into the valley. Besides, everyone was asleep."

The final blow came for me when Ernest Lipton, who spent two hours daily commuting back and forth from his house to the shop, decided to buy an economy car, a Volkswagen Beetle, and began measuring how many miles he got per gallon of gasoline. I was extremely surprised when he announced one morning that he had reached 125 miles per gallon. Being a very exact man, he qualified his statement, saying that most of his driving was not done in the city, but on the freeway, although at the peak hour of traffic, he had to slow down and accelerate quite often. A week later, he said that he had reached the 250-mile-per-gallon mark.

This marvelous event escalated until he reached an unbelievable figure: 645 miles to a gallon. His friends told him that he should enter this figure into the logs of the Volkswagen company. Ernest Lipton was as pleased as punch, and gloated, saying that he wouldn't know what to do if he reached the thousand-mile mark. His friends told him that he should claim a miracle.

This extraordinary situation went on until one morning when he caught one of his friends, who for months had been playing the oldest gag in the book on him, adding gasoline to his tank. Every morning he had been adding three or four cups so that Ernest's gas gauge was never on empty.

Ernest Lipton was nearly angry. His harshest comment was, "Gee! Is this supposed to be funny?"

I had known for weeks that his friends were playing that gag on him, but I was unable to intervene. I felt that it was none of my business. The people who were playing the gag on Ernest Lipton were his lifelong friends. I was a newcomer. When I saw his look of disappointment and hurt, and his incapacity to get angry, I felt a wave of guilt and anxiety. I was facing again an old enemy of mine. I despised Ernest Lipton, and at the same time, I liked him immensely. He was helpless.

The real truth of the matter was that Ernest Lipton looked like my father. His thick glasses and his receding hairline, as well as the stubble of graying beard that he could never quite shave completely, brought my father's features to mind. He had the same straight, pointed nose and pointed chin. But seeing Ernest Lipton's inability to get angry and punch the jokers in the nose was what really clinched his likeness to my father for me and pushed it beyond the threshold of safety.

I remembered how my father had been madly in love with the sister of his best friend. I spotted her one day in a resort town, holding hands with a young man. Her mother was with her as a chaperone. The girl seemed so happy. The two young people looked at each other, enraptured. As far as I could see, it was young love at its best. When I saw my father, I told him, relishing every instant of my recounting with all the malice of my ten years, that his girlfriend had a real boyfriend. He was taken aback. He didn't believe me.

"But have you said anything at all to the girl?" I asked him daringly. "Does she know that you are in love with her?"

"Don't be stupid, you little creep!" he snapped at me. "I don't have to tell any woman any shit of that sort!" Like a spoiled child, he looked at me petulantly, his lips trembling with rage.

"She's mine! She should know that she's my woman without my having to tell her anything!"

He declared all this with the certainty of a child who has had everything in life given to him without having to fight for it.

At the apex of my form, I delivered my punch line. "Well," I said, "I think she expected someone to tell her that, and someone has just beaten you to it."

I was prepared to jump out of his reach and run because I thought he would slash at me with all the fury in the world, but instead, he crumpled down and began to weep. He asked me, sobbing uncontrollably, that since I was capable of anything, would I please spy on the girl for him and tell him what was going on?

I despised my father beyond anything I could say, and at the same time I loved him, with a sadness that was unmatched. I cursed myself for precipitating that shame on him.

Ernest Lipton reminded me of my father so much that I quit my job, alleging that I had to go back to school. I didn't want to increase the burden that I already carried on my shoulders. I had never forgiven myself for causing my father that anguish, and I had never forgiven him for being so cowardly.

I went back to school and began the gigantic task of reintegrating myself into my studies of anthropology. What made this reintegration very difficult was the fact that if there was someone I could have worked with with ease and delight because of his admirable touch, his daring curiosity, and his willingness to expand his knowledge without getting flustered or defending indefensible points, it was someone outside my department, an archaeologist. It was because of his influence that I had become interested in fieldwork in the first place. Perhaps because of the fact that he actually went into the field, literally to dig out information, his practicality was an oasis of sobriety for me. He was the only one who had encouraged me to go ahead and do fieldwork because I had nothing to lose.

"Lose it all, and you'll gain it all," he told me once, the soundest advice that I ever got in academia. If I followed don Juan's advice, and worked toward correcting my obsession with self-reflection, I veritably had nothing to lose and everything to gain. But this possibility hadn't been in the cards for me at that time.

When I told don Juan about the difficulty I encountered in finding a professor to work with, I thought that his reaction to what I'd said was vicious. He called me a petty fart, and worse. He told me what I already knew: that if I were not so tense, I could have worked successfully with anybody in academia, or in business.

"*Warrior-travelers* don't complain," don Juan went on. "They take everything that *infinity* hands them as a challenge. A challenge is a challenge. It isn't personal. It cannot be taken as a curse or a blessing. A *warrior-traveler* either wins the challenge or the challenge demolishes him. It's more exciting to win, so win!"

I told him that it was easy for him or anyone else to say that, but to carry it out was another matter, and that my tribulations were insoluble because they originated in the incapacity of my fellow men to be consistent.

"It's not the people around you who are at fault," he said. "They cannot help themselves. The fault is with you, because you can help yourself, but you are bent on judging them, at a deep level of silence. Any idiot can judge. If you judge them, you will only get the worst out of them. All of us human beings are prisoners, and it is that prison that makes us act in such a miserable way. Your challenge is to take people as they are! Leave people alone."

"You are absolutely wrong this time, don Juan," I said. "Believe me, I have no interest whatsoever in judging them, or entangling myself with them in any way."

"You do understand what I'm talking about," he insisted doggedly. "If you're not conscious of your desire to judge them," he continued, "you are in even worse shape than I thought. This is the flaw of *warrior-travelers* when they begin to resume their journeys. They get cocky, out of hand."

I admitted to don Juan that my complaints were petty in the extreme. I knew that much. I said to him that I was confronted with daily events, events that had the nefarious quality of wearing down all my resolve, and that I was embarrassed to relate to don Juan the incidents that weighed heavily on my mind.

"Come on," he urged me. "Out with it! Don't have any secrets from me. I'm an empty tube. Whatever you say to me will be projected out into *infinity*."

"All I have are miserable complaints," I said. "I am exactly like all the people I know. There's no way to talk to a single one of them without hearing an overt or a covert complaint."

I related to don Juan how in even the simplest dialogues my friends managed to sneak in an endless number of complaints, such as in a dialogue like this one:

"How is everything, Jim?"

"Oh, fine, fine, Cal." A huge silence would follow.

I would be obliged to say, "Is there something wrong, Jim?"

"No! Everything's great. I have a bit of a problem with Mel, but you know how Mel is—selfish and shitty. But you have to take your friends as they come, true? He could, of course, have a little more consideration. But what the fuck. He's himself. He always puts the burden on you—take me or leave me. He's been doing that since we were twelve, so it's really my fault. Why in the fuck do I have to take him?"

"Well, you're right, Jim, you know Mel is very hard, yes. Yeah!"

"Well, speaking of shitty people, you're no better than Mel, Cal. I can never count on you," etc.

Another classic dialogue was:

"How are you doing, Alex? How's your married life?"

"Oh, just great. For the first time, I'm eating on time, home-cooked meals, but I'm getting fat. There's nothing for me to do except watch TV. I used to go out with you guys, but now I can't. Theresa doesn't let me. Of course, I could tell her to go and fuck herself, but I don't want to hurt her. I feel content, but miserable."

And Alex had been the most miserable guy before he got married. He was the one whose classic joke was to tell his friends, every time we ran into him, "Hey, come to my car, I want to introduce you to my bitch."

He enjoyed himself pink with our crushed expectations when we would see that what he had in his car was a female dog. He introduced his "bitch" to all his friends. We were shocked when he actually married Theresa, a long-distance runner. They met at a marathon when Alex fainted. They were in the mountains, and Theresa had to revive him by any means, so she pissed on his face. After that, Alex was her prisoner. She had marked her territory. His friends used to say, "Her pissy prisoner." His friends thought she was the true bitch who had turned weird Alex into a fat dog.

Don Juan and I laughed for a while. Then he looked at me with a serious expression.

"These are the ups and downs of daily living," don Juan said. "You win, and you lose, and you don't know when you win or when you lose. This is the price one pays for living under the rule of self-reflection. There is nothing that I can say to you, and there's nothing that you can say to yourself. I could only recommend that you not feel guilty because you're an asshole, but that you strive to end the dominion of self-reflection. Go back to school. Don't give up yet."

My interest in remaining in academia was waning considerably. I began to live on automatic pilot. I felt heavy, despondent. However, I noticed that my mind was not involved. I didn't calculate anything, or set up any goals or expectations of any sort. My thoughts were not obsessive, but my feelings were. I tried to conceptualize this dichotomy between a quiet mind and turbulent feelings. It was in this frame of mindlessness and overwhelmed feelings that I walked one day from Haines Hall, where the anthropology department was, to the cafeteria to eat my lunch.

I was suddenly accosted by a strange tremor. I thought I was going to faint, and I sat down on some brick steps. I saw yellow spots in front of my eyes. I had the sensation that I was spinning. I was sure that I was going to get sick to my stomach. My vision became blurry, and finally I couldn't see a thing. My physical discomfort was so total and intense that it didn't leave room for a single thought. I had only bodily sensations of fear and anxiety mixed with elation, and a strange anticipation that I was at the threshold of a gigantic event. They were sensations without the counterpart of thought. At a given moment, I no longer knew whether I was sitting or standing. I was surrounded by the most impenetrable darkness one can imagine, and then, I *saw* energy as it flowed in the universe.

I *saw* a succession of luminous spheres walking toward me or away from me. I *saw* them one at a time, as don Juan had always told me one *sees* them. I knew they were different individuals because of their differences in size. I examined the details of their structures. Their luminosity and their roundness were made of fibers that seemed to be stuck together. They were thin or thick fibers. Every one of those luminous figures had a thick, shaggy covering. They looked like some strange, luminous, furry animals, or gigantic round insects covered with luminous hair.

What was the most shocking thing to me was the realization that I had *seen* those furry insects all my life. Every occasion on which don Juan had made me deliberately *see* them seemed to me at that moment to be like a detour that I had taken with him. I remembered every instance of his help in making me *see* people as luminous spheres, and all of those instances were set apart from the bulk of *seeing* to which I was having access now. I knew then, beyond the shadow of a doubt, that I had perceived energy as it flows in the universe all my life, on my own, without anybody's help.

Such a realization was overwhelming to me. I felt infinitely vulnerable, frail. I needed to seek cover, to hide somewhere. It was exactly like the dream that most of us seem to have at one time or another in which we find ourselves naked and don't know what to do. I felt more than naked; I felt unprotected, weak, and I dreaded returning to my normal state. In a vague way, I sensed that I was lying down. I braced myself for my return to normality. I conceived of the idea that I was going to find myself lying on the brick walk, twitching convulsively, surrounded by a whole circle of spectators.

The sensation that I was lying down became more and more accentuated. I felt that I could move my eyes. I could see light through my closed eyelids, but I dreaded opening them. The odd part was that I didn't hear any of those people that I imagined were around me. I heard no noise at all. At last, I ventured opening my eyes. I was on my bed, in my office apartment by the corner of Wilshire and Westwood boulevards.

I became quite hysterical upon finding myself in my bed. But for some reason that was beyond my grasp, I calmed down almost immediately. My hysteria was replaced by a bodily indifference, or by a state of bodily satisfaction, something like what one feels after a good meal. However, I could not quiet my mind. It had been the most shocking thing imaginable for me to realize that I had perceived energy directly all my life. How in the world could it have been possible that I hadn't known? What had been preventing me from gaining access to that facet of my being? Don Juan had said that every human being has the potential to *see* energy directly. What he hadn't said was that every human being already *sees* energy directly but doesn't know it.

I put that question to a psychiatrist friend. He couldn't shed any light on my quandary. He thought that my reaction was the result of fatigue and overstimulation. He gave me a prescription for Valium and told me to rest.

I hadn't dared mention to anyone that I had woken up in my bed without being able to account for how I had gotten there. Therefore, my haste to see don Juan was more than justified. I flew to Mexico City as soon as I could, rented a car, and drove to where he lived.

"You've done all this before!" don Juan said, laughing, when I narrated my mind-boggling experience to him. "There are only two things that are new. One is that now you have perceived energy all by yourself. What you did was to *stop the world*, and then you realized that you have always *seen* energy as it flows in the universe, as every human being does, but without knowing it deliberately. The other new thing is that you have traveled from your *inner silence* all by yourself.

"You know, without my having to tell you, that anything is possible if one departs from *inner silence*. This time your fear and vulnerability made it possible for you to end up in your bed, which is not really that far from the UCLA campus. If you would not indulge in your surprise, you would realize that what you did is nothing, nothing extraordinary for a *warrior-traveler*.

"But the issue which is of the utmost importance isn't knowing that you have always perceived energy directly, or your journeying from *inner silence*, but, rather, a twofold affair. First, you experienced something which the sorcerers of ancient Mexico called the *clear view*, or *losing the human form*: the time when human pettiness vanishes, as if it had been a patch of fog looming over us, a fog that slowly clears up and dissipates. But under no circumstances must you believe that this is an accomplished fact. The sorcerers' world is not an immutable world like the world of everyday life, where they tell you that once you reach a goal, you remain a winner forever. In the sorcerers' world, to arrive at a certain goal means that you have simply acquired the most efficient tools to continue your fight, which, by the way, will never end.

"The second part of this twofold matter is that you experienced the most maddening question for the hearts of human beings. You expressed it yourself when you asked yourself the questions: 'How in the world could it have been possible that I didn't know that I had perceived energy directly all my life? What had been preventing me from gaining access to that facet of my being?'"

# Mud Shadows

TO SIT IN silence with don Juan was one of the most enjoyable experiences I knew. We were comfortably sitting on some stuffed chairs in the back of his house in the mountains of central Mexico. It was late afternoon. There was a pleasant breeze. The sun was behind the house, at our backs. Its fading light created exquisite shades of green in the big trees in the backyard. There were big trees growing around his house, and beyond it, which obliterated the sight of the city where he lived. This always gave me the impression that I was in the wilderness, a different wilderness than the barren Sonoran desert, but wilderness nonetheless.

"Today, we're going to discuss a most serious topic in sorcery," don Juan said abruptly, "and we're going to begin by talking about the *energy body*."

He had described the *energy body* to me countless times, saying that it was a conglomerate of energy fields, the mirror image of the conglomerate of energy fields that makes up the physical body when it is *seen* as energy that flows in the universe. He had said that it was smaller, more compact, and of heavier appearance than the luminous sphere of the physical body.

Don Juan had explained that the body and the *energy body* were two conglomerates of energy fields compressed together by some strange agglutinizing force. He had emphasized no end that the force that binds that group of energy fields together was, according to the sorcerers of ancient Mexico, the most mysterious force in the universe. His personal estimation was that it was the pure essence of the entire cosmos, the sum total of everything there is.

He had asserted that the physical body and the *energy body* were the only counterbalanced energy configurations in our realm as human beings. He accepted, therefore, no other dualism than the one between these two. The dualism between body and mind, spirit and flesh, he considered to be a mere concatenation of the mind, emanating from it without any energetic foundation.

Don Juan had said that by means of discipline it is possible for anyone to bring the *energy body* closer to the physical body. Normally, the distance between the two is enormous. Once the *energy body* is within a certain range, which varies for each of us individually, anyone, through discipline, can forge it into the exact replica of their physical body—that is to say, a three-dimensional, solid being. Hence the sorcerers' idea of the *other* or the *double*. By the same token, through the same processes of discipline, anyone can forge their three-dimensional, solid physical body to be a perfect replica of their *energy body*—that is to say, an ethereal charge of energy invisible to the human eye, as all energy is.

When don Juan had told me all about this, my reaction had been to ask him if he was describing a mythical proposition. He had replied that there was nothing mythical about sorcerers. Sorcerers were practical beings, and what they described was always something quite sober and down-to-earth. According to don Juan, the difficulty in understanding what sorcerers did was that they proceeded from a different *cognitive system*.

Sitting at the back of his house in central Mexico that day, don Juan said that the *energy body* was of key importance in whatever was taking place in my life. He *saw* that it was an *energetic fact*

216

that my *energy body*, instead of moving away from me, as it normally happens, was approaching me with great speed.

"What does it mean, that it's approaching me, don Juan?" I asked.

"It means that something is going to knock the daylights out of you," he said, smiling. "A tremendous degree of control is going to come into your life, but not your control, the *energy body's* control."

"Do you mean, don Juan, that some outside force will control me?" I asked.

"There are scores of outside forces controlling you at this moment," don Juan replied. "The control that I am referring to is something outside the domain of language. It is your control and at the same time it is not. It cannot be classified, but it can certainly be experienced. And above all, it can certainly be manipulated. Remember this: It can be manipulated, to your total advantage, of course, which again, is not your advantage, but the *energy body's* advantage. However, the *energy body* is you, so we could go on forever like dogs biting their own tails, trying to describe this. Language is inadequate. All these experiences are beyond syntax."

Darkness had descended very quickly, and the foliage of the trees that had been glowing green a little while before was now very dark and heavy. Don Juan said that if I paid close attention to the darkness of the foliage without focusing my eyes, but sort of looked at it from the corner of my eye, I would see a fleeting shadow crossing my field of vision.

"This is the appropriate time of day for doing what I am asking you to do," he said. "It takes a moment to engage the necessary attention in you to do it. Don't stop until you catch that fleeting black shadow."

I did see some strange fleeting black shadow projected on the foliage of the trees. It was either one shadow going back and forth or various fleeting shadows moving from left to right or right to left or straight up in the air. They looked like fat black fish to me, enormous fish. It was as if gigantic swordfish were flying in the air. I was engrossed in the sight. Then, finally, it scared me. It became too dark to see the foliage, yet I could still see the fleeting black shadows.

"What is it, don Juan?" I asked. "I see fleeting black shadows all over the place."

"Ah, that's the universe at large," he said, "incommensurable, nonlinear, outside the realm of syntax. The sorcerers of ancient Mexico were the first ones to see those fleeting shadows, so they followed them around. They saw them as you're seeing them, and they *saw* them as energy that flows in the universe. And they did discover something transcendental."

He stopped talking and looked at me. His pauses were perfectly placed. He always stopped talking when I was hanging by a thread.

"What did they discover, don Juan?" I asked.

"They discovered that we have a companion for life," he said, as clearly as he could. "We have a predator that came from the depths of the cosmos and took over the rule of our lives. Human beings are its prisoners. The predator is our lord and master. It has rendered us docile, helpless. If we want to protest, it suppresses our protest. If we want to act independently, it demands that we don't do so."

It was very dark around us, and that seemed to curtail any expression on my part. If it had been daylight, I would have laughed my head off. In the dark, I felt quite inhibited.

"It's pitch black around us," don Juan said, "but if you look out of the corner of your eye, you will still see fleeting shadows jumping all around you."

He was right. I could still see them. Their movement made me dizzy. Don Juan turned on the light, and that seemed to dissipate everything.

"You have arrived, by your effort alone, to what the shamans of ancient Mexico called the topic of topics," don Juan said. "I have been beating around the bush all this time, insinuating to you that something is holding us prisoner. Indeed we are held prisoner! This was an *energetic fact* for the sorcerers of ancient Mexico."

"Why has this predator taken over in the fashion that you're describing, don Juan?" I asked. "There must be a logical explanation."

"There is an explanation," don Juan replied, "which is the simplest explanation in the world. They took over because we are food for them, and they squeeze us mercilessly because we are their sustenance. Just as we rear chickens in chicken coops, *gallineros*, the predators rear us in human coops, *humaneros*. Therefore, their food is always available to them."

I felt that my head was shaking violently from side to side. I could not express my profound sense of unease and discontentment, but my body moved to bring it to the surface. I shook from head to toe without any volition on my part.

"No, no, no, no," I heard myself saying. "This is absurd, don Juan. What you're saying is something monstrous. It simply can't be true, for sorcerers or for average men, or for anyone."

"Why not?" don Juan asked calmly. "Why not? Because it infuriates you?"

"Yes, it infuriates me," I retorted. "Those claims are monstrous!"

"Well," he said, "you haven't heard all the claims yet. Wait a bit longer and see how you feel. I'm going to subject you to a blitz. That is, I'm going to subject your mind to tremendous onslaughts, and you cannot get up and leave because you're caught. Not because I'm holding you prisoner, but because something in you will prevent you from leaving, while another part of you is going to go truthfully berserk. So brace yourself!"

There was something in me which was, I felt, a glutton for punishment. He was right. I wouldn't have left the house for the world. And yet I didn't like one bit the inanities he was spouting.

"I want to appeal to your analytical mind," don Juan said. "Think for a moment, and tell me how you would explain the contradiction between the intelligence of man the engineer and the stupidity of his systems of beliefs, or the stupidity of his contradictory behavior. Sorcerers believe that the predators have given us our systems of beliefs, our ideas of good and evil, our social mores. They are the ones who set up our hopes and expectations and dreams of success or failure. They have given us covetousness, greed, and cowardice. It is the predators who make us complacent, routinary, and egomaniacal."

"But how can they do this, don Juan?" I asked, somehow angered further by what he was saying. "Do they whisper all that in our ears while we are asleep?"

"No, they don't do it that way. That's idiotic!" don Juan said, smiling. "They are infinitely more efficient and organized than that. In order to keep us obedient and meek and weak, the predators engaged themselves in a stupendous maneuver—stupendous, of course, from the point of view of a fighting strategist. A horrendous maneuver from the point of view of those who suffer it. They gave us their mind! Do you hear me? The predators give us their mind, which becomes our mind. The predators' mind is baroque, contradictory, morose, filled with the fear of being discovered any minute now.

"I know that even though you have never suffered hunger," he went on, "you have food anxiety, which is none other than the anxiety of the predator who fears that any moment now its maneuver is going to be uncovered and food is going to be denied. Through the mind, which, after all, is their mind, the predators inject into the lives of human beings whatever is convenient for them. And they ensure, in this manner, a degree of security to act as a buffer against their fear."

"It's not that I can't accept all this at face value, don Juan," I said. "I could, but there's something so odious about it that it actually repels me. It forces me to take a contradictory stand. If it's true that they eat us, how do they do it?"

Don Juan had a broad smile on his face. He was as pleased as punch. He explained that sorcerers *see* infant human beings as strange, luminous balls of energy, covered from the top to the bottom with a glowing coat, something like a plastic cover that is adjusted tightly over their cocoon of energy. He said that that *glowing coat of awareness* was what the predators consumed, and that when a human being reached adulthood, all that was left of that *glowing coat of awareness* was a narrow fringe that went from the ground to the top of the toes. That fringe permitted mankind to continue living, but only barely.

As if I had been in a dream, I heard don Juan Matus explaining that to his knowledge, man was the only species that had the *glowing coat of awareness* outside that luminous cocoon. Therefore, he became easy prey for an awareness of a different order, such as the heavy awareness of the predator.

He then made the most damaging statement he had made so far. He said that this narrow fringe of awareness was the epicenter of self-reflection, where man was irremediably caught. By playing on our self-reflection, which is the only point of awareness left to us, the predators create flares of awareness that they proceed to consume in a ruthless, predatory fashion. They give us inane problems that force those flares of awareness to rise, and in this manner they keep us alive in order for them to be fed with the energetic flare of our pseudoconcerns.

There must have been something to what don Juan was saying, which was so devastating to me that at that point I actually got sick to my stomach.

After a moment's pause, long enough for me to recover, I asked don Juan: "But why is it that the sorcerers of ancient Mexico and all sorcerers today, although they *see* the predators, don't do anything about it?"

"There's nothing that you and I can do about it," don Juan said in a grave, sad voice. "All we can do is discipline ourselves to the point where they will not touch us. How can you ask your fellow men to go through those rigors of discipline? They'll laugh and make fun of you, and the more aggressive ones will beat the shit out of you. And not so much because they don't believe it. Down in the depths of every human being, there's an ancestral, visceral knowledge about the predators' existence."

My analytical mind swung back and forth like a yo-yo. It left me and came back and left me and came back again. Whatever don Juan was proposing was preposterous, incredible. At the same time, it was a most reasonable thing, so simple. It explained every kind of human contradiction I could think of. But how could one have taken all this seriously? Don Juan was pushing me into the path of an avalanche that would take me down forever.

I felt another wave of a threatening sensation. The wave didn't stem from me, yet it was attached to me. Don Juan was doing something to me, mysteriously positive and terribly negative at the same time. I sensed it as an attempt to cut a thin film that seemed to be glued to me. His eyes were fixed on mine in an unblinking stare. He moved his eyes away and began to talk without looking at me anymore.

"Whenever doubts plague you to a dangerous point," he said, "do something pragmatic about it. Turn off the light. Pierce the darkness; find out what you can see."

He got up to turn off the lights. I stopped him.

"No, no, don Juan," I said, "don't turn off the lights. I'm doing okay."

What I felt then was a most unusual, for me, fear of the darkness. The mere thought of it made me pant. I definitely knew something viscerally, but I wouldn't dare touch it, or bring it to the surface, not in a million years!

"You saw the fleeting shadows against the trees," don Juan said, sitting back against his chair. "That's pretty good. I'd like you to see them inside this room. You're not *seeing* anything. You're just merely catching fleeting images. You have enough energy for that."

I feared that don Juan would get up anyway and turn off the lights, which he did. Two seconds later, I was screaming my head off. Not only did I catch a glimpse of those fleeting images, I heard them buzzing by my ears. Don Juan doubled up with laughter as he turned on the lights.

"What a temperamental fellow!" he said. "A total disbeliever, on the one hand, and a total pragmatist on the other. You must arrange this internal fight. Otherwise, you're going to swell up like a big toad and burst."

Don Juan kept on pushing his barb deeper and deeper into me. "The sorcerers of ancient Mexico," he said, "*saw* the predator. They called it the *flyer* because it leaps through the air. It is not a pretty sight. It is a big shadow, impenetrably dark, a black shadow that jumps through the air. Then, it lands flat on the ground. The sorcerers of ancient Mexico were quite ill at ease with the idea of when it made its appearance on Earth. They reasoned that man must have been a complete being at one point, with stupendous insights, feats of awareness that are mythological legends nowadays. And then everything seems to disappear, and we have now a sedated man."

I wanted to get angry, call him a paranoiac, but somehow the righteousness that was usually just underneath the surface of my being wasn't there. Something in me was beyond the point of asking myself my favorite question: What if all that he said is true? At the moment he was talking to me that night, in my heart of hearts, I felt that all of what he was saying was true, but at the same time, and with equal force, all that he was saying was absurdity itself.

"What are you saying, don Juan?" I asked feebly. My throat was constricted. I could hardly breathe.

"What I'm saying is that what we have against us is not a simple predator. It is very smart, and organized. It follows a methodical system to render us useless. Man, the magical being that he is destined to be, is no longer magical. He's an average piece of meat. There are no more dreams for man but the dreams of an animal who is being raised to become a piece of meat: trite, conventional, imbecilic."

Don Juan's words were eliciting a strange, bodily reaction in me comparable to the sensation of nausea. It was as if I were going to get sick to my stomach again. But the nausea was coming from the bottom of my being, from the marrow of my bones. I convulsed involuntarily. Don Juan shook me by the shoulders forcefully. I felt my neck wobbling back and forth under the impact of his grip. The maneuver calmed me down at once. I felt more in control.

"This predator," don Juan said, "which, of course, is an *inorganic being*, is not altogether invisible to us, as other *inorganic beings* are. I think as children we do see it and decide it's so horrific that we don't want to think about it. Children, of course, could insist on focusing on the sight, but everybody else around them dissuades them from doing so.

"The only alternative left for mankind," he continued, "is *discipline*. Discipline is the only deterrent. But by discipline I don't mean harsh routines. I don't mean waking up every morning at five-thirty and throwing cold water on yourself until you're blue. Sorcerers understand discipline as the capacity to face with serenity odds that are not included in our expectations. For them, discipline is an art: the art of facing *infinity* without flinching, not because they are strong and tough but because they are filled with awe."

"In what way would the sorcerers' discipline be a deterrent?" I asked.

"Sorcerers say that discipline makes the *glowing coat of awareness* unpalatable to the *flyer*," don Juan said, scrutinizing my face as if to discover any signs of disbelief. "The result is that the predators become bewildered. An inedible *glowing coat of awareness* is not part of their cognition, I suppose. After being bewildered, they don't have any recourse other than refraining from continuing their nefarious task.

"If the predators don't eat our *glowing coat of awareness* for a while," he went on, "it'll keep on growing. Simplifying this matter to the extreme, I can say that sorcerers, by means of their discipline, push the predators away long enough to allow their *glowing coat of awareness* to grow beyond the level of the toes. Once it goes beyond the level of the toes, it grows back to its natural size.

The sorcerers of ancient Mexico used to say that the *glowing coat of awareness* is like a tree. If it is not pruned, it grows to its natural size and volume. As awareness reaches levels higher than the toes, tremendous maneuvers of perception become a matter of course.

"The grand trick of those sorcerers of ancient times," don Juan continued, "was to burden the *flyers' mind* with discipline. They found out that if they taxed the *flyers' mind* with *inner silence*, the *foreign installation* would flee, giving to any one of the practitioners involved in this maneuver the total certainty of the mind's foreign origin. The *foreign installation* comes back, I assure you, but not as strong, and a process begins in which the fleeing of the *flyers' mind* becomes routine, until one day it flees permanently. A sad day indeed! That's the day when you have to rely on your own devices, which are nearly zero. There's no one to tell you what to do. There's no mind of foreign origin to dictate the imbecilities you're accustomed to.

"My teacher, the nagual Julian, used to warn all his disciples," don Juan continued, "that this was the toughest day in a sorcerer's life, for the real mind that belongs to us, the sum total of our experience, after a lifetime of domination has been rendered shy, insecure, and shifty. Personally, I would say that the real battle of sorcerers begins at that moment. The rest is merely preparation."

I became genuinely agitated. I wanted to know more, and yet a strange feeling in me clamored for me to stop. It alluded to dark results and punishment, something like the wrath of God descending on me for tampering with something veiled by God himself. I made a supreme effort to allow my curiosity to win.

"What—what—what do you mean," I heard myself say, "by *taxing the flyers' mind?*"

"Discipline taxes the foreign mind no end," he replied. "So, through their discipline, sorcerers vanquish the *foreign installation.*"

I was overwhelmed by his statements. I believed that don Juan was either certifiably insane or that he was telling me something so awesome that it froze everything in me. I noticed, however, how quickly I rallied my energy to deny everything he had said. After an instant of panic, I began to laugh, as if don Juan had told me a joke. I even heard myself saying, "Don Juan, don Juan, you're incorrigible!"

Don Juan seemed to understand everything I was experiencing. He shook his head from side to side and raised his eyes to the heavens in a gesture of mock despair.

"I am so incorrigible," he said, "that I am going to give the *flyers' mind*, which you carry inside you, one more jolt. I am going to reveal to you one of the most extraordinary secrets of sorcery. I am going to describe to you a finding that took sorcerers thousands of years to verify and consolidate."

He looked at me and smiled maliciously. "The *flyers' mind* flees forever," he said, "when a sorcerer succeeds in grabbing on to the vibrating force that holds us together as a conglomerate of energy fields. If a sorcerer maintains that pressure long enough, the *flyers' mind* flees in defeat. And that's exactly what you are going to do: hold on to the energy that binds you together."

I had the most inexplicable reaction I could have imagined. Something in me actually shook, as if it had received a jolt. I entered into a state of unwarranted fear, which I immediately associated with my religious background.

Don Juan looked at me from head to toe.

"You are fearing the wrath of God, aren't you?" he said. "Rest assured, that's not your fear. It's the *flyers'* fear, because it knows that you will do exactly as I'm telling you."

His words did not calm me at all. I felt worse. I was actually convulsing involuntarily, and I had no means to stop it.

"Don't worry," don Juan said calmly. "I know for a fact that those attacks wear off very quickly. The *flyer's mind* has no concentration whatsoever."

After a moment, everything stopped, as don Juan had predicted. To say again that I was bewildered is a euphemism. This was the first time ever, with don Juan or alone, in my life that I didn't know whether I was coming or going. I wanted to get out of the chair and walk around, but I was deathly afraid. I was filled with rational assertions, and at the same time I was filled with an infantile fear. I began to breathe deeply as a cold perspiration covered my entire body. I had somehow unleashed on myself a most godawful sight: black, fleeting shadows jumping all around me, wherever I turned.

I closed my eyes and rested my head on the arm of the stuffed chair. "I don't know which way to turn, don Juan," I said. "Tonight, you have really succeeded in getting me lost."

"You're being torn by an internal struggle," don Juan said. "Down in the depths of you, you know that you are incapable of refusing the agreement that an indispensable part of you, your *glowing coat of awareness*, is going to serve as an incomprehensible source of nourishment to, naturally, incomprehensible entities. And another part of you will stand against this situation with all its might.

"The sorcerers' revolution," he continued, "is that they refuse to honor agreements in which they did not participate. Nobody ever asked me if I would consent to be eaten by beings of a different kind of awareness. My parents just brought me into this world to be food, like themselves, and that's the end of the story."

Don Juan stood up from his chair and stretched his arms and legs. "We have been sitting here for hours. It's time to go into the house. I'm gonna eat. Do you want to eat with me?"

I declined. My stomach was in an uproar.

"I think you'd better go to sleep," he said. "The blitz has devastated you."

I didn't need any further coaxing. I collapsed onto my bed and fell asleep like the dead.

At home, as time went by, the idea of the *flyers* became one of the main fixations of my life. I got to the point where I felt that don Juan was absolutely right about them. No matter how hard I tried, I couldn't discard his logic. The more I thought about it, and the more I talked to and observed myself and my fellow men, the more intense the conviction that something was rendering us incapable of any activity or any interaction or any thought that didn't have the self as its focal point. My concern, as well as the concern of everyone I knew or talked to, was the self. Since I couldn't find any explanation for such universal homogeneity, I believed that don Juan's line of thought was the most appropriate way of elucidating the phenomenon.

I went as deeply as I could into readings about myths and legends. In reading, I experienced something I had never felt before: Each of the books I read was an interpretation of myths and legends. In each one of those books, a homogeneous mind was palpable. The styles differed, but the drive behind the words was homogeneously the same: Even though the theme was something as abstract as myths and legends, the authors always managed to insert statements about themselves. The homogeneous drive behind every one of those books was not the stated theme of the book; instead, it was self-service. I had never felt this before.

I attributed my reaction to don Juan's influence. The unavoidable question that I posed to myself was: Is he influencing me to see this, or is there really a foreign mind dictating everything we do? I lapsed, perforce, into denial again, and I went insanely from denial to acceptance to denial. Something in me knew that whatever don Juan was driving at was an *energetic fact*, but something equally important in me knew that all of that was guff. The end result of my internal struggle was a sense of foreboding, the sense of something imminently dangerous coming at me.

I made extensive anthropological inquiries into the subject of the *flyers* in other cultures, but I couldn't find any references to them anywhere. Don Juan seemed to be the only source of information about this matter. The next time I saw him, I instantly jumped to talk about the *flyers*.

"I have tried my best to be rational about this subject matter," I said, "but I can't. There are moments when I fully agree with you about the predators."

"Focus your attention on the fleeting shadows that you actually see," don Juan said with a smile.

I told don Juan that those fleeting shadows were going to be the end of my rational life. I saw them everywhere. Since I had left his house, I was incapable of going to sleep in the dark. To sleep with the lights on did not bother me at all. The moment I turned the lights off, however, everything around me began to jump. I never saw complete figures or shapes. All I saw were fleeting black shadows.

"The *flyers' mind* has not left you," don Juan said. "It has been seriously injured. It's trying its best to rearrange its relationship with you. But something in you is severed forever. The *flyer* knows that. The real danger is that the *flyers' mind* may win by getting you tired and forcing you to quit by playing the contradiction between what it says and what I say.

"You see, the *flyers' mind* has no competitors," don Juan continued. "When it proposes something, it agrees with its own proposition, and it makes you believe that you've done something of worth. The *flyers' mind* will say to you that whatever Juan Matus is telling you is pure nonsense, and then the same mind will agree with its own proposition, 'Yes, of course, it is nonsense,' you will say. That's the way they overcome us.

"The *flyers* are an essential part of the universe," he went on, "and they must be taken as what they really are—awesome, monstrous. They are the means by which the universe tests us.

"We are energetic probes created by the universe," he continued as if he were oblivious to my presence, "and it's because we are possessors of energy that has awareness that we are the means by which the universe becomes aware of itself. The *flyers* are the implacable challengers. They cannot be taken as anything else. If we succeed in doing that, the universe allows us to continue."

I wanted don Juan to say more. But he said only, "The blitz ended the last time you were here; there's only so much you could say about the *flyers*. It's time for another kind of maneuver."

I couldn't sleep that night. I fell into a light sleep in the early hours of the morning, until don Juan dragged me out of my bed and took me for a hike in the mountains. Where he lived, the configuration of the land was very different from that of the Sonoran desert, but he told me not to indulge in comparison, that after walking for a quarter of a mile, every place in the world was just the same.

"Sightseeing is for people in cars," he said. "They go at great speed without any effort on their part. Sightseeing is not for walkers. For instance, when you are riding in a car, you may see a gigantic mountain whose sight overwhelms you with its beauty. The sight of the same mountain will not overwhelm you in the same manner if you look at it while you're going on foot; it will overwhelm you in a different way, especially if you have to climb it or go around it."

It was very hot that morning. We walked on a dry riverbed. One thing that this valley and the Sonoran desert had in common was their millions of insects. The gnats and flies all around me were like dive-bombers that aimed at my nostrils, eyes, and ears. Don Juan told me not to pay attention to their buzzing.

"Don't try to disperse them with your hand," he uttered in a firm tone. "*Intend* them away. Set up an energy barrier around you. Be silent, and from your silence the barrier will be constructed. Nobody knows how this is done. It is one of those things that the old sorcerers called *energetic facts*. Shut off your internal dialogue. That's all it takes.

"I want to propose a weird idea to you," don Juan went on as he kept walking ahead of me.

I had to accelerate my steps to be closer to him so as not to miss anything he said.

"I have to stress that it's a weird idea that will find endless resistance in you," he said. "I will tell you beforehand that you won't accept it easily. But the fact that it's weird should not be a deterrent. You are a social scientist. Therefore, your mind is always open to inquiry, isn't that so?"

Don Juan was shamelessly making fun of me. I knew it, but it didn't bother me. Perhaps due to the fact that he was walking so fast, and I had to make a tremendous effort to keep up with him, his sarcasm just sloughed off me, and instead of making me feisty, it made me laugh. My undivided attention was focused on what he was saying, and the insects either stopped bothering me because I had *intended* a barrier of energy around me or because I was so busy listening to don Juan that I didn't care about their buzzing around me anymore.

"The weird idea," he said slowly, measuring the effect of his words, "is that every human being on this earth seems to have exactly the same reactions, the same thoughts, the same feelings. They seem to respond in more or less the same way to the same stimuli. Those reactions seem to be sort of fogged up by the language they speak, but if we scrape that off, they are exactly the same reactions that besiege every human being on Earth. I would like you to become curious about this, as a social scientist, of course, and see if you could formally account for such homogeneity."

Don Juan collected a series of plants. Some of them could hardly be seen. They seemed to be more in the realm of algae, moss. I held his bag open, and we didn't speak anymore. When he had enough plants, he headed back for his house, walking as fast as he could. He said that he wanted to clean and separate those plants and put them in a proper order before they dried up too much.

I was deeply involved in thinking about the task he had delineated for me. I began by trying to review in my mind if I knew of any articles or papers written on this subject. I thought that I would have to research it, and I decided to begin my research by reading all the works available on "national character." I got enthusiastic about the topic, in a haphazard way, and I really wanted to start for home right away, for I wanted to take his task to heart, but before we reached his house, don Juan sat down on a high ledge overlooking the valley. He didn't say anything for a while. He was not out of breath. I couldn't conceive of why he had stopped to sit down.

"The task of the day, for you," he said abruptly, in a foreboding tone, "is one of the most mysterious things of sorcery, something that goes beyond language, beyond explanations. We went for a hike today, we talked, because the mystery of sorcery must be cushioned in the mundane. It must stem from nothing, and go back again to nothing. That's the art of *warrior-travelers:* to go through the eye of a needle unnoticed. So, brace yourself by propping your back against this rock wall, as far as possible from the edge. I will be by you, in case you faint or fall down."

"What are you planning to do, don Juan?" I asked, and my alarm was so patent that I noticed it and lowered my voice.

"I want you to cross your legs and enter into *inner silence,*" he said. "Let's say that you want to find out what articles you could look for to discredit or substantiate what I have asked you to do in your academic milieu. Enter into *inner silence,* but don't fall asleep. This is not a journey through the *dark sea of awareness.* This is *seeing from inner silence.*"

It was rather difficult for me to enter into *inner silence* without falling asleep. I fought a nearly invincible desire to fall asleep. I succeeded, and found myself looking at the bottom of the valley from an impenetrable darkness around me. And then, I *saw* something that chilled me to the marrow of my bones. I *saw* a gigantic shadow, perhaps fifteen feet across, leaping in the air and then landing with a silent thud. I felt the thud in my bones, but I didn't hear it.

"They are really heavy," don Juan said in my ear. He was holding me by the left arm, as hard as he could.

I *saw* something that looked like a mud shadow wiggle on the ground, and then take another gigantic leap, perhaps fifty feet long, and land again, with the same ominous silent thud. I fought not to lose my concentration. I was frightened beyond anything I could rationally use as a description. I kept my eyes fixed on the jumping shadow on the bottom of the valley. Then I heard a most peculiar buzzing, a mixture of the sound of flapping wings and the buzzing of a radio whose dial has not quite picked up the frequency of a radio station, and the thud that followed was something unforgettable. It shook don Juan and me to the core—a gigantic black mud shadow had just landed by our feet.

"Don't be frightened," don Juan said imperiously. "Keep your *inner silence* and it will move away."

I was shivering from head to toe. I had the clear knowledge that if I didn't keep my *inner silence* alive, the mud shadow would cover me up like a blanket and suffocate me. Without losing the darkness around me, I screamed at the top of my voice. Never had I been so angry, so utterly frustrated. The mud shadow took another leap, clearly to the bottom of the valley. I kept on screaming, shaking my legs. I wanted to shake off whatever might come to eat me. My state of nervousness was so intense that I lost track of time. Perhaps I fainted.

When I came to my senses, I was lying in my bed in don Juan's house. There was a towel, soaked in icy-cold water, wrapped around my forehead. I was burning with fever. One of don Juan's female cohorts rubbed my back, chest, and forehead with rubbing alcohol, but this did not relieve me. The heat I was experiencing came from within myself. It was wrath and impotence that generated it.

Don Juan laughed as if what was happening to me was the funniest thing in the world. Peals of laughter came out of him in an endless barrage.

"I would never have thought that you would take *seeing* a *flyer* so much to heart," he said.

He took me by the hand and led me to the back of his house, where he dunked me in a huge tub of water, fully clothed—shoes, watch, everything.

"My watch, my watch!" I screamed.

Don Juan twisted with laughter. "You shouldn't wear a watch when you come to see me," he said. "Now you've fouled up your watch!"

I took off my watch and put it by the side of the tub. I remembered that it was waterproof and that nothing would happen to it.

Being dunked in the tub helped me enormously. When don Juan pulled me out of the freezing water, I had gained a degree of control.

"That sight is preposterous!" I kept on repeating, unable to say anything else.

The predator don Juan had described was not something benevolent. It was enormously heavy, gross, indifferent. I felt its disregard for us. Doubtless, it had crushed us ages ago, making us, as don Juan had said, weak, vulnerable, and docile. I took off my wet clothes, covered myself with a poncho, sat in my bed, and veritably wept my head off, but not for myself. I had my wrath, my *unbending intent*, not to let them eat me. I wept for my fellow men, especially for my father. I never knew until that instant that I loved him so much.

"He never had a chance," I heard myself repeating, over and over, as if the words were not really mine. My poor father, the most considerate being I knew, so tender, so gentle, so helpless.

# Starting on
# the Definitive Journey

# The Jump into the Abyss

THERE WAS ONLY one trail leading to the flat mesa. Once we were on the mesa itself, I realized that it was not as extensive as it had appeared when I had looked at it from a distance. The vegetation on the mesa was not different from the vegetation below: faded green woody shrubs that had the ambiguous appearance of trees.

At first, I didn't see the chasm. It was only when don Juan led me to it that I became aware that the mesa ended in a precipice; it wasn't really a mesa but merely the flat top of a good-sized mountain. The mountain was round and eroded on its east and south faces; however, on part of its west and north sides, it seemed to have been cut with a knife. From the edge of the precipice, I was able to see the bottom of the ravine, perhaps six hundred feet below. It was covered with the same woody shrubs that grew everywhere.

A whole row of small mountains to the south and to the north of that mountaintop gave the clear impression that they had been part of a gigantic canyon, millions of years old, dug out by a no longer existing river. The edges of that canyon had been erased by erosion. At certain points they had been leveled with the ground. The only portion still intact was the area where I was standing.

"It's solid rock," don Juan said as if he were reading my thoughts. He pointed with his chin toward the bottom of the ravine. "If anything were to fall down from this edge to the bottom, it would get smashed to flakes on the rock, down there."

This was the initial dialogue between don Juan and myself, that day, on that mountaintop. Prior to going there, he had told me that his time on Earth had come to an end. He was leaving on his *definitive journey*. His statements were devastating to me. I truly lost my grip, and entered into a blissful state of fragmentation, perhaps similar to what people experience when they have a mental breakdown. But there was a core fragment of myself that remained cohesive: the me of my childhood. The rest was vagueness, incertitude. I had been fragmented for so long that to become fragmented once again was the only way out of my devastation.

A most peculiar interplay between different levels of my awareness took place afterward. Don Juan, his cohort don Genaro, two of his apprentices, Pablito and Nestor, and I had climbed to that mountaintop. Pablito, Nestor, and I were there to take care of our last task as apprentices: to jump into an abyss, a most mysterious affair, which don Juan had explained to me at various levels of awareness but which has remained an enigma to me to this day.

Don Juan jokingly said that I should get my writing pad and start taking notes about our last moments together. He gently poked me in the ribs and assured me, as he hid his laughter, that it would have been only proper, since I had started on the *warrior-travelers'* path by taking notes.

Don Genaro cut in and said that other *warrior-travelers* before us had stood on that same flat mountaintop before embarking on their journey to the unknown. Don Juan turned to me and in a soft voice said that soon I would be entering into *infinity* by the force of my personal power, and that he and don Genaro were there only to bid me farewell. Don Genaro cut in again and said that I was there also to do the same for them.

"Once you have entered into *infinity*," don Juan said, "you can't depend on us to bring you back. Your decision is needed then. Only you can decide whether or not to return. I must also warn you that few *warrior-travelers* survive this type of encounter with *infinity*. *Infinity* is enticing beyond belief. A *warrior-traveler* finds that to return to the world of disorder, compulsion, noise, and pain is a most unappealing affair. You must know that your decision to stay or to return is not a matter of a reasonable choice, but a matter of *intending* it.

"If you choose not to return," he continued, "you will disappear as if the earth had swallowed you. But if you choose to come back, you must tighten your belt and wait like a true *warrior-traveler* until your task, whatever it might be, is finished, either in success or in defeat."

A very subtle change began to take place in my awareness then. I started to remember faces of people, but I wasn't sure I had met them; strange feelings of anguish and affection started to mount. Don Juan's voice was no longer audible. I longed for people I sincerely doubted I had ever met. I was suddenly possessed by the most unbearable love for those persons, whoever they may have been. My feelings for them were beyond words, and yet I couldn't tell who they were. I only sensed their presence, as if I had lived another life before, or as if I were feeling for people in a dream. I sensed that their outside forms shifted; they began by being tall and ended up petite. What was left intact was their essence, the very thing that produced my unbearable longing for them.

Don Juan came to my side and said to me, "The agreement was that you remain in the awareness of the daily world." His voice was harsh and authoritative. "Today you are going to fulfill a concrete task," he went on, "the last link of a long chain; and you must do it in your utmost mood of reason."

I had never heard don Juan talk to me in that tone of voice. He was a different man at that instant, yet he was thoroughly familiar to me. I meekly obeyed him and went back to the awareness of the world of everyday life. I didn't know that I was doing this, however. To me, it appeared, on that day, as if I had acquiesced to don Juan out of fear and respect.

Don Juan spoke to me next in the tone I was accustomed to. What he said was also very familiar. He said that the backbone of a *warrior-traveler* is humbleness and efficiency, acting without expecting anything and withstanding anything that lies ahead of him.

I went at that point through another shift in my level of awareness. My mind focused on a thought, or a feeling of anguish. I knew then that I had made a pact with some people to die with them, and I couldn't remember who they were. I felt, without the shadow of a doubt, that it was wrong that I should die alone. My anguish became unbearable.

Don Juan spoke to me. "We are alone," he said. "That's our condition, but to die alone is not to die in loneliness."

I took big gulps of air to erase my tension. As I breathed deeply, my mind became clear.

"The great issue with us males is our frailty," he went on. "When our awareness begins to grow, it grows like a column, right on the midpoint of our luminous being, from the ground up. That column has to reach a considerable height before we can rely on it. At this time in your life, as a sorcerer, you easily lose your grip on your new awareness. When you do that, you forget everything you have done and *seen* on the *warrior-travelers' path* because your consciousness shifts back to the awareness of your everyday life. I have explained to you that the task of every male sorcerer is to reclaim everything he has done and *seen* on the *warrior-travelers' path* while he was on new levels of awareness. The problem of every male sorcerer is that he easily forgets because his awareness loses its new level and falls to the ground at the drop of a hat."

"I understand exactly what you're saying, don Juan," I said.

"Perhaps this is the first time I have come to the full realization of why I forget everything, and why I remember everything later. I have always believed that my shifts were due to a personal pathological condition; I know now why these changes take place, yet I can't verbalize what I know."

"Don't worry about verbalizations," don Juan said. "You'll verbalize all you want in due time. Today, you must act on your *inner silence*, on what you know without knowing. You know to perfection what you have to do, but this knowledge is not quite formulated in your thoughts yet."

On the level of concrete thoughts or sensations, all I had were vague feelings of knowing something that was not part of my mind. I had, then, the clearest sense of having taken a huge step down; something seemed to have dropped inside me. It was almost a jolt. I knew that I had entered into another level of awareness at that instant.

Don Juan told me then that it is obligatory that a *warrior-traveler* say good-bye to all the people he leaves behind. He must say his good-bye in a loud and clear voice so that his shout and his feelings will remain forever recorded in those mountains.

I hesitated for a long time, not out of bashfulness but because I didn't know whom to include in my thanks. I had completely internalized the sorcerers' concept that *warrior-travelers* can't owe anything to anyone.

Don Juan had drilled a sorcerers' axiom into me: "*Warrior-travelers* pay elegantly, generously, and with unequaled ease every favor, every service rendered to them. In this manner, they get rid of the burden of being indebted."

I had paid, or I was in the process of paying, everyone who had honored me with their care or concern. I had *recapitulated* my life to such an extent that I had not left a single stone unturned. I truthfully believed in those days that I didn't owe anything to anyone. I expressed my beliefs and hesitation to don Juan.

Don Juan said that I had indeed *recapitulated* my life thoroughly, but he added that I was far from being free of indebtedness.

"How about your ghosts?" he went on. "Those you can no longer touch?"

He knew what he was talking about. During my *recapitulation*, I had recounted to him every incident of my life. Out of the hundreds of incidents that I related to him, he had isolated three as samples of indebtedness that I incurred very early in life, and added to that, my indebtedness to the person who was instrumental in my meeting him. I had thanked my friend profusely, and I had sensations that something out there acknowledged my thanks. The other three had remained stories from my life, stories of people who had given me an inconceivable gift, and whom I had never thanked.

One of these stories had to do with a man I'd known when I was a child. His name was Mr. Leandro Acosta. He was my grandfather's archenemy, his true nemesis. My grandfather had accused this man repeatedly of stealing chickens from his chicken farm. The man wasn't a vagrant, but someone who did not have a steady, definite job. He was a maverick of sorts, a gambler, a master of many trades: handyman, self-styled curer, hunter and provider of plant and insect specimens for local herbalists and curers and any kind of bird or mammal life for taxidermists or pet shops.

People believed that he made tons of money, but that he couldn't keep it or invest it. His detractors and friends alike believed that he could have established the most prosperous business in the area, doing what he knew best—searching for plants and hunting animals—but that he was cursed with a strange disease of the spirit that made him restless, incapable of tending to anything for any length of time.

One day, while I was taking a stroll on the edge of my grandfather's farm, I noticed that someone was watching me from between the thick bushes at the forest's edge. It was Mr. Acosta. He was squatting inside the bushes of the jungle itself and would have been totally out of sight had it not been for my sharp eight-year-old eyes.

"No wonder my grandfather thinks that he comes to steal chickens," I thought. I believed that no one else but me could have noticed him; he was utterly concealed by his motionlessness. I had caught the difference between the bushes and his silhouette by feeling rather than sight. I approached him. The fact that people rejected him so viciously, or liked him so passionately, intrigued me no end.

"What are you doing there, Mr. Acosta?" I asked daringly.

"I'm taking a shit while I look at your grandfather's farm," he said, "so you better scram before I get up unless you like the smell of shit."

I moved away a short distance. I wanted to know if he was really doing what he was claiming. He was. He got up. I thought he was going to leave the bush and come onto my grandfather's land and perhaps walk across to the road, but he didn't. He began to walk inward, into the jungle.

"Hey, hey, Mr. Acosta!" I yelled. "Can I come with you?"

I noticed that he had stopped walking; it was again more a feeling than an actual sight because the bush was so thick.

"You can certainly come with me if you can find an entry into the bush," he said.

That wasn't difficult for me. In my hours of idleness, I had marked an entry into the bush with a good-sized rock. I had found out through an endless process of trial and error that there was a crawling space there, which if I followed for three or four yards turned into an actual trail on which I could stand up and walk.

Mr. Acosta came to me and said, "Bravo, kid! You've done it. Yes, come with me if you want to."

That was the beginning of my association with Mr. Leandro Acosta. We went on daily hunting expeditions. Our association became so obvious, since I was gone from the house from dawn to sunset, without anybody ever knowing where I went, that finally my grandfather admonished me severely.

"You must select your acquaintances," he said, "or you will end up being like them. I will not tolerate this man affecting you in any way imaginable. He could certainly transmit to you his élan, yes. And he could influence your mind to be just like his: useless. I'm telling you, if you don't put an end to this, I will. I'll send the authorities after him on charges of stealing my chickens, because you know damn well that he comes every day and steals them."

I tried to show my grandfather the absurdity of his charges. Mr. Acosta didn't have to steal chickens. He had the vastness of that jungle at his command. He could have drawn from that jungle anything he wanted. But my arguments infuriated my grandfather even more. I realized then that my grandfather secretly envied Mr. Acosta's freedom, and Mr. Acosta was transformed for me by this realization from a nice hunter into the ultimate expression of what is at the same time both forbidden and desired.

I attempted to curtail my encounters with Mr. Acosta, but the lure was just too overwhelming for me. Then, one day, Mr. Acosta and three of his friends proposed that I do something that Mr. Acosta had never done before: catch a vulture alive, uninjured. He explained to me that the vultures of the area, which were enormous, with a five- to six-foot wingspan, had seven different types of flesh in their bodies, and each one of those seven types served a specific curative purpose. He said that the desired state was that the vulture's body not be injured. The vulture had to be killed by tranquilizer, not by violence. It was easy to shoot them, but in that case, the meat lost its curative value. So the art was to catch them alive, a thing that he had never done. He had figured out, though, that with my help and the help of his three friends he had the problem licked. He assured me that his was a natural conclusion arrived at after hundreds of occasions on which he had observed the behavior of vultures.

"We need a dead donkey in order to perform this feat, something which we have," he declared ebulliently.

He looked at me, waiting for me to ask the question of what would be done with the dead donkey. Since the question was not asked, he proceeded.

"We remove the intestines, and we put some sticks in there to keep the roundness of the belly.

"The leader of the turkey vultures is the king; he is the biggest, the most intelligent," he went on. "No sharper eyes exist. That's what makes him a king. He'll be the one who will spot the dead donkey, and the first who will land on it. He'll land downwind from the donkey to really smell that it is dead. The intestines and soft organs that we are going to draw out of the donkey's belly we'll pile by his rear end, outside. This way, it looks like a wild cat has already eaten some of it. Then, lazily, the vulture will come closer to the donkey. He'll take his time. He'll come hopping-flying, and then he will land on the dead donkey's hip and begin to rock the donkey's body. He would turn it over if it were not for the four sticks that we will stake into the ground as part of the armature. He'll stand on the hip for a while; that will be the clue for other vultures to come and land there in the vicinity. Only when he has three or four of his companions down with him will the king vulture begin his work."

"And what is my role in all this, Mr. Acosta?" I asked.

"You hide inside the donkey," he said with a deadpan expression. "Nothing to it. I give you a pair of specially designed leather gloves, and you sit there and wait until the king turkey vulture rips the anus of the dead donkey open with his enormous powerful beak and sticks his head in to begin eating. Then you grab him by the neck with both hands and don't let go.

"My three friends and I will be hiding on horseback in a deep ravine. I'll be watching the operation with binoculars. When I see that you have grabbed the king vulture by the neck, we'll come at full gallop and throw ourselves on top of the vulture and subdue him."

"Can you subdue that vulture, Mr. Acosta?" I asked him. Not that I doubted his skill, I just wanted to be assured.

"Of course I can!" he said with all the confidence in the world. "We're all going to be wearing gloves and leather leggings. The vulture's talons are quite powerful. They could break a shinbone like a twig."

There was no way out for me. I was caught, nailed by an exorbitant excitation. My admiration for Mr. Leandro Acosta knew no limits at that moment. I saw him as a true hunter—resourceful, cunning, knowledgeable.

"Okay, let's do it then!" I said.

"That's my boy!" said Mr. Acosta. "I expected as much from you."

He had put a thick blanket behind his saddle, and one of his friends just lifted me up and put me on Mr. Acosta's horse, right behind the saddle, sitting on the blanket.

"Hold on to the saddle," Mr. Acosta said, "and as you hold on to the saddle, hold the blanket, too."

We took off at a leisurely trot. We rode for perhaps an hour until we came to some flat, dry, desolate lands. We stopped by a tent that resembled a vendor's stand in a market. It had a flat roof for shade. Underneath that roof was a dead brown donkey. It didn't seem that old; it looked like an adolescent donkey.

Neither Mr. Acosta nor his friends explained to me whether they had found or killed the dead donkey. I waited for them to tell me, but I wasn't going to ask. While they made the preparations, Mr. Acosta explained that the tent was in place because vultures were on the lookout from huge distances out there, circling very high, out of sight, but certainly capable of seeing everything that was going on.

"Those creatures are creatures of sight alone," Mr. Acosta said. "They have miserable ears, and their noses are not as good as their eyes. We have to plug every hole of the carcass. I don't want you to be peeking out of any hole, because they will see your eye and never come down. They must see nothing."

They put some sticks inside the donkey's belly and crossed them, leaving enough room for me to crawl in. At one moment I finally ventured the question that I was dying to ask.

"Tell me, Mr. Acosta, this donkey surely died of illness, didn't he? Do you think its disease could affect me?"

Mr. Acosta raised his eyes to the sky. "Come on! You cannot be that dumb. Donkey's diseases cannot be transmitted to man. Let's live this adventure and not worry about stupid details. If I were shorter, I'd be inside that donkey's belly myself. Do you know what it is to catch the king of turkey buzzards?"

I believed him. His words were sufficient to set up a cloak of unequaled confidence over me. I wasn't going to get sick and miss the event of events.

The dreaded moment came when Mr. Acosta put me inside the donkey. Then they stretched the skin over the armature and began to sew it closed. They left, nevertheless, a large area open at the bottom, against the ground, for air to circulate in. The horrendous moment for me came when the skin was finally closed over my head like the lid of a coffin. I breathed hard, thinking only about the excitement of grabbing the king of vultures by the neck.

Mr. Acosta gave me last-minute instructions. He said that he would let me know by a whistle that resembled a birdcall when the king vulture was flying around and when it had landed, so as to keep me informed and prevent me from fretting or getting impatient. Then I heard them pulling down the tent, followed by their horses galloping away. It was a good thing that they hadn't left a single space open to look out from because that's what I would have done. The temptation to look up and see what was going on was nearly irresistible.

A long time went by in which I didn't think of anything. Then I heard Mr. Acosta's whistling and I presumed the king vulture was circling around. My presumption turned to certainty when I heard the flapping of powerful wings, and then suddenly, the dead donkey's body began to rock as if it were in a windstorm. Then I felt a weight on the donkey's body, and I knew that the king vulture had landed on the donkey and was not moving anymore. I heard the flapping of other wings and the whistling of Mr. Acosta in the distance. Then I braced myself for the inevitable. The body of the donkey began to shake as something started to rip the skin.

Then, suddenly, a huge, ugly head with a red crest, an enormous beak, and a piercing, open eye burst in. I yelled with fright and grabbed the neck with both hands. I think I stunned the king vulture for an instant because he didn't do anything, which gave me the opportunity to grab his neck even harder, and then all hell broke loose. He ceased to be stunned and began to pull with such force that I was smashed against the structure, and in the next instant I was partially out of the donkey's body, armature and all, holding on to the neck of the invading beast for dear life.

I heard Mr. Acosta's galloping horse in the distance. I heard him yelling, "Let go, boy, let go, he's going to fly away with you!"

The king vulture indeed was going to either fly away with me holding on to his neck or rip me apart with the force of his talons. The reason he couldn't reach me was because his head was sunk halfway into the viscera and the armature. His talons kept slipping on the loose intestines and they never actually touched me. Another thing that saved me was that the force of the vulture was involved in pulling his neck out from my clasp and he could not move his talons far forward enough to really injure me. The next thing I knew, Mr. Acosta had landed on top of the vulture at the precise moment that my leather gloves came off my hands.

Mr. Acosta was beside himself with joy. "We've done it, boy, we've done it!" he said. "The next time, we will have longer stakes on the ground that the vulture cannot yank out, and you will be strapped to the structure."

My relationship with Mr. Acosta had lasted long enough for us to catch a vulture. Then my interest in following him disappeared as mysteriously as it had appeared and I never really had the opportunity to thank him for all the things that he had taught me.

Don Juan said that he had taught me the patience of a hunter at the best time to learn it; and above all, he had taught me to draw from solitariness all the comfort that a hunter needs.

"You cannot confuse solitude with solitariness," don Juan explained to me once. "Solitude for me is psychological, of the mind. Solitariness is physical. One is debilitating, the other comforting."

For all this, don Juan had said, I was indebted to Mr. Acosta forever whether or not I understood indebtedness the way *warrior-travelers* understand it.

The second person don Juan thought I was indebted to was a ten-year-old child I'd known growing up. His name was Armando Velez. Just like his name, he was extremely dignified, starchy, a little old man. I liked him very much because he was firm and yet very friendly. He was someone who could not easily be intimidated. He would fight anyone if he needed to and yet he was not a bully at all.

The two of us used to go on fishing expeditions. We used to catch very small fish that lived under rocks and had to be gathered by hand. We would put the tiny fish we caught to dry in the sun and eat them raw, all day sometimes.

I also liked the fact that he was very resourceful and clever as well as being ambidextrous. He could throw a rock with his left hand farther than with his right. We had endless competitive games in which, to my ultimate chagrin, he always won. He used to sort of apologize to me for winning by saying, "If I slow down and let you win, you'll hate me. It'll be an affront to your manhood. So try harder."

Because of his excessively starchy behavior, we used to call him "Señor Velez," but the "Señor" was shortened to "Sho," a custom typical of the region in South America where I come from.

One day, Sho Velez asked me something quite unusual. He began his request, naturally, as a challenge to me. "I bet anything," he said, "that I know something that you wouldn't dare do."

"What are you talking about, Sho Velez?"

"You wouldn't dare go down a river in a raft."

"Oh yes I would. I've done it in a flooded river. I got stranded on an island for eight days once. They had to drift food to me."

This was the truth. My other best friend was a child nicknamed

Crazy Shepherd. We got stranded in a flood on an island once, with no way for anyone to rescue us. Townspeople expected the flood to overrun the island and kill us both. They drifted baskets of food down the river in the hope that they would land on the island, which they did. They kept us alive in this fashion until the water had subsided enough for them to reach us with a raft and pull us to the banks of the river.

"No, this is a different affair," Sho Velez continued with his erudite attitude. "This one implies going on a raft on a subterranean river."

He pointed out that a huge section of a local river went through a mountain. That subterranean section of the river had always been a most intriguing place for me. Its entrance into the mountain was a foreboding cave of considerable size, always filled with bats and smelling of ammonia. Children of the area were told that it was the entrance to hell: sulfur fumes, heat, stench.

"You bet your friggin' boots, Sho Velez, that I will never go near that river in my lifetime!" I said, yelling. "Not in ten lifetimes! You have to be really crazy to do something like that."

Sho Velez's serious face got even more solemn. "Oh," he said, "then I will have to do it all by myself. I thought for a minute that I could goad you into going with me. I was wrong. My loss."

"Hey, Sho Velez, what's with you? Why in the world would you go into that hellish place?"

"I have to," he said in his gruff little voice. "You see, my father is as crazy as you are, except that he is a father and a husband. He has six people who depend on him. Otherwise, he would be as crazy as a goat. My two sisters, my two brothers, my mother and I depend on him. He is everything to us."

I didn't know who Sho Velez's father was. I had never seen him. I didn't know what he did for a living. Sho Velez revealed that his father was a businessman, and that everything that he owned was on the line, so to speak.

"My father has constructed a raft and wants to go. He wants to make that expedition. My mother says that he's just letting off steam, but I don't trust him," Sho Velez continued. "I have seen your crazy look in his eyes. One of these days, he'll do it, and I am sure that he'll die. So, I am going to take his raft and go into that river myself. I know that I will die, but my father won't."

I felt something like an electric shock go through my neck, and I heard myself saying in the most agitated tone one can imagine, "I'll do it, Sho Velez, I'll do it. Yes, yes, it'll be great! I'll go with you!"

Sho Velez had a smirk on his face. I understood it as a smirk of happiness at the fact that I was going with him, not at the fact that he had succeeded in luring me. He expressed that feeling in his next sentence. "I know that if you are with me, I will survive," he said.

I didn't care whether Sho Velez survived or not. What had galvanized me was his courage. I knew that Sho Velez had the guts to do what he was saying. He and Crazy Shepherd were the only gutsy kids in town. They both had something that I considered unique and unheard of: courage. No one else in that whole town had any. I had tested them all. As far as I was concerned, every one of them was dead, including the love of my life, my grandfather. I knew this without the shadow of a doubt when I was ten. Sho Velez's daring was a staggering realization for me. I wanted to be with him to the bitter end.

We made plans to meet at the crack of dawn, which we did, and the two of us carried his father's lightweight raft for three or four miles out of town, into some low, green mountains to the entrance of the cave where the river became subterranean. The smell of bat manure was overwhelming. We crawled on the raft and pushed ourselves into the stream. The raft was equipped with flashlights, which we had to turn on immediately. It was pitch black inside the mountain and humid and hot. The water was deep enough for the raft and fast enough that we didn't need to paddle.

The flashlights would create grotesque shadows. Sho Velez whispered in my ear that perhaps it was better not to look at all, because it was truly something more than frightening. He was right; it was nauseating, oppressive. The lights stirred bats so that they began to fly around us, flapping their wings aimlessly. As we traveled deeper into the cave, there were not even bats anymore, just stagnant air that was heavy and hard to breathe. After what seemed like hours to me, we came to a sort of pool where the water was very deep; it hardly moved. It looked as if the main stream had been dammed.

"We are stuck," Sho Velez whispered in my ear again. "There's no way for the raft to go through, and there's no way for us to go back."

The current was just too great for us to even attempt a return trip. We decided that we had to find a way out. I realized then that if we stood on top of the raft, we could touch the ceiling of the cave, which meant that the water had been dammed almost all the way to the top of the cave. At the entrance it was cathedral-like, maybe fifty feet high. My only conclusion was that we were on top of a pool that was about fifty feet deep.

We tied the raft to a rock and began to swim downward into the depths, trying to feel for a movement of water, a current. Everything was humid and hot on the surface but very cold a few feet below. My body felt the change in temperature and I became frightened, a strange animal fear that I had never felt before. I surfaced. Sho Velez must have felt the same. We bumped into each other on the surface.

"I think we're close to dying," he said solemnly.

I didn't share his solemnity or his desire to die. I searched frantically for an opening. Floodwaters must have carried rocks that had created a dam. I found a hole big enough for my ten-year-old body to go through. I pulled Sho Velez down and showed the hole to him. It was impossible for the raft to go through it. We pulled our clothes from the raft and tied them into a very tight bundle and swam downward with them until we found the hole again and went through it.

We ended up on a water slide, like the ones in an amusement

park. Rocks covered with lichen and moss allowed us to slide for a great distance without being injured at all. Then we came into an enormous cathedral-like cave, where the water continued flowing, waist deep. We saw the light of the sky at the end of the cave and waded out. Without saying a word, we spread out our clothes and let them dry in the sun, then headed back for town. Sho Velez was nearly inconsolable because he had lost his father's raft.

"My father would have died there," he finally conceded. "His body would never have gone through the hole we went through. He's too big for it. My father is a big, fat man," he said. "But he would have been strong enough to walk his way back to the entrance."

I doubted it. As I remembered, at times, due to the inclination, the current was astoundingly fast. I conceded that perhaps a desperate, big man could have finally walked his way out with the aid of ropes and a lot of effort.

The issue of whether Sho Velez's father would have died there or not was not resolved then, but that didn't matter to me. What mattered was that for the first time in my life I had felt the sting of envy. Sho Velez was the only being I have ever envied in my life. He had someone to die for, and he had proved to me that he would do it; I had no one to die for, and I had proved nothing at all.

In a symbolic fashion, I gave Sho Velez the total cake. His triumph was complete. I bowed out. That was his town, those were his people, and he was the best among them as far as I was concerned. When we parted that day, I spoke a banality that turned out to be a deep truth when I said, "Be the king of them, Sho Velez. You are the best."

I never spoke to him again. I purposely ended my friendship with him. I felt that this was the only gesture I could make to denote how profoundly I had been affected by him.

Don Juan believed that my indebtedness to Sho Velez was imperishable, that he was the only one who had ever taught me that we must have something we could die for before we could think that we have something to live for.

"If you have nothing to die for," don Juan said to me once, "how can you claim that you have something to live for? The two go hand in hand, with death at the helm."

The third person don Juan thought I was indebted to beyond my life and my death was my grandmother on my mother's side. In my blind affection for my grandfather—the male—I had forgotten the real source of strength in that household: my very eccentric grandmother.

Many years before I came to their household, she had saved a local Indian from being lynched. He was accused of being a sorcerer. Some irate young men were actually hanging him from a tree on my grandmother's property. She came upon the lynching and stopped it. All the lynchers seemed to have been her godsons and they wouldn't dare go against her. She pulled the man down and took him home to cure him. The rope had already cut a deep wound on his neck.

His wounds healed, but he never left my grandmother's side. He claimed that his life had ended the day of the lynching, and that whatever new life he had no longer belonged to him; it belonged to her. Being a man of his word, he dedicated his life to serving my grandmother. He was her valet, majordomo, and counselor. My aunts said that it was he who had advised my grandmother to adopt a newborn orphan child as her son, something that they resented more than bitterly.

When I came into my grandparents' house, my grandmother's adopted son was already in his late thirties. She had sent him to study in France. One afternoon, out of the blue, a most elegantly dressed husky man got out of a taxi in front of the house. The driver carried his leather suitcases to the patio. The husky man tipped the driver generously. I noticed in one glance that the husky man's features were very striking. He had long, curly hair, long, curly eyelashes. He was extremely handsome without being physically beautiful. His best feature was, however, his beaming, open smile, which he immediately turned on me.

"May I ask your name, young man?" he said with the most beautiful stage voice I had ever heard.

The fact that he had addressed me as young man had won me over instantly. "My name is Carlos Aranha, sir," I said, "and may I ask in turn what is yours?"

He made a gesture of mock surprise. He opened his eyes wide and jumped backward as if he had been attacked. Then he began to laugh uproariously. At the sound of his laughter, my grandmother came out to the patio. When she saw the husky man, she screamed like a small girl and threw her arms around him in a most affectionate embrace. He lifted her up as if she weighed nothing and twirled her around. I noticed then that he was very tall. His huskiness hid his height. He actually had the body of a professional fighter. He seemed to notice that I was eyeing him. He flexed his biceps.

"I've done some boxing in my day, sir," he said, thoroughly aware of what I was thinking.

My grandmother introduced him to me. She said that he was her son Antoine, her baby, the apple of her eye; she said that he was a dramatist, a theater director, a writer, a poet.

The fact that he was so athletic was his winning ticket with me. I didn't understand at first that he was adopted. I noticed, however, that he didn't look at all like the rest of the family. While every one of the members of my family were corpses that walked, he was alive, vital from the inside out. We hit it off marvelously. I liked the fact that he worked out every day, punching a bag. I liked immensely that not only did he punch the bag, he kicked it, too, in the most astounding style, a mixture of boxing and kicking. His body was as hard as a rock.

One day Antoine confessed to me that his only fervent desire in life was to be a writer of note.

"I have everything," he said. "Life has been very generous to me. The only thing I don't have is the only thing I want: talent. The muses do not like me. I appreciate what I read, but I cannot create anything that I like to read. That's my torment; I lack the discipline or the charm to entice the muses, so my life is as empty as anything can be."

Antoine went on to tell me that the one reality that he had was his mother. He called my grandmother his bastion, his support, his twin soul. He ended up by voicing a very disturbing thought to me. "If I didn't have my mother," he said, "I wouldn't live."

I realized then how profoundly tied he was to my grandmother. All the horror stories that my aunts had told me about the spoiled child Antoine became suddenly very vivid for me. My grandmother had really spoiled him beyond salvation. Yet they seemed so very happy together. I saw them sitting for hours on end, his head on her lap as if he were still a child. I had never heard my grandmother converse with anybody for such lengths of time.

Abruptly, one day Antoine started to produce a lot of writing. He began to direct a play at the local theater, a play that he had written himself. When it was staged, it became an instant success. His poems were published in the local paper. He seemed to have hit a creative streak. But only a few months later it all came to an end. The editor of the town's paper publicly denounced Antoine; he accused him of plagiarism and published in the paper the proof of Antoine's guilt.

My grandmother, of course, would not hear of her son's misbehavior. She explained it all as a case of profound envy. Every one of those people in that town was envious of the elegance, the style of her son. They were envious of his personality, of his wit. Indeed, he was the personification of elegance and savoir faire. But he was a plagiarist for sure; there was no doubt about it.

Antoine never explained his behavior to anyone. I liked him too much to ask him anything about it. Besides, I didn't care. His reasons were his reasons, as far as I was concerned. But something was broken; from then on, our lives moved in leaps and bounds, so to speak. Things changed so drastically in the house from one day to the next that I grew accustomed to expect anything, the best or the worst. One night my grandmother walked into

Antoine's room in a most dramatic fashion. There was a look of hardness in her eyes that I had never seen before. Her lips trembled as she spoke.

"Something terrible has happened, Antoine," she began.

Antoine interrupted her. He begged her to let him explain.

She cut him off abruptly. "No, Antoine, no," she said firmly. "This has nothing to do with you. It has to do with me. At this very difficult time for you, something of greater importance yet has happened. Antoine, my dear son, I have run out of time.

"I want you to understand that this is inevitable," she went on. "I have to leave, but you must remain. You are the sum total of everything that I have done in this life. Good or bad, Antoine, you are all I am. Give life a try. In the end, we will be together again anyway. Meanwhile, however, do, Antoine, do. Whatever, it doesn't matter what, as long as you do."

I saw Antoine's body as it shivered with anguish. I saw how he contracted his total being, all the muscles of his body, all his strength. It was as if he had shifted gears from his problem, which was like a river, to the ocean.

"Promise me that you won't die until you die!" she shouted at him.

Antoine nodded his head.

My grandmother, the next day, on the advice of her sorcerer-counselor, sold all her holdings, which were quite sizable, and turned the money over to her son Antoine. And the following day, very early in the morning, the strangest scene that I had ever witnessed took place in front of my ten-year-old eyes: the moment in which Antoine said good-bye to his mother. It was a scene as unreal as the set of a moving picture; unreal in the sense that it seemed to have been concocted, written down somewhere, created by a series of adjustments that a writer makes and a director carries out.

The patio of my grandparents' house was the setting. Antoine was the main protagonist, his mother the leading actress. Antoine was traveling that day. He was going to the port. He was going to catch an Italian liner and go over the Atlantic to Europe on a leisurely cruise. He was as elegantly dressed as ever. A taxi driver was waiting for him outside the house, blowing the horn of his taxi impatiently.

I had witnessed Antoine's last feverish night when he tried as desperately as anyone can try to write a poem for his mother.

"It is crap," he said to me. "Everything that I write is crap. I'm a nobody."

I assured him, even though I was nobody to assure him, that whatever he was writing was great. At one moment, I got carried away and stepped over certain boundaries I should never have crossed.

"Take it from me, Antoine," I yelled. "I am a worse nobody than you! You have a mother. I have nothing. Whatever you are writing is fine."

Very politely, he asked me to leave his room. I had succeeded in making him feel stupid, having to listen to advice from a nobody kid. I bitterly regretted my outburst. I would have liked him to keep on being my friend.

Antoine had his elegant overcoat neatly folded, draped over his right shoulder. He was wearing a most beautiful green suit, English cashmere.

My grandmother spoke. "You have to hurry up, dear," she said. "Time is of the essence. You have to leave. If you don't, these people will kill you for the money."

She was referring to her daughters, and their husbands, who were beyond fury when they found out that their mother had quietly disinherited them, and that the hideous Antoine, their arch-enemy, was going to get away with everything that was rightfully theirs.

"I'm sorry I have to put you through all this," my grandmother apologized. "But, as you know, time is independent of our wishes."

Antoine spoke with his grave, beautifully modulated voice. He sounded more than ever like a stage actor. "It'll take but a minute, Mother," he said. "I'd like to read something that I have written for you."

It was a poem of thanks. When he had finished reading, he paused. There was such a wealth of feeling in the air, such a tremor.

"It was sheer beauty, Antoine," my grandmother said, sighing. "It expressed everything that you wanted to say. Everything that I wanted to hear." She paused for an instant. Then her lips broke into an exquisite smile.

"Plagiarized, Antoine?" she asked.

Antoine's smile in response to his mother was equally beaming. "Of course, Mother," he said. "Of course."

They embraced, weeping. The horn of the taxi sounded more impatient yet. Antoine looked at me where I was hiding under the stairway. He nodded his head slightly, as if to say, "Good-bye. Take care." Then he turned around, and without looking at his mother again, he ran toward the door. He was thirty-seven years old, but he looked like he was sixty, he seemed to carry such a gigantic weight on his shoulders. He stopped before he reached the door, when he heard his mother's voice admonishing him for the last time.

"Don't turn around to look, Antoine," she said. "Don't turn around to look, ever. Be happy, and do. Do! There is the trick. Do!"

The scene filled me with a strange sadness that lasts to this day—a most inexplicable melancholy that don Juan explained as my first-time knowledge that we do run out of time.

The next day my grandmother left with her counselor/manservant/valet on a journey to a mythical place called Rondonia, where her sorcerer-helper was going to elicit her cure. My grandmother was terminally ill, although I didn't know it. She never returned, and don Juan explained the selling of her holdings and giving them to Antoine as a supreme sorcerers' maneuver executed by her counselor to detach her from the care of her family. They were so angry with Mother for her deed that they didn't care whether or not she returned. I had the feeling that they didn't even realize that she had left.

On the top of that flat mountain, I recollected those three events as if they had happened only an instant before. When I expressed my thanks to those three persons, I succeeded in bringing them back to that mountaintop. At the end of my shouting, my loneliness was something inexpressible. I was weeping uncontrollably.

Don Juan very patiently explained to me that loneliness is inadmissible in a warrior. He said that *warrior-travelers* can count on one being on which they can focus all their love, all their care: this marvelous Earth, the mother, the matrix, the epicenter of everything we are and everything we do; the very being to which all of us return; the very being that allows *warrior-travelers* to leave on their *definitive journey.*

Don Genaro proceeded to perform then an act of magical *intent* for my benefit. Lying on his stomach, he executed a series of dazzling movements. He became a blob of luminosity that seemed to be swimming, as if the ground were a pool. Don Juan said that it was Genaro's way of hugging the immense earth, and that in spite of the difference in size, the earth acknowledged Genaro's gesture. The sight of Genaro's movements and the explanation of them replaced my loneliness with sublime joy.

"I can't stand the idea that you are leaving, don Juan," I heard myself saying. The sound of my voice and what I had said made me feel embarrassed. When I began to sob, involuntarily, driven by self-pity, I felt even more chagrined. "What is the matter with me, don Juan?" I muttered. "I'm not ordinarily like this."

"What's happening to you is that your awareness is on your toes again," he replied, laughing.

Then I lost any vestige of control and gave myself fully to my feelings of dejection and despair.

"I'm going to be left alone," I said in a shrieking voice. "What's going to happen to me? What's going to become of me?"

"Let's put it this way," don Juan said calmly. "In order for me to leave this world and face the unknown, I need all my strength, all my forbearance, all my luck; but above all, I need every bit of a *warrior-traveler's* guts of steel. To remain behind and fare like a *warrior-traveler*, you need everything of what I myself need. To venture out there, the way we are going to, is no joking matter, but neither is it to stay behind."

I had an emotional outburst and kissed his hand.

"Whoa, whoa, whoa!" he said. "Next thing you're going to make a shrine for my *guaraches*!"

The anguish that gripped me turned from self-pity to a feeling of unequaled loss. "You are leaving!" I muttered. "My god! Leaving forever!"

At that moment don Juan did something to me that he had done repeatedly since the first day I had met him. His face puffed up as if the deep breath he was taking inflated him. He tapped my back forcefully with the palm of his left hand and said, "Get up from your toes! Lift yourself up!"

In the next instant, I was once again coherent, complete, in control. I knew what was expected of me. There was no longer any hesitation on my part, or any concern about myself. I didn't care what was going to happen to me when don Juan left. I knew that his departure was imminent. He looked at me, and in that look his eyes said it all.

"We will never be together again," he said softly. "You don't need my help anymore; and I don't want to offer it to you, because if you are worth your salt as a *warrior-traveler*, you'll spit in my eye for offering it to you. Beyond a certain point, the only joy of a *warrior-traveler* is his aloneness. I wouldn't like you to try to help me, either. Once I leave, I am gone. Don't think about me, for I won't think about you. If you are a worthy *warrior-traveler*, be impeccable! Take care of your world. Honor it; guard it with your life!"

He moved away from me. The moment was beyond self-pity or tears or happiness. He shook his head as if to say good-bye, or as if he were acknowledging what I felt.

"Forget the self and you will fear nothing, in whatever level of awareness you find yourself to be," he said.

He had an outburst of levity. He teased me for the last time on this Earth.

"I hope you find love!" he said.

He raised his palm toward me and stretched his fingers like a child, then contracted them against the palm.

"*Ciao,*" he said.

I knew that it was futile to feel sorry or to regret anything, and that it was as difficult for me to stay behind as it was for don Juan to leave. Both of us were caught in an irreversible energetic maneuver that neither of us could stop. Nevertheless, I wanted to join don Juan, follow him wherever he went. The thought crossed my mind that perhaps if I died, he would take me with him.

I *saw* then how don Juan Matus, the nagual, led the fifteen other seers who were his companions, his wards, his delight, one by one to disappear in the haze of that mesa, toward the north. I *saw* how every one of them turned into a blob of luminosity, and together they ascended and floated above the mountaintop like phantom lights in the sky. They circled above the mountain once, as don Juan had said they would do: their last survey, the one for their eyes only; their last look at this marvelous Earth. And then they vanished.

I knew what I had to do. I had run out of time. I took off at my top speed toward the precipice and leaped into the abyss. I felt the wind on my face for a moment, and then the most merciful blackness swallowed me like a peaceful subterranean river.

# The Return Trip

I WAS VAGUELY aware of the loud noise of a motor that seemed to be racing in a stationary position. I thought that the attendants were fixing a car in the parking lot at the back of the building where I had my office/apartment. The noise became so intense that it finally caused me to wake up. I silently cursed the boys who ran the parking lot for fixing their car right under my bedroom window. I was hot, sweaty, and tired. I sat up on the edge of my bed, then had the most painful cramps in my calves. I rubbed them for a moment. They seemed to have contracted so tightly that I was afraid that I would have horrendous bruises. I automatically headed for the bathroom to look for some liniment. I couldn't walk. I was dizzy. I fell down, something that had never happened to me before. When I had regained a minimum of control, I noticed that I wasn't worried at all about the cramps in my calves. I had always been a near hypochondriac. An unusual pain in my calves such as the one I was having now would ordinarily have thrown me into a chaotic state of anxiety.

I went then to the window to close it, although I couldn't hear the noise anymore. I realized that the window was locked and that it was dark outside. It was night! The room was stuffy. I opened the windows. I couldn't understand why I had closed them. The night air was cool and fresh. The parking lot was empty. It occurred to me that the noise must have been made by a car accelerating in the alley between the parking lot and my building. I thought nothing of it anymore, and went to my bed to go back to sleep. I lay across it with my feet on the floor. I wanted to sleep in this fashion to help the circulation in my calves, which were very sore, but I wasn't sure whether it would have been better to keep them down or perhaps lift them up on a pillow.

As I was beginning to rest comfortably and fall asleep again, a thought came to my mind with such ferocious force that it made me stand up in one single reflex. I had jumped into an abyss in Mexico! The next thought that I had was a quasi-logical deduction: Since I had jumped into the abyss deliberately in order to die, I must now be a ghost. How strange, I thought, that I should return, in ghostlike form, to my office/apartment on the corner of Westwood and Wilshire in Los Angeles after I had died. No wonder my feelings were not the same. But if I were a ghost, I reasoned, why would I have felt the blast of fresh air on my face, or the pain in my calves?

I touched the sheets of my bed; they felt real to me. So did its metal frame. I went to the bathroom. I looked at myself in the mirror. By the looks of me, I could easily have been a ghost. I looked like hell. My eyes were sunken, with huge black circles under them. I was dehydrated, or dead. In an automatic reaction, I drank water straight from the tap. I could actually swallow it. I drank gulp after gulp, as if I hadn't drunk water for days. I felt my deep inhalations. I was alive! By god, I was alive! I knew it beyond the shadow of a doubt, but I wasn't elated, as I should have been.

A most unusual thought crossed my mind then: I had died and revived before. I was accustomed to it; it meant nothing to me. The vividness of the thought, however, made it into a quasi-memory. It was a quasi-memory that didn't stem from situations in which my life had been endangered. It was something quite different from that. It was, rather, a vague knowledge of something that had never happened and had no reason whatsoever to be in my thoughts.

There was no doubt in my mind that I had jumped into an abyss in Mexico. I was now in my apartment in Los Angeles, over three thousand miles from where I had jumped, with no recollection whatsoever of having made the return trip. In an automatic fashion, I ran the water in the tub and sat in it. I didn't feel the warmth of the water; I was chilled to the bone. Don Juan had taught me that at moments of crisis, such as this one, one must use running water as a cleansing factor. I remembered this and got under the shower. I let the warm water run over my body for perhaps over an hour.

I wanted to think calmly and rationally about what was happening to me but I couldn't. Thoughts seemed to have been erased from my mind. I was thoughtless yet I was filled to capacity with sensations that came to my whole body in barrages that I was incapable of examining. All I was able to do was to feel their onslaughts and let them go through me. The only conscious choice I made was to get dressed and leave. I went to eat breakfast, something I always did at any time of the day or night, at Ship's Restaurant on Wilshire, a block away from my office/apartment.

I had walked from my office to Ship's so many times that I knew every step of the way. The same walk this time was a novelty for me. I didn't feel my steps. It was as if I had a cushion under my feet, or as if the sidewalk were carpeted. I practically glided. I was suddenly at the door of the restaurant after what I thought might have been only two or three steps. I knew that I could swallow food because I had drunk water in my apartment. I also knew that I could talk because I had cleared my throat and cursed while the water ran on me. I walked into the restaurant as I had always done. I sat at the counter and a waitress who knew me came to me.

"You don't look too good today, dear," she said. "Do you have the flu?"

"No," I replied, trying to sound cheerful. "I've been working too hard. I've been up for twenty-four hours straight writing a paper for a class. By the way, what day is today?"

She looked at her watch and gave me the date, explaining that she had a special watch that was a calendar, too, a gift from her daughter. She also gave me the time: 3:15 A.M.

I ordered steak and eggs, hash browned potatoes, and buttered white toast. When she went away to fill my order, another wave of horror flooded my mind: Had it been only an illusion that I had jumped into that abyss in Mexico, at twilight the previous day? But even if the jump had been only an illusion, how could I have returned to L.A. from such a remote place only ten hours later? Had I slept for ten hours? Or was it that it had taken ten hours for me to fly, slide, float, or whatever to Los Angeles? To have traveled by conventional means to Los Angeles from the place where I had jumped into the abyss was out of the question, since it would have taken two days just to travel to Mexico City from the place where I had jumped.

Another strange thought emerged in my mind. It had the same clarity of my quasi-memory of having died and revived before, and the same quality of being totally foreign to me: My continuity was now broken beyond repair. I had really died, one way or another, at the bottom of that gully. It was impossible to comprehend my being alive, having breakfast at Ship's. It was impossible for me to look back into my past and see the uninterrupted line of continuous events that all of us see when we look into the past.

The only explanation available to me was that I had followed don Juan's directives; I had moved my *assemblage point* to a position that prevented my death, and from my *inner silence* I had made the return journey to L.A. There was no other rationale for me to hold on to. For the first time ever, this line of thought was thoroughly acceptable to me, and thoroughly satisfactory. It didn't really explain anything, but it certainly pointed out a pragmatic procedure that I had tested before in a mild form when I met don Juan in that town of our choice, and this thought seemed to put all my being at ease.

Vivid thoughts began to emerge in my mind. They had the unique quality of clarifying issues. The first one that erupted had to do with something that had plagued me all along. Don Juan had described it as a common occurrence among male sorcerers: my incapacity to remember events that had transpired while I was in states of heightened awareness.

Don Juan had explained heightened awareness as a minute displacement of my *assemblage point*, which he achieved, every time I saw him, by actually pushing forcefully on my back. He helped me, with such displacements, to engage energy fields that were ordinarily peripheral to my awareness. In other words, the energy fields that were usually on the edge of my *assemblage point* became central to it during that displacement. A displacement of this nature had two consequences for me: an extraordinary keenness of thought and perception, and the incapacity to remember, once I was back in my normal state of awareness, what had transpired while I had been in that other state.

My relationship with my cohorts had been an example of both of these consequences. I had cohorts, don Juan's other apprentices, companions for my *definitive journey*. I interacted with them only in heightened awareness. The clarity and scope of our interaction was supreme. The drawback for me was that in my daily life they were only poignant quasi-memories that drove me to desperation with anxiety and expectations. I could say that I lived my normal life on the perennial lookout for somebody who was going to appear all of a sudden in front of me, perhaps emerging from an office building, perhaps turning a corner and bumping into me. Wherever I went, my eyes darted everywhere, ceaselessly and involuntarily, looking for people who didn't exist and yet existed like no one else.

While I sat at Ship's that morning, everything that had happened to me in heightened awareness, to the most minute detail, in all the years with don Juan became again a continuous memory without interruption. Don Juan had lamented that a male sorcerer who is the nagual perforce had to be fragmented because of the bulk of his energetic mass. He said that each fragment lived a specific range of a total scope of activity, and the events that he experienced in each fragment had to be joined someday to give a complete, conscious picture of everything that had taken place in his total life.

Looking into my eyes, he had told me that that unification takes years to accomplish, and that he had been told of cases of naguals who never reached the total scope of their activities in a conscious manner and lived fragmented.

What I experienced that morning at Ship's was beyond anything I could have imagined in my wildest fantasies. Don Juan had said to me time after time that the world of sorcerers was not an immutable world, where the word is final, unchanging, but that it's a world of eternal fluctuation where nothing should be taken for granted. The jump into the abyss had modified my cognition so drastically that it allowed now the entrance of possibilities both portentous and indescribable.

But anything that I could have said about the unification of my cognitive fragments would have paled in comparison to the reality of it. That fateful morning at Ship's I experienced something infinitely more potent than I did the day that I *saw* energy as it flows in the universe, for the first time—the day that I ended up in the bed of my office/apartment after having been on the campus of UCLA without actually going home in the fashion my cognitive system demanded in order for the whole event to be real. In Ship's, I integrated all the fragments of my being. I had acted in each one of them with perfect certainty and consistency, and yet I had had no idea that I had done that. I was, in essence, a gigantic puzzle, and to fit each piece of that puzzle into place produced an effect that had no name.

I sat at the counter at Ship's, perspiring profusely, pondering uselessly, and obsessively asking questions that couldn't be answered: How could all this be possible? How could I have been fragmented in such a fashion? Who are we really? Certainly not the people all of us have been led to believe we are. I had memories of events that had never happened, as far as some core of myself was concerned. I couldn't even weep.

"A sorcerer weeps when he is fragmented," don Juan had said to me once. "When he's complete, he's taken by a shiver that has the potential, because it is so intense, of ending his life."

I was experiencing such a shiver! I doubted that I would ever meet my cohorts again. It appeared to me that all of them had left with don Juan. I was alone. I wanted to think about it, to mourn my loss, to plunge into a satisfying sadness the way I had always done. I couldn't. There was nothing to mourn, nothing to feel sad about. Nothing mattered. All of us were *warrior-travelers*, and all of us had been swallowed by *infinity*.

All along, I had listened to don Juan talk about the *warrior-traveler*. I had liked the description immensely, and I had identified with it on a purely emotional basis. Yet I had never felt what he really meant by that, regardless of how many times he had explained his meaning to me. That night, at the counter of Ship's, I knew what don Juan had been talking about. I was a *warrior-traveler*. Only *energetic facts* were meaningful for me. All the rest were trimmings that had no importance at all.

That night, while I sat waiting for my food, another vivid thought erupted in my mind. I felt a wave of empathy, a wave of identification with don Juan's premises. I had finally reached the goal of his teachings: I was one with him as I had never been before. It had never been the case that I was just fighting don Juan or his concepts, which were revolutionary for me because they didn't fulfill the linearity of my thoughts as a Western man. Rather, it was that don Juan's precision in presenting his concepts had always scared me half to death. His efficiency had appeared to be dogmatism. It was that appearance that had forced me to seek elucidations, and had made me act, all along, as if I had been a reluctant believer.

Yes, I had jumped into an abyss, I said to myself, and I didn't die because before I reached the bottom of that gully I let the *dark sea of awareness* swallow me. I surrendered to it, without fears or regrets. And that *dark sea* had supplied me with whatever was necessary for me not to die, but to end up in my bed in L.A. This explanation would have explained nothing to me two days before. At three in the morning, in Ship's, it meant everything to me.

I banged my hand on the table as if I were alone in the room. People looked at me and smiled knowingly. I didn't care. My mind was focused on an insoluble dilemma: I was alive despite the fact that I had jumped into an abyss in order to die ten hours before. I knew that such a dilemma could never be resolved. My normal cognition required a linear explanation in order to be sat-isfied, and linear explanations were not possible. That was the crux of the interruption of continuity. Don Juan had said that that interruption was sorcery. I knew this now, as clearly as I was capable of. How right don Juan had been when he had said that in order for me to stay behind, I needed all my strength, all my forbearance, and above all, a *warrior-traveler's* guts of steel.

I wanted to think about don Juan, but I couldn't. Besides, I didn't care about don Juan. There seemed to be a giant barrier between us. I truly believed at that moment that the foreign thought that had been insinuating itself to me since I had woken up was true: I was someone else. An exchange had taken place at the moment of my jump. Otherwise, I would have relished the thought of don Juan; I would have longed for him. I would have even felt a twinge of resentment because he hadn't taken me with him. That would have been my normal self. I truthfully wasn't the same. This thought gained momentum until it invaded all my being. Any residue of my old self that I may have retained vanished then.

A new mood took over. I was alone! Don Juan had left me inside a dream as his agent provocateur. I felt my body begin to lose its rigidity; it became flexible, by degrees, until I could breathe deeply and freely. I laughed out loud. I didn't care that people were staring at me and weren't smiling this time. I was alone, and there was nothing I could have done about it!

I had the physical sensation of actually entering into a passageway, a passageway that had a force of its own. It pulled me in. It was a silent passageway. Don Juan was that passageway, quiet and immense. This was the first time ever that I felt that don Juan was void of physicality. There was no room for sentimentality or longing. I couldn't possibly have missed him because he was there as a depersonalized emotion that lured me in.

The passageway challenged me. I had a sensation of ebullience, ease. Yes, I could travel that passageway, alone or in company, perhaps forever. And to do this was not an imposition for me, nor was it a pleasure. It was more than the beginning of the *definitive journey*, the unavoidable fate of a *warrior-traveler*, it was the beginning of a new era. I should have been weeping with the realization that I had found that passageway, but I wasn't. I was facing *infinity* at Ship's! How extraordinary! I felt a chill on my back. I heard don Juan's voice saying that the universe was indeed unfathomable.

At that moment, the back door of the restaurant, the one that led to the parking lot, opened and a strange character entered: a man perhaps in his early forties, disheveled and emaciated, but with rather handsome features. I had seen him for years roaming around UCLA, mingling with the students. Someone had told me that he was an outpatient of the nearby Veterans' Hospital. He seemed to be mentally unbalanced. I had seen him time after time at Ship's, huddled over a cup of coffee, always at the same end of the counter. I had also seen how he waited outside, looking through the window, watching for his favorite stool to become vacant if someone was sitting there.

When he entered the restaurant, he sat at his usual place, and then he looked at me. Our eyes met. The next thing I knew, he had let out a formidable scream that chilled me, and everyone present, to the bone. Everyone looked at me, wide-eyed, some of them with unchewed food in their mouths. Obviously, they thought I had screamed. I had set up the precedents by banging the counter and then laughing out loud. The man jumped off his stool and ran out of the restaurant, turning back to stare at me while, with his hands, he made agitated gestures over his head.

I succumbed to an impulsive urge and ran after the man. I wanted him to tell me what he had seen in me that had made him scream. I overtook him in the parking lot and asked him to tell me why he had screamed. He covered his eyes and screamed again, even louder. He was like a child, frightened by a nightmare, screaming at the top of his lungs. I left him and went back to the restaurant.

"What happened to you, dear?" the waitress asked with a concerned look. "I thought you ran out on me."

"I just went to see a friend," I said.

The waitress looked at me and made a gesture of mock annoyance and surprise.

"Is that guy your friend?" she asked.

"The only friend I have in the world," I said, and that was the truth, if I could define "friend" as someone who sees through the veneer that covers you and knows where you really come from.